☙ Hot Stuff

Hot Stuff

A Cookbook in Praise of the Piquant

Jessica B. Harris

Atheneum New York 1985

To my father, **Jesse B. Harris,**
who taught me how to eat hot stuff.

And my mother, **Rhoda A. Harris,**
who taught me how to cook it.

Drawings by Sylvia Duke

Library of Congress Cataloging in Publication Data

Harris, Jessica B.
Hot stuff.

Includes index.
1. Cookery (Peppers) 2. Cookery, International.
I. Title.
TX803.P46H37 1985 641.6′384 84-45047
ISBN 0-689-11483-4

Published simultaneously in Canada by Collier Macmillan Canada, Inc.
Composition by Maryland Linotype Composition Co., Inc.,
Baltimore, Maryland
Manufactured by Fairfield Graphics, Fairfield, Pennsylvania
Designed by Cathryn S. Aison
First Edition

Acknowledgments

NO COOKBOOK WRITER can claim dominion over a collection of recipes; we've all had help. Help from people known and unknown. Help from those who created recipes and techniques that became traditional. Who created guacamole or Thiebou Dienne? Who invented whisking eggs for an omelette? Thanks goes first to all those who went before.

A large thank you then goes to the tourist offices that have helped in arranging trips to the corners of the world where I gathered recipes, to nameless women in markets around the world who patiently answered questions about spices and dishes, and to my international extended family, particularly Nicole N'Dongo in Senegal, Theodore Komaclo in the Ivory Coast, and Regina Celi Corbacho, Antonio Luis Figueiredo, Nair, Carmen, Maria, Regina Adalgisa, Daria and others in Bahia, Brazil, who translated the questions and offered recipes.

A particular thank you goes to my New York friends: Richard Alleman, June Bobb, Stephanie Curtis, Linda Cohen, Karen Kopta, Darrell Leo, Martha Jones and Oumar Thiam who came, ate, and commented.

To Judith Kern, my editor, and Carole Abel, my agent, who got *Hot Stuff* out of the kitchen and into the book stores.

Finally, a thank you to my mother, Rhoda, and to my father, Jesse, who died while the book was being written.

Contents

Hot Stuff

◆§ Hot Stuff

A FEW DECADES AGO if people were asked to name a favorite American dish, they probably would have replied chicken pot pie or chipped beef on toast. Today, the reply is more likely to be pizza, chile, or even tacos! Americans are tiring of bland, underseasoned food; the country is growing up in its tastes. A recent column in a culinary magazine signaled an American demand for more authoritative flavors as a trend for the 1980s.

One does not have to be a cook or even a food authority to note that American taste for the hot and spicy is increasing. Restaurants featuring piquant foods from the Szechwan and Hunan provinces of China have made inroads into the popularity of the blander Cantonese cuisine. The spicy cooking of southern Italy is enjoying a renaissance, and Indian restaurants are multiplying with the alacrity of rabbits. In major metropolitan areas immigrants from Asia, Mediterranean Europe, the Caribbean, Latin America, and Africa are bringing their cuisines with them, and it is now possible to find such items as fresh ginger and hot chiles in neighborhood markets throughout the country. The regional cuisines of this country are gaining importance, and with their growing acceptance pickled jalapeño chiles and Louisiana hot sauces are appearing on supermarket shelves.

Pepper in all its forms—both the fruit of the *piper nigrum* vine, which produces black, white, and green pepper, and the myriad members of the capsicum family, which include the bell peppers, paprika, and hot chiles—is being rediscovered and re-evaluated as a culinary element that blends successfully with almost all others to create new tastes.

In its true form, *piper nigrum*, and in the capsicum form that has adopted its name, the history of pepper is one of exploration, discovery, and greed. There is enough melodrama in the search for the securing of pepper to make several television miniseries, and the spice and its history are a leitmotif running through the history of the modern world.

THE PEPPER STORY

Spices have been around ever since early man bit into an aromatic berry or ground up a bit of the bark of a special tree to flavor his food. Pepper, however, is the "master spice" whose uses and history are as exotic as the history of the world.

Pepper was traded to the pharonic Egyptians and to the ancient Greeks and Romans by Arab merchants. The merchants, however, refused to divulge the source of the marvelous spice and thus shrouded its origins in mystery and legend for hundreds of years.

The Romans were the first truly to fall under its spell. The Emperor Domitian (A.D. 81–96) had a special spice market built, which he named the *horrea piperataria* in honor of the master spice. This market, which was later replaced by Trajan's market, sold all manner of exotic spices. Both markets must have prefigured the noisy open-air markets in many parts of the modern world, where spices are piled in kaleidoscopic abundance and hawked by vendors to those who wish to enhance the taste of their food. One of the major spices sold was pepper, and already the little black berries had become so important that they were used instead of gold to pay rents and ransoms.

Without modern refrigeration, food spoiled rapidly and cooking a meal usually meant making the best of aged meats. Salt and pepper, then, assumed great importance. Salt, although not readily available, was relatively common, for it could be obtained from the sea. Pepper was mysterious . . . and rare. It was so rare that in A.D. 410, when Alaric and the Visigoth hordes arrived in the imperial city of Rome, part of the ransom they demanded was three thousand pounds of pepper The spice was, in those days, indeed an imperial ransom.

By the Middle Ages, pepper had assumed even greater importance. It was used as currency because, unlike gold, it could not be short-weighted, adulterated, or alloyed. Dock workers who unloaded pepper shipments suffered inspections not unlike those given diamond workers in South Africa. The pockets of their clothes were sewn up so that not one of the precious little black grains could be taken.

In those years pepper was king. In fact, a pound of pepper could buy a serf his freedom in France. In England a pound of the spice was the equivalent of three weeks' wages for a farm worker. At some times the value of the spice was so high that a pound of pepper was equal in worth to a pound of gold. A man's wealth was measured not only by the amount of gold in his coffers but also by the amount of pepper in his cupboards. The term "pepper bags" became the medieval equivalent of today's moneybags.

The Crusades contributed to pepper's preeminence. Crusaders had traditionally brought spices back from their wars in the Middle East. In fact, Venetian and Genoese seafarers, who transported Crusaders to the Holy Land, established their supremacy in the pepper trade by returning with their ships laden with spices and pepper to sell in European markets. Europe's appetite for pepper was voracious. During parts of the Middle Ages the Continent consumed 6.6 million pounds of pepper annually.

The year 1271 marked the end of the "darkness" of the Middle Ages. The year signaled the beginning of the last of the Crusades and also the beginning of a journey that would change the pepper trade and the map of the known world.

That year two Venetians, Nicolo and Maffeo Polo accompanied by Nicolo's young son, Marco, embarked on their second trip to the Orient, which would last twenty-four years. Marco's tales of his journey, published after his return, finally demystified pepper's origins. His writings would initiate direct trade with the

Orient and assure Venetian supremacy in that area for years. They would lead, incidentally, to the discovery of the New World and of another plant that would also come to be named pepper.

In his tales Marco Polo spoke of Java, where is obtained "the greatest part of the spices that are distributed throughout the world," of the kingdom of Dely (today's India), which produced "great quantity of pepper," and of other exotic kingdoms that grew the master spice.

Polo marveled at towns like Kin-sai, where one of the Khan's customs officers informed him that "the daily load of pepper bought was forty-three loads, each load being two hundred and forty-three pounds." The figure is astronomical even today and must have been truly awe-inspiring to Marco Polo, who knew the value of pepper in the medieval European market. The young Polo also visited the Malabar coast of India, producer of Tellicherry, the *summum* of today's black peppers. He remarked on the vast abundance there of pepper and other spices.

Marco Polo's writings were at first dismissed as the ravings of a madman. Later, they would set off a race between European monarchs for a safe route to the Spice Islands (today's Moluccas) ; the race would last for two centuries.

Outside Lisbon today, facing a desolate and seemingly endless Atlantic Ocean, there stands a monument of King Henry the Navigator. Henry, although not himself a seafaring explorer, was the mentor of many voyages of exploration. His establishment of a naval college in 1418 and his underwriting of successive systematic explorations of the African coast would lead Portugal to the circumnavigation of the African continent and to the discovery of a sea route to the Spice Islands. When Vasco da Gama arrived on the Malabar Coast in 1498, he established Portuguese preeminence in the pepper trade.

Changes in the domination of the pepper trade read like a microcosm of the history of the European world. First came the Arabs, who were followed by the Italians. The Spanish briefly owned trading rights to the Spice Islands, which they ceded to the Portuguese in return for dominance in the New World. The era of expansion and exploration in the late fifteenth and early sixteenth centuries ended with the Portuguese handing over the reins to the Dutch. The Dutch East India Company proved so greedy that in one year the price of pepper on the London market almost trebled. The Dutch maintained their dominance in the field, as one history book put it, by "ruthlessly restricting production, even if this meant pulling up plants, cutting down trees and killing natives who objected."

The British and the Dutch vied for domination of the pepper trade, but the Dutch maintained control over the Spice Islands, Java, and Sumatra, until well into the twentieth century. The British were forced to look elsewhere.

The British East India Company was formed in 1600 for the purpose of expanding Britain's territories in the East. Soon British gains included major footholds in what would become the jewel in the crown of empire—India. But pepper did not dominate Britain's trade with India. By 1680, in fact, that trade was centered on textiles; the British had left the pepper trade to others.

The French also entered the fray, though they never attained the predominance of either the British or the Dutch. The French East India Company, though under the direction of a gentleman with an incredibly fortuitous name—Pierre Poivre (Peter Pepper)—never really gained ground.

The race for pepper and the race for territory went hand in hand through history. By the end of the eighteenth century pepper was still the predominant spice in the Western world.

Meanwhile, on the other side of the Atlantic, other pepper developments were taking place. If Christopher Columbus's voyages of discovery had not been a winning financial proposition from the pepper merchant's point of view, they had introduced another "pepper" to the world. Columbus's misconception that he had reached the East Indies led him to give the name "pepper" to the wide variety of small fruits that the natives of the islands he visited added to their food for piquancy. In his search for black pepper, Columbus had given the world the myriad varieties of capsicum pepper. He had also created eternal confusion among lovers of pepper of both types. In English, for example, the word "pepper" can apply to either the black, white, or green grains of the *piper nigrum* plant or to the many varieties of the capsicum genus. There is, however, no botanical relationship between the two peppers. Other languages, such as French, do not have this confusion, and no self-respecting French person would ask for *piment* (hot capsicum pepper) when *poivre* (black or white or green peppercorns) was wanted.

Capsicum peppers have been used for millennia in the New World. Archaeological evidence has established that the natives of Peru and Brazil began eating capsicums, which grew wild, between 6500 and 5000 B.C. By the time of the Aztecs and the Incas, multiple varieties of this piquant fruit had been cultivated and were the favored foods of the Americas.

The chile, as many members of the capsicum family are called, was precious in Mexico, where it was used in tribute and was part of the sums paid to the city of Tenochititlan (today's Mexico City) by conquered peoples.

There are hundreds (possibly even thousands) of varieties of capsicum peppers. They range from the mild green peppers that are stuffed with a variety of fillings and served as garnishes on salads to the ultra hot chiles, eaten in parts of Latin America and Asia, that can literally sear the palates of those unaccustomed to eating them.

Although capsicum peppers are the New World's gastronomical gift to the world, they have, in an ironic reversal, become an integral part of the cuisines of the world's black-pepper-producing countries. The cooking of Southeast Asia and India would be unthinkable without the bite of the fiery red and green chiles, which arrived in India in 1611.

The pepper story, however, does not end with the discovery of capsicum peppers and their export to India, Asia, Africa, and Europe. (Paprika is also a member of the capsicum family; it has made the cuisine of Hungary famous.) Black pepper and the pepper trade also figured in the early history of the United States.

Although Salem, Massachusetts, is better known for its witch trials, it was for many years the pepper capital of the New World. Taking advantage of Salem's location on the New England coast and of the seafaring talents of the New Englanders, Americans outwitted Dutch trading monopolies and negotiated trade agreements for pepper directly with the Sumatrans. The one-hundred-ton brig *Cadet*, which sailed out of Salem harbor in 1788 bound for Southeast Asia, was only the first of many ships to sail that route. By the early nineteenth century, the New England area had imported so much pepper that it was reexporting it to Europe. It had already reexported 7.5 million pounds of pepper by that time, and the import duties alone were enough to pay 5 percent of the new country's government expenses. Many of this country's first millionaires, among them Eli Yale, founder of Yale University, made their fortunes in the pepper trade.

Pepper is still the world's most popular spice, and chiles are the backbone of many of the world's cuisines. Innovative uses for pepper are still being discovered. Although unknown in the West before World War II, green peppercorns have been adopted with a vengeance by the nouvelle cuisine, whose chefs have made it a hallmark of their cooking.

In tropical kitchens of the pepper- and chile-growing areas around the world, pepper and pepper products are being used in ways that may one day be commonplace on Western tables.

MEDICAL CLAIMS FOR PEPPER

Peppers, both *piper nigrum* and the capsicums, have always been recognized as having medical as well as culinary uses. Such uses are mentioned in Sanskrit literature more than three thousand years old, and in fact the word "pepper" is thought to be a derivative of the Sanskrit word *pipali.* Black pepper appears in early Brahamanic texts in India in which it is mentioned in the treatment of urinary complaints, liver disorders, hemorrhoids, jaundice, and overweight. It was also used as a carminative, a stimulant, a digestive, and to treat diarrhea, cholera, and arthritis. The Hindu *Ayurveda* recommends chiles as an aid to digestion and as a cure for paralysis.

Today in Brazil, doctors who specialize in pepper and its uses are known as *pimentologos*. Their claims for chiles are backed up because capsicums are rich in vitamins A and C. In an article in *Viva Bahia*, Brazilian gastroenterologist Dr. Paulo Duarte attested to the value of chiles in aiding the flow of gastric juices and promoting digestion when taken in moderation. Modern medical studies are taking a second look at old wives' tales and finding out that many are not all hokum. Some, indeed, have a basis in fact. Medical claims made for pepper and chiles over the years range from the plausible to the outrageous.

❧ Black pepper was originally considered a medical remedy. It was prescribed for everything from aching loins (nine peppercorns were said to relieve the pain) to ague. (For ague the remedy was simple—one peppercorn a day took the place of the proverbial apple and was reputed to keep the doctor away.)

❧ The Mesopotamian manuscript of Dioscorides (1222–23) describes the preparation of a *shirab* (drink) for catarrhs, coughs, and stomach ailments. It calls for one-quarter measure of white pepper.

❧ Both black and capsicum peppers have been known to "persuade" those with loss of appetite back to food, and some doctors recommend a more highly spiced diet for those with listless appetites.

❧ In the tropics it is claimed that capsicum peppers act as a natural thermostat; pepper raises the body's temperature, produces perspiration, and therefore makes an individual feel cooler. This rationale is also used in Africa, where a "good" pepper is one that makes the eater sweat profusely.

❧ The English herbalist John Gerard noted in the sixteenth century that "all pepper heateth, provoketh, digesteth, draweth, disperseth and cleanseth the dimness of sight."

❧ Chiles are used by Oriental herbalists to prevent digestive diseases.

Tincture of cayenne is an old-fashioned remedy for chilblains; it was applied to them as a warming agent.

In some parts of the South, ground-up chiles are placed in the toes of one's socks to keep the feet warm.

Pepper also serves as a natural preservative. It works by retarding the oxidation process in fats.

Chiles are rich in vitamins A and C. One two-ounce chile has more than twice the daily requirement of vitamin A established by the federal government.

A recipe from the *Farmer's Advocate* of London, Ontario, Canada, for October 1876 suggested that one cup of honey, half a cup of vinegar, and a small teaspoon of cayenne pepper made a good gargle for a sore throat.

A less likely cure is the tenth-century Anglo-Saxon recipe that mixes pepper and wine as an eyewash.

In 1747, Reverend John Wesley recommended chewing five or six peppercorns and then swallowing them as a cure for heartburn. If it didn't work, at least you knew what was burning!

A Texas remedy for rheumatism calls for a mixture of nine red chiles, coal oil, salt, and gasoline to be rubbed on the afflicted joints.

A spray to repel garden insects can be made from ground red pepper pods and water. It is sprayed on the plants to keep pepper-hating insects at bay.

Readers of the 1888 *Farmer's and Housekeeper's Cyclopedia* sprinkled cayenne pepper in nooks and crannies to keep ants away. This one really works; I've tried it with squirrels that took over a summer cottage.

❧ More recently, a book on natural beauty cures published in the French West Indies suggested using red bird peppers to prevent hair from falling. Five of the small chiles are left to macerate in two cups of oil. The oil is then massaged into the scalp.

❧ Finally, chiles have long been considered an aphrodisiac. They are supposed to cure indifference to romance. Rumor also has it that those who eat spicy foods and love hot stuff are hot stuff themselves!

THE VOCABULARY OF PEPPER

The vocabulary of pepper is complex and confusing. Brazil's malagueta peppers are often confused with melegueta pepper or grains of paradise although they are not related. Mexico's habañero chiles are known as Guinea pepper in Africa, ancho peppers in England, Bonda Man Jacques (Madame Jacques's behind) in Guadeloupe, and simply as large hot peppers in Guyana. In the United States, New Mexico green chile is also called Chile verde; it is similar to California green chile but the former is hotter. Both, incidentally are also known as Anaheim. And that's only the beginning; the confusion rages on, for peppers and dried and fresh chiles are known by a variety of national and regional names.

For the purposes of this book, pepper refers to *piper nigrum* in its white, black, or green form; mild capsicums are referred to as green or red bell peppers, and red and green hot capsicums are called red or green chiles. In recipes, chiles will be referred to by their local names. When a particular chile is not readily available, a substitution will be suggested or a mail order source listed at the end of the book.

The following list includes some of the most common names for *piper nigrum*, bell peppers, and chiles. It also includes a catalog of some common and uncommon pepper products and some false friends—spices called pepper that are not true pepper.

TYPES OF *PIPER NIGRUM*

PEPPERCORNS

Brazil—very mild. Brazil is one of the major new pepper-producing areas of the world. Brazil pepper, however, is frequently included in blends and is rarely sold under its own name. Visitors to Brazil will find the black peppercorns available in spice stalls in markets such as Bahia's Feira de São Joaquin.

Green pepper—hot. Neither black nor white pepper, this is the ultimate fresh pepper. Soft enough to be mashed, it has become the hallmark of nouvelle cuisine. It is found frozen, packed in brine, freeze-dried, and occasionally fresh in specialty gourmet shops. Because of its short life span as a fresh product, it is frequently sold preserved, in cans. (Clear bottles would allow light to contaminate the pepper.) This pepper is a specialty of Mangalore on the Malabar coast of India. Madagascar, in the Indian Ocean, also exports green pepper, which is mainly available canned. As ubiquitous as green pepper may seem to those who frequent restaurants specializing in nouvelle cuisine, it was virtually unknown to Western cooks before World War II.

Lampong—very hot. This black pepper is named for the district on the Indonesian island of Sumatra where it is grown. Although Sumatra is better known for its white pepper, Lampong peppercorns are very pungent, relatively hard, and very black.

ൟ Malabar—medium hot. The Malabar coast of India is *piper nigrum*'s home territory. It was here that the climbing vine originally grew. Malabar pepper is similar to Tellicherry pepper, but its grains are neither as large nor as even in size.

ൟ Mignonette pepper—hot. Not actually a pepper, but rather a coarse mixture of black and white peppercorns, it is frequently used in French cooking.

ൟ Muntok—mildly hot. Native to the Indonesian island of Bangka, this pepper is always sold white. White pepper comes from the same berry as black pepper, but it has been processed and the hull removed to reveal the inner white core. The processing makes white pepper more expensive than similar grades of black pepper. White pepper is milder than black pepper; it is frequently used in English and Scandinavian cooking and in sauces in which black pepper is considered unsightly.

ൟ Sarawak—mildly hot. The north coast of the island of Borneo gives its name to this pungent pepper. The berries are brownish black, small, and uneven in size.

ൟ Tellicherry—hot. Named for a seaport on the Malabar coast in southwestern India, this pepper is considered to be the *summum* of black pepper. Its pungent, large, even-sized berries have a slightly smoky taste. Gourmets consider it the best in the world.

CAPSICUM PEPPERS

There are hundreds (and some say thousands) of varieties of capsicum peppers. They are almost impossible to classify because the names by which they are known change from region to region. The confusion is complicated because capsicums cross-pollinate fairly simply so that new varieties are always being discovered. Capsicums form a botanical genus of the *Solanacae*, the nightshade family. The red, green, yellow, and even purple fruits are used in seasoning and in cooking. Varieties include *capsicum cerasiforme* (cherry peppers), *capsicum conoides* (tabasco peppers), and *capsicum grossum* (mild bell or sweet peppers), among others. According to the *Encyclopaedia Britannica* all of the above peppers, and indeed all garden peppers, are derived from *capsicum frutescens*, an indigenous South American plant.

Although to the uninitiated, all chiles are hot, they vary in taste and in piquancy. Some are relatively mild while others will literally sear the tongues of the unaccustomed. One does, however, develop a tolerance for hot chiles. If you use them frequently, you'll find that you'll soon want to add two instead of one, three instead of two, and so forth. Brazilians, pepper lovers all, are known to add one or two hot malagueta peppers to sandwiches, and a Guyanese friend of mine likes nothing better than to make a sandwich of wiri-wiri peppers and bread!

It is difficult to rate the "heat" of a chile. Dr. Roy Nakayama of New Mexico State University near Las Cruces, New Mexico, has developed a rating system for the piquancy of chiles. The scale, which was published as part of an article in *Santa Fe Magazine*, goes from one (mildest) to ten (hottest), as follows:

1—New Mexico or Anaheim
2—Rio Grande
3—Numex Big Jim
4—Hot Ancho
5—Sandia
6—Española or Cayenne
7—Jalapeño
8—Tabasco
9—Santaca (Japanese)
10—Bahamian

Although not all the peppers on Dr. Nakayama's list are readily available, many varieties can be found under different names throughout the United States. The following list includes some of the myriad varieties of chiles.

❧ Anaheim—mildly hot. Sometimes called California green, this vivid green chile is generally about seven inches long and an inch and a half wide. It will usually have a rounded tip. It is readily available throughout the United States.

❧ Bell peppers—mild. These fleshy varieties are sometimes called bullnose peppers or simply red or green peppers. They are available all year-round but are considered "in season" between June and November. They are widely used both raw and cooked and are frequently found in Middle Eastern cuisine. Some varieties are California Wonder, a large, smooth, chunky pepper that is deep green when immature and ripens to deep red; Ruby King, a long, thin, thick-fleshed variety; and Sunnybrook, a pepper that looks like a flattened tomato.

BELL

Bird peppers—hot. These small hot peppers are similar to the Brazilian malagueta pepper. They are found in the ubiquitous Caribbean pepper sauces and in many other Caribbean dishes. They can be found preserved in vinegar or sherry in West Indian grocery stores.

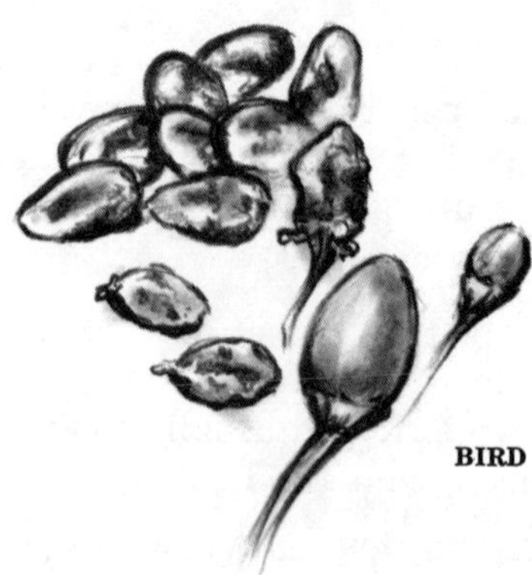

BIRD

❧ Bonda Man Jacques—hot. This small, shriveled, lantern-shaped red pepper from Guadeloupe goes by a rather rude name, which means Madame Jacques's behind in Creole. It is similar to the habañero chiles found in the markets in major U.S. cities.

❧ California green chile—Anaheim.

❧ Chile cayenne—hot. This long, thin green chile is available throughout the United States all-year-round. It can be substituted for fresh serranos or jalapeños when those varieties are unavailable. This chile is thought to have originated in Cayenne, Guyana, South America. In its ripe state, the dried chile is ground with other chiles to produce cayenne pepper, a term that has become synonymous with hot dried pepper powder.

❧ Chile verde—New Mexico green chile.

❧ Fresno—very hot. This is a California-only chile, which is similar to the jalapeño chile.

❧ Güero—very hot. This yellow chile is similar in size and shape to the jalapeño. Its average length is about four or five inches.

❧ Habañero—very hot. This light green or red chile looks like a miniature lantern or a small bell pepper. It is known by a variety of names. Called ancho in England, it should not be confused with the dried American ancho. It goes by the names Bonda Man Jacques in Guadeloupe in its red form and in a deep purple variant is called piment negresse (Negress pepper) on the same island. In West Africa it is known as Guinea pepper. It can be found fresh in the United States in the markets of Latin American neighborhoods.

❧ Jalapeño—very hot. This chile is generally about two inches long by one inch wide and has a smooth green skin. Jalapeños are available throughout the United States, either fresh or pick-

JALAPEÑO

led in brine. They are probably the most familiar of all chiles because of their use in Mexican and Tex-Mex foods.

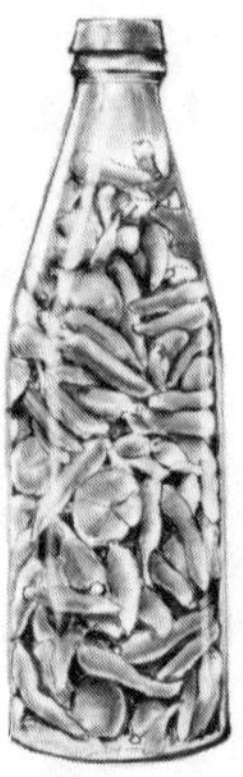

MALAGUETA

❧ Malagueta pepper—very hot. Bright red and green and about one inch long, these chiles are used in Brazilian cooking. They are especially featured in the cuisine of Bahia and are a standard condiment in Brazilian restaurants. Unavailable fresh in the United States, they can be purchased preserved in vinegar in Brazilian stores or by mail. This pepper is not to be confused with melegueta pepper or grains of paradise, which is not pepper at all.

❧ Mulato—Poblano.

❧ New Mexico green chile—mildly hot. This chile is bright green and similar to the Anaheim, its California cousin. The New Mexico green chile is, however, slightly hotter than its California counterpart. It is known by a variety of names, the most common of which is chile verde.

❧ Pimento de cheiro—hot. This hot chile, similar to the habeñero, is used in Brazilian cooking.

❧ Pequin—very hot. These chiles are small, oval, bright red, and about half an inch long.

❧ Poblano—mild to mildly hot. A large, dark green chile frequently used for stuffed peppers, it is sometimes referred to as Mulato.

SERRANO

❧ Serrano—very hot. Lighter green in color and slightly longer and narrower in shape than a jalapeño, this chile averages two inches in length and one-half inch in width. Serrano chiles are readily found in parts of the country where there are large Mexican and Hispanic populations.

❧ Tabasco—very hot. Smooth-skinned and bright red, this tapered chile averages one and a half inches in length. It is sold bottled whole and fresh. In spite of its name, it is not an ingredient of Tabasco sauce.

☙ Wiri-wiri—hot. These peppers are small cherrylike, red-skinned chiles. In Guyana, they are grown in pots on windowsills by cooks who want their spices readily available. They are also sold preserved in vinegar.

☙ DRIED AND PRESERVED CHILES

☙ Ancho—mildly hot. This is the ripe, dried form of the Poblano chile. It is wrinkled, ovoid in shape, and ranges in color from deep maroon to almost black; after soaking it becomes a deep terra-cotta. It averages five inches in length and three inches in width. This is *the* chile con carne chile and is a major ingredient in many prepared chile powders. It adds color and mild heat.

☙ California chile—mildly hot. This is the dried form of the chile that is sold fresh under the name Anaheim. The long pod, which has been allowed to ripen before drying, is bright red in color and has a smooth skin. It is readily available and is frequently used in wreaths and *ristras* (chains), which are available by mail order.

☙ Chipotle—very hot. This is a smoked, dried form of the jalapeño chile. The name comes from the Nahuatl words *chil* (meaning chile) and *potli* (meaning smoke). The chile is brick red in color, about two and a half inches long, and one-half inch wide. It is available canned at stores specializing in Mexican food products and is also occasionally found fresh in some markets.

☙ Japonés—very hot. This thin red chile, sometimes called Hontaka (or simply Oriental chile pepper), is the dried form of the Serrano chile. It is grown mainly in Japan; hence its name, which means "Japanese" in Spanish. It is used in both Oriental and Latin American cooking. Sold dried in jars or cellophane packages, it is widely available.

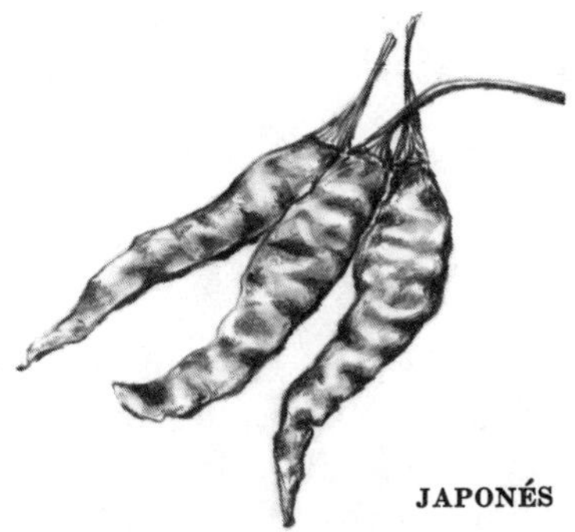

JAPONÉS

Mulato—hot. This dried chile is frequently confused with the ancho chiles, but it is usually larger and is slightly more reddish in color. Ancho and mulato chiles are frequently used interchangeably.

Mirasol Colorado—mild. This chile, which is similar to the California Anaheim or the New Mexican green chile, is widely used in Peruvian cooking.

New Mexico red—mildly hot to hot. This chile is also known as *chile de ristra* for it, like its California cousin the Anaheim, is frequently used in making wreaths and *ristras*. Brick red in color, pod-shaped, and smooth-skinned, it is readily available in the Southwest and can be purchased by mail order throughout the United States.

RISTRAS

Pequin—very hot. This is the dried form of the small red chile of the same name which is sold fresh.

PEPPER PRODUCTS

Some Common

Cayenne—hot to very hot. Cayenne, when not specifically referring to a particular chile, applies to a powder made from various dried chiles. It can range in color from terra-cotta to deep maroon depending on the mixture of chiles. It can have a range of flavors from pungent to smoky. One constant, however, is that it is always hot.

Chile powder—mildly hot to very hot. There is no homogeneity among chile powders. The flavor depends on the brand. The more common brands tend to have the least flavor; they contain a mixture of dried chile peppers, garlic, cumin, oregano, and salt. Local brands and specialty brands have more character and, depending on the ingredients, can range from mildly hot to ultra hot.

Chile sauce—mild to hot. Despite the name, commercial chile sauces have little to do with chile peppers. They are simply a catsup base doctored up with horseradish, garlic powder, and possibly a dash or two of chile powder. When considering a specialty brand or a homemade chile sauce, watch out! The mixture might be anything from supermarket bland to Tex-Mex four-alarm hot.

Curry powder—mildly hot to very hot. There is no such thing as curry powder in India. There spices are ground specifically for the dish being prepared. What is sold here as curry powder is a mixture of black pepper, dried chiles, turmeric, cardamom, coriander, mustard, and cumin, with occasional other spices. The proportions of the spices and the piquancy of the curry powder vary from brand to brand. When cooking, verify the taste as you go and add additional spices to taste.

❧ Hot sauces—mildly hot to very hot. This all-purpose term covers a wide range of pepper sauces (as they are called in the Caribbean). They range in taste from mildly hot to incendiary. Louisiana Red and Green sauces in their familiar long, narrow bottles are probably the best known in the United States to aficionados of hot food. Tabasco is known the world over. Visitors to the Caribbean and adventurous shoppers will find names like Bellos, a red-hot, fiery mixture from Dominica; Esther's, a turmeric-hued pepper sauce from Barbados; and Goya's rosy salsa piquante from Puerto Rico as well as an infinite variety of local brands. Recipes for pepper sauces are included in the recipe section of the book.

❧ Paprika—mild to mildly hot. Paprika peppers belong to the capsicum genus. When dried, paprika yields a mild powder used mainly to add color to various dishes. Paprikas, however, add a definite flavor as well, and some paprikas can be quite piquant. Hungary, where the transplanted capsicum has virtually become the national spice, produces the most flavorful and vivid of the paprikas.

❧ Pepperoncini—mildly hot to hot. Also called Tuscan peppers, these small, light green peppers are packaged in brine. They are frequently used in Italian salads and antipasti.

❧ Pickled peppers—hot. These are small red and green chiles that have been cured in vinegar. A table condiment found along with salt and pepper in many Cajun, Creole, and Soul Food restaurants, these hot chiles—and they are hot—add extra bite to any dish. The flavored liquid is good for adding zest to soups and stews and can be replenished by adding cider vinegar to the bottle.

❧ Pimiento—mild. These skinned, roasted red bell peppers are readily available throughout the United States and are widely used both as a garnish and in such dishes as anchovies and peppers. They are found in supermarkets or in Italian groceries.

❧ Pizza peppers—hot. This is a mixture of dried chiles designed to be sprinkled on pizza.

❧ Red pepper jelly—mildly hot. Sweet and piquant tastes are combined in this preparation, which can be either homemade or mass-produced. It is perfect on freshly baked cornbread.

❧ Tabasco sauce—hot. This is, to many people, the *summum* of hot sauces. It is a patented mixture of vinegar, spices, and the tiny red, green, and yellow peppers that grow in the salty soil of Avery Island in New Iberia, Louisiana. The aged mixture is a prerequisite for the perfect Bloody Mary and is readily available throughout the United States.

Some Not So Common

❧ Chinese hot oil—very hot. This mixture of hot chile peppers and oil is used to add bite to many dishes from the Szechwan and Hunan provinces of China.

❧ Harissa—very hot. Pulverized dried chile peppers, cumin, and salt make up this fiery Tunisian paste used to flavor couscous. It can be made at home or purchased canned in specialty shops.

❧ Pickapepper sauce—hot. This Jamaican condiment is similar in color and texture to Worcestershire sauce. The difference is in the taste. Pickapepper sauce, which is made of a mixture of hot peppers, sugar, salt, and spices, is hot.

❧ Quatre Epices—mildly hot. Four spices—white peppercorns, nutmeg, cloves, and cinnamon—combine in this frequently used French seasoning.

❧ Ras El Hanout—mildly hot to hot. The name is Arabic for top of the shop. The mixture includes a variety of spices from black peppercorns and cayenne to such nonpepper peppers as Jamaica pepper and grains of paradise. Dried rosebuds, tumeric, mace, lavender, and even Spanish Fly may be added at the discretion of the shop owner. The mixture can be approximated at home and is used in many Moroccan dishes.

❧ Recaito—mild. This condiment is frequently called for in Puerto Rican cooking. A green sauce redolent of coriander, onion, garlic, and bell pepper, it jazzes up dishes from beans to stews. A prepared version is bottled by Goya Foods.

❧ Shichimitogarashi—hot. This is a Japanese "on-the-table" condiment made from seven spices—ground hot red peppers, sesame, mustard, poppy seeds, dried tangerine peel, rape, and *sansho* (Japanese pepper leaf).

❧ Sofrito—mild. Bell peppers, onions, tomatoes, pork, and spices form the basis of this preparation, which is the foundation of much Hispanic cooking. It is used as a seasoning for fricasees, stews, asopaos, and other dishes. It can be made at home or purchased prepared in the specialty area of the supermarket.

❧ Tea spice—mildly hot. This is a powder made of ground ginger, black pepper, mint, pepper root, cardamom, cloves, and nutmeg. In India it is used, as the name suggests, to season tea.

FALSE FRIENDS

When Is a Pepper Not a Pepper?

Here are some peppers that are really not pepper at all.

❧ Anise pepper—mildly hot. The berries of an indigenous Chinese tree, *xanthoyxlum pipertum*, these are used in five-spice powder. They are also called Szechwan pepper.

❧ Brazil pepper—mildly hot. Not a member of the *piper nigrum* family, this plant, which is sometimes called Florida holly, produces a berry that is marketed as pink peppercorns.

Extremely popular in nouvelle cuisine dishes several years ago, it declined in popularity when it was discovered that it could cause a severe allergic reaction.

Cubebs—mild. Once used for seasoning and mentioned in the Bible, this form of the *piper* genus is now used only in medicine.

Grains of paradise—hot. This name has been used to refer to a variety of spices. It is frequently applied to the spicy brown seeds of the West African plant *Aframomum melegueta*, which is related to cardamom and allspice. The grains are used as a substitute for pepper. This spice is also known as Guinea pepper and melegueta pepper (not to be confused with the West African habañero chiles known as Guinea peppers and the Brazilian chiles known as malagueta pepper).

Jamaica pepper—mild. This is simply another name for allspice, which is used in baking and preserving. It is also called pimiento and toute épice.

Long pepper—mildly hot to hot. This spice, genus *piper* but species *longum*, also produces peppercorns, which are longer and more oval than those of the *piper nigrum*. The berries are sweeter and not as pungent. This spice was much used in classical times for it was thought of by the ancients as pepper. Today it is rarely used as a spice, but it still occasionally turns up in mixtures like Morocco's Ras el Hanout.

Monk's pepper—mildly hot. This ironically named spice is used infrequently and is reputed to be an aphrodisiac.

PURCHASING AND PRESERVING PEPPER, BELL PEPPERS, AND CHILES

PEPPER

The most important thing to remember when buying peppercorns is that preground pepper is only spicy dust. Its flavor does not resemble the piquant taste of freshly ground pepper. It has lost its pungency and is frequently even adulterated with such items as ground date pits. No true lover of hot stuff would ever use preground white or black pepper.

Many types of black and white pepper with different flavors are available on the market. The major variable in purchasing pepper is freshness. Home grinding, therefore, is essential. It takes only a few seconds, and the rewards are infinite. When purchasing peppercorns, look for those that are even in color, not too hard, even in size, aromatic, and free from dust.

To preserve peppercorns, store them in an airtight container in a cool place.

☙ HOW TO PURCHASE A PEPPER MILL

A good working pepper mill is a must for any good cook. Finding one can be more difficult than one would think because of the profusion of designs, which can confuse the buyer. A good pepper mill is simple. It should be easy to fill, hold an adequate quantity of pepper, have a stainless steel grinding mechanism that can be adjusted from coarse to fine grain, and be easy to use. Above all, a pepper mill should not look like the pillar from the front porch of a Victorian gingerbread house or a hand-turned balustrade. There are no design prerequisites; however, stainless steel, pewter, glass, plastic, and wood seem to be the most common materials used.

In you have a transparent pepper mill, a mixture of black and white peppercorns with a few grains of allspice turns it into a decorative item.

☙ BELL PEPPERS

When purchasing red, green, or yellow bell peppers, look for firm, well-shaped, thick-fleshed specimens. Pale-colored bell peppers are immature and therefore not as flavorful. Shriveled, blemished, limp, or bruised ones should be discarded.

Unripe, or green, bell peppers and their ripe red and yellow counterparts are a good source of vitamin C and also contain some vitamin A. (Red peppers contain more vitamins than green ones.) They also contain small amounts of calcium, phosphorus, iron, sodium, magnesium, thiamin, riboflavin, and niacin. A three-and-a-half-ounce raw serving of green peppers contains about 22 calories. A similar-sized serving of raw red bell pepper has approximately 32 calories, making it an ideal snack food for dieters.

☙ FRESH CHILES

As with bell peppers, chiles must be carefully examined before purchase. The same caveats apply. If you're buying in bulk, pick over the chiles and be sure to remove ripening or soft ones for immediate use. Chiles will keep up to four weeks if wrapped in a paper towel in a moisture-free area of the refrigerator. Plastic bags are anathema because they will retain the moisture the chiles produce and cause them to rot. Check the chiles periodically, removing those that are softening for use.

Fresh green chiles, like the chile Serrano, the New Mexico green chile, and the Anaheim, may be frozen. They should be boiled for about ten minutes or toasted before freezing. Fresh green chiles should never be frozen raw because they will lose their bite and taste.

To roast chiles or bell peppers. Place the peppers or chiles on the boiler rack and cook them, turning frequently until the skins blister and char. Remove them and place them in a paper bag for a few minutes. (The moisture will accumulate and make peeling easier.) Remove from the paper bag and peel, core, and seed the chiles according to the recipe directions. Be sure to read the chile caveats that follow before handling hot chiles.

Many people find it easy to preserve fresh red chiles in already prepared sauces, which can be either refrigerated or frozen. One method produces a hot paste that is then added to dishes during cooking. (See below.)

☙ HOT CHILE PASTE

Grind fresh red chiles in a food processor or blender with a small amount of salt until the mixture becomes a thick paste. Place the chile paste in small freezer packages of about four tablespoons each. (One tablespoon of paste is the equivalent of two chiles.) Store the packages in the freezer. When ready to use, allow the paste to thaw, drain off any liquid, and use in cooking as you would fresh chiles.

Other red chile sauces are listed in the recipe section.

◆§ DRIED CHILES

Chiles are best sun-dried. Some, like the Chipotle, are even dried and then smoked. Outside of the Southwest, however, it is difficult to determine what method of drying was used. When selecting dried chiles, it is essential to pick them over to be sure they are free of insects and maggots, have a glossy red color, and are free of spots.

If the chiles are in good shape when purchased, they will last for an indefinite period of time, but they should be picked over periodically to remove any that have spoiled. Dried chiles should be kept in a cool, dry place.

Even when purchasing ready-made dried red chile wreaths or *ristras* be sure to check them over and remove any imperfect ones so that they do not adulterate the others.

Some forms of dried chile pods are marketed in cellophane bags. They, too, should be checked for color and insects. To ensure freshness, you may, if you dare, ask the shop owner how long they've been on the shelf. These too, should be stored in a cool, dark place.

CHILE CAVEATS—LET THE USER BEWARE

Chiles contain highly volatile oils that can irritate and even burn skin and eyes. For this reason, it is important to wear rubber gloves when working with chiles. Be sure not to touch your face or eyes while working and when through, wash your hands thoroughly with warm, soapy water.

If you feel that rubber gloves are impossible to work in, rub your hands with cooking oil before handling chiles. The oil protects the skin.

If, despite warnings, you should feel the tingling irritation that is a sign of a chile burn, soak your hands in milk to soothe the irritation. Again, be sure not to touch your eyes. If the chile has come into contact with your eyes or mucous membranes, however, flush them immediately with cold water. Alternately, sugar can be rubbed on oiled hands to neutralize chile burns.

Finally, when working with dried chiles, be sure to use only cold water. Hot water poured on dried chiles may produce fumes that can irritate the nose and eyes.

LOWERING THE THERMOSTAT

Sometimes even the most avid lover of hot stuff will find it necessary to temper the heat of a chile or chile sauce. Here are a few methods of beating the heat. The most simple, of course, is to diminish the number of chiles used in the recipe, but the heat is not always evident at the early stages of cooking.

❧ Removing the ribs and all seeds from a chile before using it will diminish the heat. The seeds are the hottest part of the chile.

❧ Fresh chiles can be tempered by soaking them in cold water or in a five-to-one mixture of water and vinegar for three-quarters of an hour.

❧ Placing chiles in a pot of cold water and bringing it to a boil will also attenuate the heat of a chile.

❧ For dried chile sauces, combining the chile powder with paprika will lower the heat. Alternatively, you can increase the amount of tomato product used in the sauce base.

❧ Fresh bell pepper pulp can also be used to lower the thermostat in red and green chile sauces.

PUTTING OUT THE FIRE

If despite all precautions you take a bite that is just too darned hot, don't despair. Eat a bit of banana or avocado or a piece of bread. Try a mouthful of bland pasta or potato. Drink wine or beer and not the cold water you'd think would do the job. You'll feel better.

The recipes in *Hot Stuff* explore the myriad culinary possibilities of *piper nigrum* and the capsicum family. They can be used as condiments, as spices, as vegetables, and as all-around food enhancers. The recipes range from mild to incendiary. As with any cookbook, the recipes are blueprints. Novice cooks will want to follow them exactly; more experienced cooks may wish to experiment and add their own variations. As a taste for hot stuff develops, you may find that another grinding of pepper or another chile or two slipped into the stew will add a bit of piquancy.

All the recipes in *Hot Stuff* are graded with a rating of one to four peppers so that the uninitiated will not sear their palates.

One pepper = mild stuff
Two peppers = mildly hot stuff
Three peppers = hot stuff
Four peppers = very hot stuff

◆§ Hot Stuff in Africa

I WAS STARING at several pieces of unidentifiable brown meat floating in a murky green liquid with bits of red pepper. The whole was covered with a bright orange slick of palm oil. It was called Soupikandia, a delicacy from the Casamance region of Senegal, and it was my introduction to African cooking. My heart sank, but because I was eating at a friend's home, I gamely tackled a few mouthfuls, thankful that the slippery palm oil aided its rapid descent to my stomach without requiring me to chew. I washed it down with gallons of the accompanying tamarind juice, but no one had informed me of its prodigious laxative powers. The next day it was clear that I would have to tackle African cuisine in another manner.

Undaunted, though cautious, I tried again, the next time in the home of some friends in the Ivory Coast. Foutou (pounded bananas) with Sauce Claire was on the menu, and it was just my luck to get the fish eye. The Foutou was not too bad—it had the consistency and taste of old banana bubble gum—and the tomatoey fish sauce was quite good. The fish eye slid down the same way the Soupikandia had. There just had to be more to African cooking than slippery, unidentifiable things in murky sauces.

My third time I won. It was on a Sunday evening in Senegal. "Poulet Yassa," my friends said, "marinated chicken with lemon, onion, and pepper." It sounded delicious. It came steaming and hot, accompanied by fluffy short-grained Senegalese rice. It looked appetizing—no palm oil floated on top. Could I have found the right African dish? I tasted. The chicken was succulent, delicately flavored with lemon, and the onions were lightly sautéed to a golden brown and redolent with peppery oil. Indeed, the yassa was a success, and it started me on an African culinary odyssey that hasn't stopped yet.

African menus usually consist of fried foods, stews served over starches, and grilled dishes. Although many areas have adopted sophisticated Western culinary techniques, the traditional dishes are frequently cooked over open fires, and this method usually serves best.

Pepper is a hallmark of African cooking. In Ghana a "good" pepper is one that makes eaters break out in a sweat and mop their brows. Marketplaces from Marrakech to Abidjan to Kinshasa to Mombasa, from the Cape to Cairo, all have a section where pepper is sold. Pepper seasons Kilichili, the dried meat that means Niger to some; it mixes with tomatoes to form Senegal's national dish, Thiebou Dienne (rice and fish stew). It combines with chicken, onion, tomatoes, and ginger to form the Ivory Coast's Kedjenou, and it turns up in Ghana's Groundnut Stew. Ethiopia's cooking would be bland were it not for Berberé, a red pepper and spice paste. Harissa puts the bite into Tunisian and Moroccan Couscous, and no self-respecting Togolese would think of eating a meal without an accompanying plate of Pili Pili.

African food covers such a range of tastes that everyone is bound to find something to love. Those familiar with black cooking in the Americas will recognize many dishes. Benin's Akkra and Brazil's Acarajé, for example, are twin sisters separated only by the Atlantic. Benin's Sauce Feuilles bears a striking resemblance to collard greens but is served with smoked fish instead of smoked pork. Senegal's Thiebou Nop Niébé is nothing more than Hoppin' John or the Caribbean's Peas and Rice. In Africa, where the communal aspect of a meal still carries weight, eating takes time. Tastes tend to be a bit strong, and the recipes in *Hot Stuff* have been adjusted to accommodate the American palate. Senegalese cooks use more oil than weight and health-conscious

Americans would consume, and a strangled cry for water would be heard throughout the land if we added as much pepper as is used by most African cooks.

The following are traditional African recipes adapted for Western tastes and Western kitchens. Substitutions have been made for African products that are not readily available. Mail order sources for some less common products are listed at the end of the book. As with all of the recipes in *Hot Stuff*, these may be considered blueprints. African cooks will readily substitute one spice for another when the first is not available; they will add another chile or reduce the number to cater to the tastes of the guests. In short, they will improvise each time to respond to the ingredients available and to individual palates.

Before proceeding with any recipes calling for hot chiles, refer to the Chile Caveats in the front of the book.

SOUPE D'AVOCAT
(WEST AFRICA)

This chilled avocado soup with a spicy twist is made in many parts of West Africa. It is a perfect dish for the summer season when avocados are plentiful and cooking is anathema.

SERVES SIX

2 ripe avocados
4 cups cold chicken broth
2 tablespoons freshly squeezed lime juice
$\frac{1}{4}$ teaspoon cayenne pepper
Salt and freshly ground black pepper to taste

Peel the avocados and mash them in a food processor or blender until they are a smooth paste. Add the paste to the chicken broth, stirring well so the soup is homogeneous. Add the remaining ingredients, mix thoroughly, and chill in the refrigerator for at least 1 hour before serving. Garnish with freshly chopped chives and diced avocado bits and serve cold.

PEANUT SOUP
(WEST AFRICA)

The peanut is one of the major starches in Africa. It abounds in African cooking and is found in dishes ranging from Senegalese Mafe to Ghanian Groundnut Stew. It is only natural, therefore, that this root should have found its way into the cooking pots of Africa as a peanut soup.

SERVES SIX

2 teaspoons cornstarch
3 cups milk
3 cups chicken broth
2 cups crunchy peanut butter
2 tablespoons grated onion
½ cup parsley, chopped
Salt and freshly ground black pepper to taste
¼ teaspoon cayenne pepper

Mix the cornstarch and the milk until smooth. Place the mixture in a soup ketttle or a large saucepan and add the other ingredients, reserving ¼ cup of the parsley for garnishing the soup. Bring the soup to a boil while stirring constantly. Then lower the heat and simmer for 15 minutes while continuing to stir. Strain the soup and serve it hot. Garnish each bowl with a sprinkling of freshly chopped parsley.

SOUPE CASAMANÇAIS
(SENEGAL)

The Casamance region in the south of Senegal has maintained many African traditions. It is the home of such favorite Senegalese recipes as Poulet Yassa (page 89). Soupe Casamançais is a fish soup. If the quantity of water is reduced, the same mixture can be served over white rice as a main dish.

SERVES FOUR TO SIX

1 large onion, chopped
2 tablespoons peanut oil
2 pounds fresh fish fillets (cod, haddock, or another meaty white fish)
½ tablespoon hot red chile, chopped
Salt and freshly ground black pepper to taste
1 quart cold water (1 pint if using as a main course)
Juice of 4 lemons

Fry the onion in the oil until golden. Add the fish fillets and the chopped chile and cook for 5 minutes. Add the salt and pepper and the cold water. Let the mixture simmer over low heat for 20 minutes. Add the lemon juice and cook for an additional 5 minutes. Serve hot as a soup or over rice as a main dish stew.

SPICY OYSTERS (BENIN)

Both sea oysters and large mangrove oysters abound in West Africa. Sweet and succulent, they are the basis for this dish, which is similar to Togolese Azi Dessi Sauce.

SERVES SIX

6 dozen oysters
⅓ cup freshly squeezed lemon juice
1 teaspoon powdered ginger
½ teaspoon cayenne pepper
5 ripe tomatoes, peeled and seeded
¼ cup peanut oil
1 medium onion, chopped fine
Salt and freshly ground black pepper to taste

Shuck the oysters and place them in a deep dish. Cover them with the lemon juice and powder lightly with the ginger and the cayenne.

Peel and seed the tomatoes and grind them into a fine paste in a food processor or blender. In a small saucepan, heat the oil, add the tomato paste, and cook over low heat, stirring constantly with a wooden spoon until it has the consistency of catsup. Add the onion, salt, and pepper. Place the oysters in the sauce and simmer on a low flame for 5 to 10 minutes. Serve immediately with white rice.

OEUFS DIABLO
(SENEGAL)

In Senegal, a dinner frequently begins with a plate of fresh hors d'oeuvres. Grated carrots vinaigrette, ripe red tomatoes covered with minced garlic and dressed with a drizzle of oil and vinegar, smooth, creamy potato salad, and Oeufs Diablo are favorites for such a plate.

SERVES SIX AS AN APPETIZER

6 eggs
3 tablespoons freshly made mayonnaise
2 hot red guinea pepper type chiles
1 teaspoon dry mustard
1 tablespoon Cocktail Sauce (see page 54)

Boil the eggs until hard and then plunge them into cold water. Peel the eggs and cut them in half lengthwise. Remove the yolks and reserve the white intact. In a small bowl, mix the other ingredients until they form a smooth paste. Add the egg yolks and continue to mix well. Pile the mixture into the egg whites. (You may wish to use a pastry bag to give this dish an added fillip.) Garnish with hot Hungarian paprika and serve as part of an appetizer plate.

AKKRA
(BENIN)

Akkra is a traditional West African appetizer. Originating in Benin, the dish is now ubiquitous throughout West Africa, where women in almost any major city can be seen sitting behind caldrons frying Akkras. The appetizer has even migrated to the

French Antilles, where it is known as Accra and made with codfish or other ingredients, and to Brazil, where it is called Acarajé and made with black-eyed peas and served not only as an appetizer but as a ritual dish for the goddess Yansan in the Candomblé religion.

SERVES SIX AS AN APPETIZER

1½ cups dried white beans
½ cup water with 2 teaspoons salt added
3 cups peanut oil for frying (A mixture of two parts peanut oil to one part galm oil gives a more authentic taste.)

Wash and soak the beans and cook them according to package directions. When cooked, drain them and place them in a blender with the salted water. Blend until they form a thick, doughlike paste. Heat the oil to 350 to 375 degrees in a deep, heavy saucepan or a deep fat fryer. Drop in the mixture one teaspoon at a time and fry until it is golden brown. Drain the fritters on paper towels and serve while hot with Hot Sauce for Akkra (below).

HOT SAUCE FOR AKKRA (BENIN)

This all-purpose hot sauce can be served with Akkra, the small bean fritters that mean Benin to some, or with almost anything that can use a dash of liquid fire.

YIELD = 1½ CUPS

3 tablespoons peanut oil
1 medium onion, chopped fine
2 small hot red chiles, diced fine
½ cup tomato paste
½ cup water
Salt and freshly ground black pepper to taste

Heat the oil and fry the onion until it is browned. Add the diced hot chiles. Combine the tomato paste and the water and add to the mixture. Let the sauce simmer for 5 minutes; add salt and freshly ground black pepper to taste, then cool. Serve with appetizers such as Boulettes de Poisson (page 41) and Akkra (pages 37–38).

CRUDITÉS À LA TUNISIENNE (TUNISIA)

This is a North African variation of crudités. It uses cream cheese (as found in American supermarkets) and Harissa (page 60), the pepper paste that is the traditional accompaniment to couscous. To make a milder version the quantity of Harissa may be diminished.

SERVES EIGHT AS AN APPETIZER

1 (8-ounce) package cream cheese
1 tablespoon milk
1 tablespoon Harissa
2 tablespoons tomato paste
Salt to taste
3 bell peppers—1 green, 1 yellow, 1 red
1 bunch celery hearts
6 carrots
1 cucumber
2 bunches scallions
1 small cauliflower

In a bowl, mix the cream cheese, milk, Harissa, and tomato paste. Taste the mixture and add salt and more tomato paste or Harissa as desired. The cheese should have a deep rosy hue. Chill the mixture in the refrigerator before serving.

Wash the vegetables and place them in iced water for a quarter of an hour so they will be crisp. Remove and drain them. Then cut the peppers into long strips; separate the celery into stalks, discarding the tough ones; and cut the carrots and cucumber into long strips. Trim and tail the scallions and separate the cauliflower into florets.

Arrange the vegetables on a platter around the bowl holding the dip. Serve as an appetizer course or with cocktails.

FISH CAKES À L'AFRICAINE (IVORY COAST)

Fish is a major staple of the Ivory Coast. In addition to being served in stews and soups and grilled, it appears in fish cakes. These are a spicy addition to any fish repertoire.

SERVES FOUR

2 pounds fish fillets (any firm, white-fleshed fish will do)
2 eggs, beaten
1 clove garlic, minced
2 tablespoons salt
1 teaspoon ground, hot red chile
2 tablespoons flour
1 cup peanut oil for frying

Poach the fish fillets in water to cover for about 5 minutes or until they are tender. Drain and chop them fine. Add the eggs, garlic, salt, chile, and flour and mix thoroughly. Form the mixture into 3-inch cakes. In a heavy frying pan or a deep fat fryer heat the oil to 350 to 375 degrees and fry the cakes until they are golden brown and crisp on both sides. Drain on paper towels and serve them warm. The fish cakes can be accompanied by Cocktail Sauce (page 54), Pili Pili Sauce (page 58), or Sauce for Fish Cakes (below).

SAUCE FOR FISH CAKES (IVORY COAST)

SERVES FOUR TO SIX

2 medium-sized onions, chopped coarse
2 cloves garlic, chopped

- 4 large ripe tomatoes, peeled, seeded, and chopped
- 1 (6-ounce) can tomato paste
- 1 teaspoon ground hot red chile
- ½ teaspoon freshly ground black pepper

Place all the ingredients in the bowl of a blender or food processor and grind until they form a well-mixed, thick sauce. Place the sauce in a saucepan and cook it over low heat for 20 minutes. Serve as soon as the sauce is cooked and the fish cakes are prepared.

BOULETTES DE POISSON (SENEGAL)

I first tasted Boulettes de Poisson at a restaurant called the Niani overlooking the water in Dakar, Senegal. Somehow, the taste of the fish balls mingled with the view of Gorée Island in the distance and the vast Atlantic Ocean beyond stretching to the Americas. The crispy fish balls, dipped in a hot sauce, quickly became a daily dish, and this was one of the first West African recipes I learned how to cook.

SERVES FOUR TO SIX

- 1 cup coarse French bread crumbs
- 1 cup boiling water
- 2 pounds red snapper fillets (or any non-oily white-meat fish), cut into small pieces
- ¼ cup parsley and scallions, mixed half and half, chopped fine
- 1 teaspoon garlic, chopped fine
- Salt and freshly ground white pepper to taste
- 1 cup flour
- 3 or more cups peanut oil for deep frying
- 2 lemons cut into wedges

Put the bread crumbs in a bowl and pour the boiling water over them. Soak the bread for 5 minutes and let it cool. Squeeze the bread to remove the water and discard the liquid. In a large bowl, combine the bread, fish, parsley, scallions, garlic, salt, and pepper. Combine the ingredients in a blender or food processor, a bit at a time, until the mixture becomes a thick, smooth paste. Transfer the paste to a clean bowl. With floured hands, roll the mixture, approximately 2 tablespoons at a time, into 1-inch balls. Place the fish balls on heavily floured waxed paper and refrigerate for 1 hour. Pour the peanut oil into a heavy frying pan or deep fat fryer to a depth of 3 inches and heat to 350 to 375 degrees. Fry the fish balls, a few at a time, for about 7 minutes or until they are cooked through and golden brown. Serve immediately, garnished with lemon wedges. The Boulettes de Poisson can be accompanied by a Pili Pili Sauce (page 58) or by Spicy Tomato Sauce (below).

SPICY TOMATO SAUCE
(SENEGAL)

This sauce is a traditional accompaniment for Boulettes de Poisson. The mixture of crunchy fish balls and piquant tomato sauce brings together the tang of the sea and the spicy side of West African cooking.

YIELD = 2½ CUPS

2 cups tomatoes, peeled, seeded, and chopped coarse
1 medium-sized onion, chopped coarse
1 tablespoon fresh ginger, minced
1 small hot red chile, seeded and chopped fine
Salt and freshly ground black pepper to taste

Mix all the ingredients in a blender or food processor until they form a paste. Serve with Boulettes de Poisson (page 41) or any other grilled fish or meat dish.

YAM FRITTERS
(ALL AFRICA)

Fritters are found throughout Africa. Fried in bubbling black caldrons in the marketplaces, they are served as accompaniments to main dish stews and as special treats for children after school. Yam Fritters also make excellent appetizers when served with a spicy cocktail sauce or a piquant Pili Pili.

SERVES FOUR TO SIX

- 1½ pounds yams
- 1 medium-sized onion, chopped fine
- 1 medium-sized tomato, peeled, seeded, and chopped fine
- ½ hot green chile, seeded and chopped fine
- 3 or more cups peanut oil for frying
- ¼ teaspoon thyme
- ¼ teaspoon cayenne pepper
- ¼ teaspoon freshly ground black pepper
- ½ teaspoon salt
- 1 egg, beaten
- ½ cup freshly made bread crumbs

Boil the yams in their skins about 25 minutes or until they are tender. Peel them and mash them in a food mill until they are smooth. Sauté the chopped onion, tomato, and chile in a few tablespoons of the oil until they are brown. Add the spices and the sautéed mixture to the mashed yams. Add the beaten egg and the bread crumbs and work the mixture until all ingredients are well blended. Form the paste into small balls. In a heavy pot or a deep fat fryer, heat the oil to 350 to 375 degrees and drop in the yam balls one at a time. Fry them until they are browned and crisp on all sides. Drain them on paper towels and serve immediately with Pili Pili Sauce (page 58).

BANANA SNACKS
(ALL AFRICA)

Bananas come in all sizes and shapes in Africa. Tiny ones no longer than baby fingers make sweet and succulent snacks. Larger plantains, too harsh to be eaten raw, are served only cooked or mashed into Foufou balls (page 62). Other bananas are eaten, as ours, either raw or cooked. This is the variety that goes into the making of banana snacks.

SERVES FOUR

2 large ripe bananas
1 small onion, chopped fine
1 tomato, seeded, peeled, and chopped fine
½ small red chile, seeded and chopped fine
Salt and freshly ground black pepper to taste
1 teaspoon grated fresh ginger
1 cup wheat flour
⅛ cup water
3 or more cups peanut oil for frying

Peel the bananas and mash them in a food processor or a food mill. Add the chopped onion, tomato, and chile and continue to mash. Then add the salt, pepper, and ginger. Combine the flour and water and add to the mixture while you continue to mash. In a heavy saucepan or a deep fat fryer, heat the oil to 350 to 375 degrees. Drop the banana mixture, ½ teaspoon at a time, into the oil. Fry the mixture until it is golden brown and crisp on both sides. Banana snacks should be soft on the inside and crisp on the outside. They can be served hot or cold or as an alternative starch with any of the main dish stews.

AVOCAT EPICÉ
(IVORY COAST)

When it's avocado season on the Ivory Coast, the markets in Treicheville, Cocody, and Adjamé, districts of the capital, Abidjan, are filled with smooth, ripe, eggplant-hued avocados. They're smaller than the ones we usually see on the East Coast of the United States, but they're as rich as cream in consistency and delicious when prepared in any number of ways. One way is Avocat Epicé, an appetizer that is similar to Mexico's guacamole, but without the coriander.

SERVES FOUR

- 2 avocados, ripe but not overripe
- 1 small onion, chopped fine
- 1 small tomato, chopped fine
- 1½ tablespoons peanut oil
- 2 small hot red chiles, chopped fine
- Juice of one lime
- Salt and freshly ground black pepper to taste

Halve the avocados lengthwise. Remove and reserve the meat but leave the shell intact to serve as a dish for each portion. Mash the reserved avocado with all the other ingredients to form a thick paste. Return the mixture to the shell. Squeeze a bit of lime juice over them and serve immediately. This is a perfect light, spicy summer first course.

SALADE D'AVOCAT ET CRABE (IVORY COAST)

Those preferring shellfish may wish to try this alternative to Avocat Epicé. Or, for a gala dinner, make a bit of each and give your guests a choice.

SERVES FOUR

- 2 large, ripe avocados
- Juice of one lemon
- ½ pound fresh crabmeat
- ½ cup cucumber, peeled and chopped
- 1 cup Cocktail Sauce (page 54)

Cut the avocados in half lengthwise. Remove and reserve the meat, leaving the shell intact to serve as a dish. Rub the lemon juice over the cut shells to keep the avocado from discoloring. Dice the reserved meat into ¼-inch pieces. Mix the avocado, crabmeat, cucumber, and Cocktail Sauce and heap the mixture into the shells. Serve chilled. This dish should be made just before serving so that the avocado does not discolor. Lobster, shrimp, or any cooked white fish may be substituted for the crabmeat.

SLATA FILFIL
(MOROCCO)

This Moroccan salad is a cooling accompaniment to any grilled dish.

SERVES SIX

1 pound green bell peppers
2 tablespoons olive oil
1 tablespoon peanut oil
2 tablespoons freshly squeezed lemon juice
1 teaspoon cumin
1 tablespoon flat-leaf parsley, chopped fine
Salt and freshly ground black pepper to taste

Grill the peppers in the broiler, turning them until they are charred on the outside. Remove the charred skin. Core and cut the peppers into long, thin strips and place them in a serving dish. Mix the remaining ingredients and pour over the peppers. Mix the peppers and the dressing well and serve.

COOKED CARROT SALAD
(NORTH AFRICA)

SERVES FOUR

6 to 8 carrots, cleaned and scraped
2 cups salt water
1 teaspoon sweet paprika

¼ teaspoon cayenne pepper
1 teaspoon cumin
2 tablespoons peanut oil
2 tablespoons white wine vinegar
1 tablespoon parsley, chopped fine (the flat Italian type is preferable)
Salt and freshly ground black pepper to taste

Wash the carrots; peel them and cut them into ¼-inch rounds. Place them in a saucepan with two cups of salt water and the garlic clove. Cook the carrots for 15 minutes, drain well, and set aside. Mix the paprika, cayenne, cumin, peanut oil, vinegar, and parsley in a small bowl. Pour the dressing over the carrots. Leave the salad warm or chill it in the refrigerator and serve it cold. This salad is an excellent summer dish and a good accompaniment to grilled meats and spicy stews.

MECHOUIA
(TUNISIA)

Not to be confused with the Senegalese Mechoui—a spit-grilled whole baby lamb—this is a simple salad made with tomatoes, eggs, and, naturally, pepper.

SERVES SIX

4 firm, ripe tomatoes
8 green bell peppers
3 hot chiles (habañero type)
4 cloves garlic
4 tablespoons olive oil
1 teaspoon dried coriander
Juice of 1 lemon
Salt and freshly ground pepper to taste
1 dozen black olives (Niçoise-type)
4 hard-boiled eggs

Grill the tomatoes, bell peppers, chiles, and garlic in the broiler, turning them frequently. When brown, peel and seed the tomatoes; core, peel, and seed the bell peppers and the chiles; peel the garlic. Place the vegetables in a food processor and chop them fine. Place them in a salad bowl. Add the olive oil, coriander, lemon juice, salt, and pepper. Mix well and adjust for taste. Decorate with black olives and slices of hard-boiled egg. This salad can be served warm or cold.

Alternately, this salad can be made with julienned strips of the grilled vegetables. (To facilitate peeling the bell peppers and the chiles after grilling, wrap them individually in paper towels. The peppers' skins will swell slightly and come off more easily.)

CARROT SAMBAL (EAST AFRICA)

The culinary traditions of East Africa not only incorporate the dishes of the African continent, they also display the influences of colonial powers and the tastes brought to the area by immigrants from Malaysia and the Indies. Carrot Sambal is testimony to just such tastes. It can be served as a salad or as an accompaniment to curries and grilled dishes.

SERVES SIX

1 pound carrots
Sugar syrup made from 1½ cups of sugar boiled with ½ cup of water
1 tablespoon ginger, minced
1 clove garlic, minced
Seeds from 2 cardamom pods, ground
1½ teaspoons ground hot red chile
1 teaspoon salt
¾ cup distilled white vinegar

Scrape and mince the carrots. Bring the water and sugar to a boil. Add the carrots, chile, ginger, garlic, cardamom seeds, and salt. Cook for 15 minutes. Add the vinegar and cook, stirring constantly, until thick. Chill and serve to accompany curries and grilled meats.

CUCUMBER SAMBAL
(EAST AFRICA)

Southeast Asia's influence on East Africa is found in the sambals and chutneys that accompany curried dishes. This sambal uses cucumbers and hot chiles to create an accompaniment for chicken curry.

SERVES SIX

3 fresh cucumbers, peeled
1 teaspoon salt
1 tablespoon distilled white vinegar
½ teaspoon dried red chiles

Grate the cucumbers into a bowl. Sprinkle them with the salt and let them stand for 1 hour, then drain. Add the distilled vinegar and the dried chiles. Mix well and serve chilled. This is a good accompaniment to any curry dish, but it goes particularly well with chicken curry.

SAALOUK SALAD
(MOROCCO)

SERVES SIX

2 small eggplant
3 small zucchini
1 large clove garlic, minced
1 teaspoon salt
½ cup peanut oil
1 teaspoon mild paprika
4 firm, ripe tomatoes
2 small hot red chiles

Wash and peel the eggplant and zucchini and cut them into 1-inch dice. Place them in a saucepan with the garlic, salt, oil, and paprika. Cover with water. Peel, seed, and quarter the tomatoes.

Add them to the saucepan. Let the mixture cook over medium heat for 5 minutes, stirring constantly. When almost done, grill the hot chiles in the broiler; when charred, remove them from the heat, place in a paper bag for a few minutes, and then peel and seed them. Dice them and add them to the mixture as it cooks. Allow the Saalouk to boil down until no liquid is left. The salad can be eaten warm or chilled and served cold. It will keep for 2 or 3 days in the refrigerator.

MOROCCAN PEPPER SALAD
(MOROCCO)

Sweet bell peppers find their way into many North African salads. This one, from Morocco, is similar to the Tunisian Mechouia (page 47), but with a twist—a hint of lemon juice.

SERVES SIX

1 pound sweet green and red bell peppers
Salt to taste
1 teaspoon cumin
3 tablespoons freshly squeezed lemon juice
2 tablespoons olive oil
1 tablespoon peanut oil
2 teaspoons chopped parsley
¼ teaspoon ground hot red chile

Grill the peppers in the broiler until they are charred. Remove them from the oven and place them in a brown paper bag. Peel and cut them into ½-inch dice. Add salt, cumin, lemon, oils, parsley, and chile. Mix the ingredients well and serve cold.

FRIED BELL PEPPER AND TOMATO SALAD
(MOROCCO)

SERVES FOUR

2 red bell peppers
2 green bell peppers

4 tablespoons olive oil
4 ripe tomatoes, halved and seeded
3 tablespoons freshly squeezed lemon juice
1 teaspoon cumin
Salt and freshly ground black pepper to taste

Wash and dry the peppers. Heat the oil in a frying pan and fry the tomato halves and the peppers. Reserve the frying fat. Peel the vegetables after they are fried. Cut the peppers in half lengthwise and arrange them on a platter alternating red peppers, green peppers, and tomatoes. Prepare a dressing of 4 tablespoons of the frying fat, the lemon juice, the cumin, and salt and freshly ground black pepper to taste. Mix the ingredients well and pour them over the salad. Allow it to cool before serving. You may wish to garnish this dish with chopped parsley.

PEANUT SAUCE (ALL AFRICA)

Sauces are used in Africa to accompany starches and to spice up grilled dishes. This one combines the crunch of the peanut and the bite of hot pepper.

SERVES FOUR

1 cup crunchy peanut butter
2 cups water
Salt to taste
½ teaspoon dried red chile, crushed
2 tablespoons minced onion
1 tablespoon peanut oil

Place the peanut butter, water, salt, and chile in a saucepan. Simmer the mixture, stirring well, for 10 minutes. Sauté the onion in the oil until it is golden and add it to the sauce. Continue to stir well and simmer the mixture for another 10 minutes. Serve the sauce warm in a gravy boat as an accompaniment to mashed potatoes, Foufou (page 62), or any of the other African starches.

DYNAMITE
(WEST AFRICA)

Peppers are a way of life in West Africa. So, when cooks find excellent ones in the local market, they make large purchases and take them home to transform them into something that American expatriates have aptly named "Dynamite." Dynamite will not keep in the refrigerator for more than a month; however, it can be frozen in small quantities and then thawed and used in place of fresh chiles as needed.

YIELD = 2 CUPS

- 1 pound small hot chiles (in Africa they are usually the lantern-shaped Guinea pepper)
- ¼ cup peanut oil
- 1 tablespoon salt

Wash the chiles, following the directions for handling peppers on page 29. Remove the stems and mince the chiles in a food processor. You can do this by hand, but it's time-consuming and you run the risk of chile burns. When the chiles are minced, add the oil, bit by bit. (You may not need all of it because you simply want to moisten the chiles. The type of chile you use will determine how much oil you need.) Add the salt and stir the mixture well. Remove a bit and reserve it for the first month's use. Place the rest, in small quantities, in freezer bags. The mixture will keep in the freezer for up to a year. It can be thawed to heat up any dish. When thawing, drain off any excess water before using.

CHERMOLA
(NORTH AFRICA)

This is a fish marinade that is used throughout the continent. The fish is washed and prepared for cooking. Then incisions are made in the skin and the whole fish is allowed to soak in the marinade so it takes on the mixture of flavors.

❧❧ **YIELD = 2½ CUPS**

1 cup peanut oil
¾ cup water
1 tablespoon mild paprika
½ tablespoon cayenne pepper
½ tablespoon cumin
3 cloves garlic, minced
1 lemon
⅓ cup fresh coriander, chopped

Mix the ingredients in a deep dish. Wash and dry the fish of your choice, make small diagonal incisions in the skin, and place the fish in the marinade. Allow the fish to marinate for 30 to 40 minutes, then prepare according to recipe directions.

PEPPER RELISH (BENIN)

This relish is good with grilled meats or as a spread on just about anything.

❧❧ **YIELD = ½ CUP**

3 large green bell peppers
1 hot chile
1 or more tablespoons olive oil
2 teaspoons cumin
Salt to taste

Bake the green bell peppers and the hot chile in a 400-degree oven for 20 minutes, or until brown. Plunge them into a bowl of cold water. Remove the charred skins, core, seed, and chop them fine. Add enough olive oil to obtain a paste of spreading consistency. Add the cumin and salt to taste and mix again. Store the relish in a jar in the refrigerator

COCKTAIL SAUCE
(ALL AFRICA)

This homemade cocktail sauce will add zest to almost any dish. It is also a part of the dressing for Salade d'Avocat et Crabe (page 45).

YIELD = 1½ CUPS

½ cup freshly made mayonnaise
½ cup catsup
2 teaspoons freshly grated horseradish
2 small hot chiles, chopped fine
1 tablespoon freshly squeezed lime juice
1 tablespoon Worcestershire sauce
Salt and freshly ground black pepper to taste

Mix the first six ingredients well. Season with salt and pepper. Serve chilled.

PALAVA SAUCE
(WEST AFRICA)

I always thought that this dish was called palaver sauce. It was a name I thought originated because every time this dish was served, folks spent a great deal of time discussing the food and the making of the dish. Imagine my surprise when I discovered the name had nothing to do with the word "palaver" at all. In Sierra Leone, they make their Palava Sauce with tripe, but this version simply calls for spinach and chopped meat.

SERVES FOUR TO SIX

1 pound fresh spinach
1 cup beef bouillon

2 medium-sized onions, chopped
2 fresh tomatoes, peeled, seeded, and chopped
2 small hard-boiled eggs, minced
1 hot green chile, seeded and chopped fine
4 tablespoons unsalted butter
½ cup cooked ground beef
½ cup smoked fish (trout, butterfish, or similar fish), chopped
1 teaspoon salt
¼ teaspoon mild paprika
Freshly ground black pepper

Wash and chop the spinach. Be sure to get rid of all the grit. Cook the spinach in the bouillon until it is tender. Pour off the stock and reserve it. Sauté the chopped onions, tomatoes, eggs, and chile in the butter for 10 minutes. Add the ground beef and the fish. Season with salt and pepper and add the spinach, stock, and paprika. Stir well and allow it to simmer for 15 minutes. Serve as a sauce over any of the West African starches.

BERBERÉ
(ETHIOPIA)*

Berberé is the name of Ethiopia's hot sauce. Made with red wine, pepper, spices, and 2 cups of paprika, it gives Ethiopian food its particular taste.

YIELD = 2 CUPS

1 teaspoon ground ginger
½ teaspoon ground cardamom
½ teaspoon ground coriander
½ teaspoon fenugreek seeds
¼ teaspoon ground nutmeg, preferably freshly grated
⅛ teaspoon ground cloves
⅛ teaspoon ground cinnamon

* From *Time/Life Foods of the World: African Cooking*, copyright © 1970 Time-Life Books, Inc.

- 1/8 teaspoon ground allspice
- 2 tablespoons onion, chopped fine
- 1 tablespoon garlic, chopped fine
- 2 tablespoons salt
- 3 tablespoons dry red wine
- 2 cups paprika
- 2 tablespoons ground hot red pepper
- 1/2 teaspoon freshly ground black pepper
- 1 1/2 cups water
- 1 to 2 tablespoons vegetable oil

In a heavy 2- to 3-quart saucepan (preferably one with an enameled or nonstick cooking surface), toast the ginger, cardamom, coriander, fenugreek, nutmeg, cloves, cinnamon, and allspice over low heat for a minute or so, stirring constantly until they are heated through. Then remove the pan from the heat and let the spices cool for 5 to 10 minutes.

Combine the toasted spices, onion, garlic, 1 tablespoon of the salt, and the wine in the jar of an electric blender and blend at high speed until the mixture is a smooth paste. (To make the paste with a mortar and pestle or in a bowl with the back of a spoon, pound the toasted spices, onion, garlic, and 1 tablespoon of salt together until pulverized. Add the wine and continue pounding until the mixture is a moist paste.)

Combine the paprika, red pepper, black pepper, and the remaining tablespoon of salt in the saucepan and toast them over low heat for a minute or so, until they are heated through, shaking the pan and stirring the spices constantly. Stir in the water, 1/4 cup at a time, then add the spice and wine mixture. Stirring vigorously, cook over the lowest possible heat for 10 to 15 minutes.

With a rubber spatula, transfer the Berberé to a jar or crock and pack it in tightly. Let the paste cool to room temperature, then dribble enough oil over the top to make a film at least 1/4-inch thick. Cover with foil or plastic wrap and refrigerate until ready to use. If you replenish the film of oil on top each time you use Berberé, it will keep in the refrigerator for 5 or 6 months.

NITER KEBBEH (ETHIOPIA)*

The Indians use ghee, the French butter, and the West Africans peanut oil, but Ethiopians use a spiced butter called Niter Kebbeh in much of their cooking. It can be made in advance and kept for up to 3 months.

YIELD = 2 CUPS

- 2 pounds unsalted butter, cut into small pieces
- 1 small onion, peeled and chopped coarse
- 3 tablespoons garlic, chopped fine
- 4 teaspoons fresh ginger root, chopped fine
- 1½ teaspoons turmeric
- 1 cardamom pod, slightly crushed with the flat of a knife, or a pinch of cardamom seeds
- 1 piece of stick cinnamon, 1 inch long
- 1 whole clove
- ⅛ teaspoon ground nutmeg, preferably freshly grated

In a heavy 4- to 5-quart saucepan, heat the butter over moderate heat, turning it about with a spoon to melt it slowly and completely without letting it brown. Then increase the heat and bring the butter to a boil. When the surface is completely covered with white foam, stir in the onion, garlic, ginger root, turmeric, cardamom, cinnamon, clove, and nutmeg. Reduce the heat to the lowest possible point and simmer uncovered and undisturbed for 45 minutes, or until the milk solids on the bottom of the pan are a golden brown and the butter on top is transparent.

Slowly pour the clear liquid Niter Kebbeh into a bowl, straining it through a fine sieve lined with a linen towel or four layers of dampened cheesecloth. Discard the seasonings. If there are any solids left in the Niter Kebbeh, strain it again to prevent it from becoming rancid later.

* From *Time/Life Foods of the World: African Cooking*, copyright © 1970 Time-Life Books, Inc.

Pour the Niter Kebbeh into a jar, cover tightly, and store in the refrigerator or at room temperature until ready to use. Niter Kebbeh will solidify when chilled. It can be kept safely, even at room tmperature, for 2 to 3 months.

PILI PILI SAUCE
(ALL AFRICA)

Pili Pili Sauce is found throughout Africa. The hot peppers are mixed with onions and garlic to form a sauce that is as widely used as catsup is in the United States. Batches are made up and then stored in the refrigerator. The sauce goes particularly well with grilled meats and with chilled seafoods such as shrimp or prawns.

YIELD = 2½ CUPS

2 cups tomato sauce
¼ cup onion, minced
1 clove garlic, minced
Juice of one lemon
2 small hot red chiles, minced
½ tablespoon freshly grated horseradish

Mix all the ingredients together thoroughly. Store in a tightly covered jar in the refrigerator. Serve with grilled meats, chilled fish dishes, or whenever you have an urge for something extra hot.

PILI PILI MAYONNAISE
(ALL AFRICA)

If Pili Pili Sauce is the equivalent of catsup, Pili Pili Mayonnaise is the equivalent of cocktail sauce. It has more of a bite than the red glop that comes out of jars, and the other advantage is that you make it yourself from scratch so that you know what went into it.

YIELD = 1 CUP

1 tablespoon Pili Pili Sauce
1 cup freshly made mayonnaise

Mix the ingredients together and serve as a dressing on cold fish salads and with summer dishes you wish to spice up.

OKRA SAUCE
(ALL AFRICA)

The ubiquitous okra pod appears again in this Okra Sauce, which can be served as an accompaniment to any of the African starches.

SERVES SIX

1 pound okra, chopped fine
½ cup water
1 teaspoon salt
1 medium-sized tomato, chopped coarse
½ teaspoon dried red chile

Prepare the okra by washing it, removing the tops and tails, and chopping it fine. Then place the okra in a saucepan and add the water, salt, tomato, and chile. Simmer the sauce for 10 minutes. Serve it hot in a gravy boat or a decorated calabash as an accompaniment to any of the African "mashes" or starch dishes.

PÂTÉ DE PIMENTS
(BENIN)

This is a simple Beninois version of the ubiquitous pepper sauce. It will keep for up to 6 months in the refrigerator when placed in a jar and covered with a ¼-inch film of oil.

YIELD = 2½ CUPS

2 cups hot red peppers, minced (seed if you wish a milder sauce)

HOT STUFF

1 medium-sized onion
One 1-inch piece of ginger, minced
Salt to taste

Purée all the ingredients in a food mill, food processor, or blender until they form a fine paste. Place the paste in a clean jar and cover with a layer of oil. This sauce is that simple. And it is a pepper lover's dream when it accompanies grilled meats, chicken or fish, and, of course, African sauces.

HARISSA
(TUNISIA)

This is a homemade Tunisian hot sauce that adds bite to couscous and makes grilled North African dishes sing with cayenne pepper.

YIELD = ¾ CUP

- ½ cup cayenne pepper
- ¼ cup ground cumin
- 2 tablespoons salt
- 3 tablespoons peanut oil

Combine all the dry ingredients in a small bowl and blend them thoroughly. Drizzle the oil into the mixture until it forms a thick paste. Place it in a small jar or bottle with a tight-fitting lid. Store in the refrigerator until ready to use. Remember—as they said in the hairdressing advertisements of the 1970s—"a little dab'l do ya." Use the Harissa sparingly because it will go a long way.

ALOCO
(IVORY COAST)

This Ivorian dish is a treat that is eaten by farm workers. It can also be purchased ready-made in the night market at Cocody, a part of the capital, Abidjan. There, by the light of kerosene lamps, women lean over heavy black iron caldrons cooking Aloco. The smell of frying blends with the aroma of wood smoke. Freshly fried, placed in your own dishes, and wrapped in brightly colored African cloth, the Aloco rarely arrives at home without someone's having a taste.

SERVES EIGHT TO TEN

8 firm, ripe plantains
3 cups palm oil
3 cups peanut oil

Peel the plantains and cut them into slices. Keep the slices about 1/8 inch thick so that you do not end up with plantain chips! Heat the oils in a heavy saucepan to 325 degrees. Fry the plantain slices in the oil until they are golden on the outside but still soft on the inside. Drain them and serve warm, accompanied by the following hot sauce.

SAUCE ALOCO

YIELD = 1/4 CUP

3 hot red chiles (Guinea pepper type)
2 small onions
4 tablespoons palm oil
Salt to taste

In a blender or food processor, grind the chiles and onions to a thick paste. You may have to add a teaspoon of water to help it blend. Heat the paste in a skillet along with the palm oil. Cook, mixing well, until the sauce is thoroughly warmed. Salt to taste and serve with Aloco or with any other dish.

Occasionally, Aloco is also eaten with sugar. In this case, omit the sauce and sweeten the fried plantains with a sprinkling of granulated sugar.

FOUFOU
(IVORY COAST)

These banana balls are traditionally served with many of the Ivorian sauces. They are easy to prepare, requiring few ingredients and a lot of elbow grease. They are pounded in a mortar while moving the pestle in a horizontal side-to-side manner. Pounding the ingredients in the usual up-and-down manner will result in a more elastic paste, which is also served and is called foutou. When made with plantains, this paste is called "koko tcha" in Ebrie, one of the many languages of the Ivory Coast.

SERVES FOUR TO SIX

4 or 5 slightly ripe plantains
2 or more tablespoons palm oil

Peel the plantains and cook them in a pot of lightly salted boiling water for 20 to 30 minutes. Drain the plantains and, while they are still warm, mash them in a mortar using a side-to-side motion. When they are smooth and creamy, mix in the palm oil. Make balls by sprinkling a bit of cold water on your hands and rolling ¼ cup of the plantain and palm oil mixture between your palms until it is a smooth, firm ball. Keep moistening your hands as you form each ball.

The Foufou should be served at once, although it can be covered with foil and left at room temperature for up to 2 hours before serving.

UGALI
(EAST AFRICA)

An East African alternative to the foufous and rice of West Africa, Ugali is a cornmeal porridge that is eaten with various stews. A portion is rolled into a ball and an indentation is made so that the stew can flavor the balls. Ugali is similar to the coocoos and cornmeal mushes of the Caribbean and the corn pones and cornmeal mushes of the Deep South. Clearly, they too crossed the ocean to find a culinary home in the New World.

SERVES SIX

1½ cups cornmeal (yellow or white)
2 cups boiling water
Salt and freshly ground black pepper to taste

Slowly add the cornmeal to the boiling water while stirring constantly. Add the salt and pepper and continue to stir. Cook the mixture while stirring until it becomes thick and has the consistency of a stiff porridge. (It will take a great deal of elbow grease to stir the porridge.) Serve warm to accompany any of the African stews.

MAIS GRILLE
(IVORY COAST)

All along the roads leading out of Abidpan, women can be seen sitting by braziers fanning the flames and grilling ears of fresh corn. This dish is a treat for children, who purchase it for a few cents and munch on it as they return home from school. It can also be served with many of the sauces found on the Ivory Coast.

SERVES ONE

1 or 2 ears of fresh corn with the silk removed but with the husk intact

Place the corn on a barbecue grill over medium heat. Turn the corn and let it cook for 15 minutes. Remove the corn, husk it, and eat it fresh or accompanied by any of the Ivoirian sauces. It makes an interesting alternative to the usual barbecue fare.

Or serve it with a dash of cayenne pepper instead of the usual salt. The pepper turns even corn into hot stuff.

GOMBOS À LA SENEGALAISE
(SENEGAL)

Gombo is the Swahili word for okra, and the vegetable is used in many different ways throughout Africa. This version is a vegetable stew that bears a slight resemblance to the New Orleans Creole dish that goes by the name gumbo.

SERVES EIGHT

1 pound okra
1 medium onion, chopped coarse
2 tablespoons peanut oil
2 medium tomatoes, peeled, seeded, and chopped coarse
1 small hot red chile, seeded and chopped
1 green bell pepper, chopped coarse
Salt and freshly ground black pepper to taste
⅓ cup tomato paste
2 medium-sized white potatoes, peeled and chopped

Place the okra in a bowl, cover it with salted water, and let it stand for 1 hour. Meanwhile, fry the onion in the peanut oil until soft, about 5 minutes. Drain the okra, reserving the liquid. Add the okra to the onion and then add the tomatoes, hot chile, and green bell pepper. Season with salt and pepper to taste. Measure the soaking liquid and add 3 cups of it to the ingredients. If there is not enough, add water to make 3 cups. Stir in the tomato paste, add the potatoes, cover, and simmer for about 30 minutes or until the vegetables are tender.

NTOMO KRAKO
(GHANA)

Fritters are a way of life in West Africa—banana fritters, bean fritters, and even yam fritters. These, from Ghana, can be eaten as a vegetable dish or as a starch with any of the West African sauces.

SERVES SIX

- 1 pound yams or sweet potatoes
- 2 eggs, beaten
- 1/4 cup light cream
- 1 onion, grated
- 1 tablespoon flour
- 1/4 teaspoon ground cloves
- 1/4 teaspoon freshly grated nutmeg
- 1/2 teaspoon freshly ground black pepper
- Flour for dredging fritters
- 3 or more cups peanut oil for frying

Place the yams in a pot of rapidly boiling water and boil for 20 minutes or until tender. Drain the yams, peel them, and trim off any discolored spots. Mash them in a food mill until they are smooth. Add the eggs, cream, grated onion, and flour and mix thoroughly. Season with the spices to taste. (You may find that you wish to add a bit more of one spice or less of another to suit your own taste.) Shape the fritters into small cakes, then dredge them lightly in flour. Pour the oil into a heavy saucepan or a fryer to at least 1/4-inch depth and heat it to 350 to 375 degrees. Add a few fritters to the oil and fry them until they are crisp and brown (about 8 minutes on each side). Remove the fritters, drain them, and keep them warm. Repeat the process until all the fritters are fried. Transfer them to a heated platter and serve immediately.

SPICY RICE
(ALL AFRICA)

Rice is one of the main starches of Africa. It finds itself under the Soupikandia of Senegal and the Groundnut Stew of Ghana. It is covered by the curries of East Africa and the Malay dishes of the South. This recipe is for a spicy rice dish that holds up next to the African sauces and yet can stand by itself with grilled meats or fish.

SERVES SIX

- 1½ cups long-grain rice
- 4 tablespoons butter
- 4 tablespoons peanut oil
- 2 medium-sized onions, chopped
- 1 hot green chile, seeded and chopped
- 3 cups chicken broth
- 2 teaspoons salt
- 1 teaspoon freshly ground black pepper

Wash the rice thoroughly and drain it. Heat 2 tablespoons of the butter and 2 tablespoons of the oil in a heavy saucepan and sauté the rice, stirring constantly, until it is light brown. Sauté the onions and chile in the remaining butter and oil until the onions are golden and tender. Add them to the rice. Add the broth, salt, and pepper and mix well. Cover and bake in a 350-degree oven for 30 to 40 minutes, or until the broth has been absorbed and the rice is tender and golden.

KENYA CORN (KENYA)

Mombasa, on Kenya's Indian Ocean coast, is an enchanted city. There, African and Arab cultures have combined to produce the Swahili culture. Kipling notwithstanding, East and West do meet in Mombasa; Indian temples are next door to whitewashed houses out of the Arabian nights and all are bathed in the glow of the African sun. The cuisine on Kenya's coast also reflects a mixture of cultures. Curries abound, and even corn, a staple in the corn pones and cornmeal mushes of the Kenyan people, takes on an exotic flavor.

SERVES EIGHT TO TEN

- 1 tablespoon salted butter
- 1 medium-sized onion, chopped coarse

1 clove garlic, minced
4 cups fresh corn cut off the cob
2 teaspoons cornstarch
1½ cups coconut milk (see below)
1 medium-sized tomato, chopped coarse
1 (2-ounce) can pimentos, drained and chopped coarse
¼ teaspoon curry powder
Salt and freshly ground white pepper to taste
Juice of half a lemon
¼ cup fresh Chinese parsley, minced

Melt the butter in a heavy saucepan. Add the onion and the garlic and sauté them until golden. Add the corn. Combine the cornstarch with 1 cup of the coconut milk, stirring well, then add it to the mixture along with the tomato, pimentos, curry powder, and salt and pepper. Cook uncovered, stirring often until the juice is absorbed. Add the remaining coconut milk and the lemon juice. Stir. Garnish with the parsley and serve as an accompaniment to any main dish.

COCONUT MILK
(ALL AFRICA)

The liquid that comes out of the coconut when you open it is coconut water. To make coconut milk, heat the coconut in a medium oven for 10 minutes so it will be easier to open. Break it open with a hammer. Reserve the liquid and remove the meat. With a paring knife, scrape off the brown peel and grate the coconut meat. (Using a food processor prevents skinned fingers.) Add 1 cup of boiling water or boiling reserved coconut water for each cup of grated coconut meat. Allow the mixture to stand for half an hour, then strain the liquid through cheesecloth, squeezing the pulp to get all of the coconut milk. Alternately, unsweetened coconut milk may be obtained from some of the stores specializing in Latin American ingredients listed at the end of the book.

THIEBOU DIENNE (SENEGAL)

This spicy stew is the national dish of Senegal. When it is served in other African countries it goes under the name of Senegalese rice. It is a fish stew with cabbage, eggplant, pumpkin, and other vegetables, served over a base of rice reddened with tomato sauce. It is a dish for celebrations and a dish for every day. Some of my friends in Senegal jokingly say that their version of the Lord's Prayer goes, "Give us this day our daily thieb." No matter what, almost every Senegalese eats thieb rice at least once a week if not once a day. In Senegal, Thiebou Dienne is eaten from a communal bowl. Family and guests assemble on a floor on a mat or cloth around a basin full of the fish and rice. Each person eats out of the section of the basin that is in front of him. The hostess sees that the guest's section is always filled with savory pieces of fish and the vegetables that the guest prefers. If he wishes, the guest can spice up his section of rice with a piece of hot pepper. One eats only with the right hand, although some households use big spoons.

SERVES EIGHT TO TEN

2 large onions, chopped fine
1 cup peanut oil
One 3-inch piece of smoked fish (butterfish, trout, or other fish)
1 (6-ounce) can tomato paste
1 bouquet of parsley, trimmed
1 large clove garlic
Salt
2 hot chiles (Guinea pepper type)
3 scallions
One 3-pound sea bream tail (or the tail of another firm-fleshed fish) cut into steaks 1½ inches thick and then cut in half). You may also wish to add the fish head, which is reputed to give the Thiebou Dienne a better taste.

- 9 cups cold salted water
- ½ pound pumpkin, cut into 1-inch dice
- ½ pound manioc root, peeled and sliced into 1-inch slices
- 2 small eggplants, cut into 1-inch slices
- 4 carrots
- 4 small purple turnips, quartered
- 1 medium-sized green cabbage, cut into eighths
- 4 sweet potatoes, quartered
- 6 to 8 okra pods, topped and tailed
- 2 pounds short-grain rice

In a large stew pot, brown the onion in 4 tablespoons of the oil. Add the smoked fish and the tomato paste, diluted with ¼ cup of water. Pulverize the parsley, garlic, a pinch of salt, half of one chile, and the scallions in a food processor until they are a fine paste. This paste is the stuffing for the fish pieces. Make slits in the fish and insert the stuffing in the slits.

Place the fish in the stew pot and allow it to simmer for a few minutes. Salt it to taste and add 9 cups of salted cold water. When the mixture comes to a boil, reduce the heat and add the vegetables. Add the hard ones first and the more tender ones later as the stew cooks. (The order in which the ingredients are given here is a good one to try.) Finally, add one crushed chile.

After 20 minutes of cooking, remove the fish and keep it warm. Cover it with a bit of the sauce. Continue to cook the stew. After an additional 15 minutes of cooking the vegetables should be tender. Remove them and add them to the fish. Keep them warm.

Reserve 2 cups of the stewing liquid to make sauces to accompany the dish. Return the remaining liquid to a boil, add the rice, and cook for 20 minutes or until all the liquid is absorbed.

Place 1 cup of the reserved liquid in a small saucepan with the remaining half chile. Cook over low heat for a few minutes and place in a sauce boat. The other cup of reserved liquid will go into another sauce boat. You will have a spicy sauce and a plain sauce.

Place the rice on one serving platter and the vegetables and fish on another. Serve hot with the two sauces. To make this dish truly festive you may add Boulettes de Poisson (see page 41) to the platter before you serve the dish. You may also serve the Thiebou Dienne accompanied by pickles (see below). To serve Thiebou Dienne in the traditional manner, place a tablecloth on the floor, mound the fish and vegetables on top of the rice in a communal basin, and eat with a soup spoon.

PICKLES POUR THIEBOU DIENNE SOUS VERRE (SENEGAL)

In Senegal, a very popular type of traditional painting is called sous verre (under glass). A stew called Thiebou Dienne (page 68) that is enriched with numerous side dishes and condiments is called Thiebou Dienne Sous Verre. One of the popular accompaniments is pickles, though Boulettes de Poisson may also be added.

SERVES EIGHT AS A CONDIMENT

5 green bell peppers
Distilled white vinegar
Water
2 hot green chiles, chopped coarse
2 cloves garlic, chopped coarse
1 tablespoon sugar
6 peppercorns
1 tablespoon salt

Quarter the peppers and place them in boiling water for 5 minutes. Drain them, remove the seeds and cores, and slice them into strips. Allow the peppers to cool. Place them in a jar and cover with a mixture of half distilled white vinegar and half water. Add the chiles, garlic, sugar, peppercorns, and salt. Let stand for a week and then serve to accompany roasts and, of course, Thiebou Dienne Sous Verre.

KEDJENOU
(IVORY COAST)

Kedjenou, sometimes called chicken in a pot, is always cooked in a terra-cotta pot called a canari. The dish can be duplicated using any of the terra-cotta cookers on the market, or it can be made in any heavy casserole with a lid. In the Ivoirian bush, the canari is occasionally replaced by a banana leaf and the dish is cooked under the ashes of a fire. You may try this method, but I make no guarantees.

SERVES EIGHT TO TEN

2 frying chickens cut into pieces
4 medium onions, chopped
6 ripe tomatoes, peeled, seeded, and chopped coarse
2 hot chiles (Guinea pepper type), chopped coarse
1 large clove garlic, chopped coarse
1 tablespoon fresh ginger, minced
1 bay leaf
Salt and freshly ground black pepper to taste

Place all the ingredients in a canari, terra-cotta cooker, or heavy casserole. Cover the cooker with a lid that is heavy enough so that no steam escapes. Place the cooker over medium-high heat and cook until you hear the contents begin to simmer. (The lid must not be lifted at any time during the cooking process so that the dish can cook in its own juices.) While cooking, shake the pot gently from time to time so that the food does not stick. Shake every 5 minutes or so for 35 to 40 minutes, by which time the Kedjenou is cooked. Serve hot with Foufou balls (page 62) or white rice.

SHRIMP MINA
(GHANA)

Smoked shrimp give this dish its savor. It takes its name from the Mina Coast, which is in turn named for the fort of San Jorge del Mina (St. George of the Mines). The fort was established as a Portuguese bastion in West Africa in 1482. The mines referred to were the gold mines of the old Gold Coast.

SERVES EIGHT

5 large ripe tomatoes
40 large, fresh shrimp
1 pound dried smoked shrimp*
½ cup peanut oil
2 medium onions, chopped fine
Salt, as needed
1 teaspoon powdered ginger
3 small hot cherry peppers

Peel and seed the tomatoes and mash them into a paste in a food processor. Shell and devein the shrimp; wash and drain them. Pulverize the shrimp in a food processor. In a frying pan, heat the oil slightly and add the tomatoes and onions. Let the mixture simmer for 15 minutes while stirring with a wooden spoon. Add the shrimp. Let the dish continue to cook for another 10 minutes or so. Taste and add salt, if necessary. Add the ginger and the cherry peppers. Prick the peppers so that they will not explode during cooking. Continue to cook the mixture for a few more minutes. You may add ½ cup of water or bouillon if the sauce is too thick. Serve over white rice or with Foufou (page 62). You might even wish to try this as an unusual sauce for pasta.

* Dried smoked shrimp can be obtained in Chinese markets or from suppliers of Asian ingredients. See the list of mail order sources at the end of the book.

CRABE BENINOISE
(BENIN)

This baked dish reflects Benin's mixture of African and French colonial culinary influence.

SERVES SIX

1½ pounds fresh crabmeat
1 cup chopped scallions, including some of the green part

½ cup chopped parsley
1 cup chopped tomato
2 eggs
2 cloves garlic, minced
1 stalk of celery, minced
1 tablespoon Hot Sauce for Akkra (see page 38)
½ cup bread crumbs

Combine all the ingredients except ¼ cup of the bread crumbs. Mix thoroughly and place into well-washed crab shells or individual baking dishes. Cover the top of each dish with a dusting of the remaining bread crumbs. Bake for 20 to 30 minutes in a 350-degree oven until golden brown on the top. Serve hot.

DORO WAT
(ETHIOPIA)

Ethiopia is a country where they like their hot stuff hot! In some areas of the country, the spicy taste of a woman's Berberę Sauce is enough to win her a husband, and cooks jealously guard the secrets of their spicy stews. One of these stews, hallmark of Ethiopian cooking, is Doro Wat. It is a spicy chicken dish, redolent of garlic, cardamom, ginger, and pepper.

SERVES FOUR TO SIX

2½ cups water
Salt to taste
Juice of one lemon
1 medium-sized chicken, cut into pieces
2 medium-sized onions, chopped
2 cloves garlic, minced
3 tablespoons salted butter
5 tablespoons tomato paste
¼ teaspoon cardamom powder
1 teaspoon cayenne pepper
2 tablespoons chile powder
1 teaspoon minced fresh ginger
5 hard-boiled eggs, peeled and pierced with a fork

Place the water, salt, and lemon juice in a heavy saucepan or stew pot. Add the chicken pieces and simmer, covered, for half an hour. Remove the chicken and the stock from the heat and reserve. In a small frying pan, sauté the onions and garlic in the butter until they are golden; add them to the stock and the chicken and heat to boiling. Add the tomato paste and spices and stir well. Simmer the stew over low heat until the chicken is tender, about 20 minutes. Add the pierced eggs to the stew during the final 10 minutes of cooking. Serve on a platter garnished with the eggs. This dish can be made even hotter with the addition of a dash of Pili Pili Sauce (page 58).

MAFE
(SENEGAL)

There are as many ways to make Mafe as there are cooks in Senegal. This way is both quick and easy.

SERVES FOUR TO SIX

1 large onion, minced
2 tablespoons peanut oil
1½ pounds meat (beef, lamb, or chicken), cut into ½-inch cubes
½ cup creamy peanut butter, diluted with 1½ cups water
½ cup tomato paste
2 carrots cut into 1-inch slices
2 small white turnips cut into 1-inch dice
1 small hot red chile, minced
½ teaspoon thyme
Salt and freshly ground black pepper to taste

Fry the onion in the oil until it is browned. Add the meat and cook until it is lightly browned. Pour the peanut butter and water mixture over the meat. Add the tomato paste and stir well. Finally, add the carrots, turnips, chile, and spices. Taste the stew for seasoning and cook slowly for 45 minutes. Check the liquid; you may wish to add more water during the cooking process (as much as a cup). Serve over white or saffron rice.

FRESH TUNA DISH
(TUNISIA)

This is a winter dish that is served during the Chanukah season by the Sephardic Jews of Tunisia.

SERVES SIX

3 pounds fresh tuna
½ cup freshly squeezed lemon juice
3 tablespoons flour
Salt and freshly ground black pepper to taste
One 1-pound can of peeled tomatoes
1 hot red chile, minced
1 tablespoon capers

Purchase thick slices of tuna or tuna steaks so that the fish will not fall apart during cooking. Marinate the tuna in the lemon juice for half an hour. Dry it and dredge in flour seasoned with salt and black pepper. In a heavy casserole brown the fish in the peanut oil for 5 minutes on each side.

Meanwhile, drain the tomatoes, removing as many seeds as possible, and put them through a food mill. Add the puréed tomatoes and the minced chile to the mixture in the casserole. Allow the mixture to cook over a low flame for half an hour. Then add the capers. Serve this savory stew with boiled white potatoes. The spiciness of the stew contrasts well with the sweetness of the new potatoes.

BIOKOSSO
(IVORY COAST)

This dish from the southern Ivory Coast is usually wrapped in banana leaves, although a reliable version can be made with aluminum foil.

SERVES FOUR TO SIX

5 tomatoes, seeded, peeled, and chopped coarse
2 large onions, chopped
2 hot chiles (Guinea pepper type)
4 or 6 small red snappers (one per person)

Grind the tomatoes, onions, and chiles in a food processor or blender until they are a coarse paste. In a 1-foot-square piece of aluminum foil, place ¼ cup of the paste, one fish, and an additional tablespoon of the paste. Close the packages of aluminum foil tightly. Then steam or grill the packages for 20 minutes. The dish is served with plantains or white rice.

SAUCE CLAIRE
(IVORY COAST)

Sauce Claire was the first dish of Ivorian food I ever ate. The fish is served whole in the Ivory Coast, but after contending with one fish eye, I make it with fish steaks. The dish can be made with various ingredients and is composed according to what is available in the market on any particular day. Meat, smoked fish, or fresh fish can be used. This version, made with fresh fish, closely approximates the dish I first tasted at a friend's home—lacking fish eye, of course. Although it is called a sauce, it becomes more like a stew when served with rice or Foufou and therefore is included in the main dish section.

SERVES SIX

2 pounds fresh fish steaks (halibut, swordfish, or another thick, white fish)
4 medium onions, chopped
1 tablespoon peanut oil
5 cups cold salted water
½ pound fresh tomatoes, peeled, seeded, and chopped
1 medium eggplant, peeled and cut into ½-inch dice
2 hot chiles (Guinea pepper type)

½ pound fresh crabmeat
5 to 8 dried smoked shrimp*

Place the fish in a heavy cooking pot along with the chopped onions and peanut oil. Let the fish cook for a few minutes, then add the water. When the water begins to boil, add the tomatoes, eggplant, and chiles (prick them with a fork so that they do not explode while cooking). Let the mixture stew for half an hour, then remove the eggplant and the chiles; chop them fine in a food processor or run them through a food mill. Replace the chiles and the eggplant in the sauce and taste for seasoning. Add the crabmeat and the smoked shrimp. Let the mixture cook for an additional 30 minutes, stirring occasionally.

Serve the sauce while it is hot with Foufou (page 62) or white rice.

* See note, page 72.

GRILLED SHRIMP TUNISIAN STYLE (TUNISIA)

Hot pepper, Harissa, and garlic all go into making this Tunisian dish of grilled shrimp with spicy sauce.

SERVES EIGHT

40 medium-sized shrimp
4 ripe tomatoes, peeled and seeded
1 bunch of parsley
1 clove garlic
2 teaspoons Harissa (page 60)
1 teaspoon cayenne pepper
3 tablespoons olive oil
2 tablespoons boiling water
Juice of one lemon
Salt and freshly ground black pepper to taste

Clean and devein the shrimp. In a food processor, chop the tomatoes, parsley, and garlic. Add the Harissa, cayenne pepper, salt, oil, water, and lemon juice. Place the mixture in a small saucepan and cook it over low heat for 20 minutes.

Meanwhile, season the shrimp with salt and black pepper. Grill them over a barbecue grill or in the broiler for 15 minutes, turning so that they cook evenly on both sides.

When ready, serve the shrimp with the sauce, which is known as Kerkennaise Sauce in Tunisia. The sauce can be served with any grilled fish and for any lover of hot stuff is better than catsup on a hamburger.

OYSTERS AZI DESSI
(TOGO)

SERVES FOUR

24 large fresh oysters
1 cup lemon juice
2 cups peanut oil
1 cup flour
½ teaspoon cayenne pepper
Salt and freshly ground black pepper to taste

Open the oysters, detach them from their shells, and drop them into the lemon juice. In a heavy saucepan, heat the oil to 325 degrees for frying. Drain the oysters, dry them, and dredge them in a mixture of flour, cayenne, salt, and black pepper. Fry them rapidly, turning them until they are crisp and cooked (about 10 minutes). Drain and serve immediately with Azi Dessi Sauce (below).

AZI DESSI SAUCE

SERVES FOUR

1 pound tomatoes
3 tablespoons palm oil
2 medium-sized onions
1 hot red chile, chopped fine

1 clove garlic
½ pound smoked dried shrimp
1 teaspoon powdered ginger
2 tablespoons creamy peanut butter

Peel and seed the tomatoes and grind them in a blender or food processor until puréed. Place the mixture in a frying pan, add the oil and cook the mixture over low heat until it has a catsup-like consistency (about 15 minutes). Chop the onions, chile, and garlic in a food processor or blender; add them to the sauce and cook for 5 minutes. Pulverize the dried shrimp and add it and the ginger to the sauce. Cook for 10 minutes, stirring well to mix all the ingredients. Stir in the peanut butter just before serving.

This version of Azi Dessi calls for the oysters and sauce to be served separately. Frequently, in Togo, where this dish originates, the oysters are cooked in the sauce, making a luxurious oyster and tomato stew that is served with Foufou (page 62) or white rice.

KOPE
(BAULE IVORY COAST)

This dish is a fresh okra stew. Although Baule in origin, it is eaten throughout the Ivory Coast. Made with meat, okra, crab, onions, and tomatoes, it, like many African dishes, bears a resemblance to the Creole gumbos of New Orleans.

SERVES SIX

2 pounds stewing beef, cut in 1-inch cubes
1 large onion, chopped coarse
3 tablespoons peanut oil
8 cups water
1 smoked butterfish, carefully boned and shredded
2 large ripe tomatoes, chopped coarse
Salt to taste
1 pound fresh okra (select only young pods)
2 tablespoons dried smoked shrimp*

2 tablespoons dried mushrooms
½ pound fresh crabmeat
2 hot chiles

In a large, heavy saucepan, brown the meat and the onion in the peanut oil for 15 minutes. Cover with the water and add the smoked fish, tomatoes, and salt. Cover the pot and allow it to simmer for half an hour.

Meanwhile, in a second saucepan, bring 3 cups of water to a boil. Top and tail the okra and slice it into ¼-inch rounds. Add it to the water and bring it to a boil. Then, grind the shrimp and the mushrooms and add them to the okra. Finally, add the crabmeat and the hot chiles. (Prick the chiles with a fork to be sure they do not burst during cooking.) Continue to cook over medium heat for 10 minutes, stirring gently from time to time so as not to break the okra. Pour the okra mixture into the saucepan with the meat. Lower the heat and continue to cook for 10 minutes or until the meat is thoroughly cooked. Serve over white rice or with Foufou (page 62).

* See note, page 72.

CRAB GUMBO
(WEST AFRICA)

The humble okra pod is a culinary staple in many African countries. People appreciate not only its taste but also its consistency, which binds sauces together and holds them. Here's a crab gumbo that can also be made with either chicken or shrimp. Again, New Orleans is brought to mind by such ingredients as onion, tomatoes, okra, and, of course, pepper.

SERVES SIX TO EIGHT

3½ pounds fresh crabmeat
2 medium-sized onions, chopped coarse
4 medium-sized tomatoes, peeled, seeded, and chopped coarse

1 quart chicken broth
1 teaspoon salt
1 teaspoon cayenne pepper
1 pound okra, tailed, topped, and cut into rounds
1 tablespoon flour

Place the crabmeat, onions, tomatoes, chicken broth, salt, and pepper in a heavy saucepan or stew pot. Simmer, covered, for 20 minutes. Add the okra and continue to simmer over low heat until the okra is tender. Thicken the gumbo with flour and serve it hot, over white rice.

GROUNDNUT STEW
(GHANA)

Groundnuts are peanuts, which grow in abundance in West Africa. Groundnut Stew is almost the national dish of Ghana. It was one of the first African dishes I ever tasted. The year was 1972, and the place was a small restaurant in Accra, Ghana, called the Black Pot. My love affair with African cooking had begun. Here is a version that incorporates not only peanuts and the national culinary bird of Africa, the chicken, but also calls for 6 cups of beer—a ubiquitous Ghanian drink.

SERVES SIX

1 medium-sized chicken cut into pieces
2 medium-sized onions, chopped coarse
6 cups lager beer
1 cup creamy peanut butter
1 (6-ounce) can tomato paste
1 red bell pepper, diced
1 cup sliced carrots
1 cup sliced okra
2 hot red chiles (Guinea pepper type)

Simmer the chicken and onions in the beer for about 45 minutes. Remove the cooked chicken and set it aside. Place the peanut butter in a bowl and whisk in 1 cup of the chicken-beer broth. Add the peanut butter liquid and the remaining ingredients to the original pot and simmer for 20 minutes. Meanwhile, remove the chicken meat from the bones and cut it in 1-inch cubes. Return the chicken to the pot and cook for an additional 5 minutes. Serve the stew hot, in bowls or in a tureen. For an authentic African serving dish, try a decorated calabash gourd. White or saffron rice is a good accompaniment.

KALLAI FIL
(TCHAD)

Kallai Fil is a Tchadian barbecue. Chicken, lamb, or rabbit can be used. The meat is stuffed and marinated before it is placed in a clay pot or canari to be cooked in the ashes of an open fire. This version calls for chicken and uses a clay cooker; these pots are readily available. It is made in the oven, but the courageous may wish to try it at an outdoor barbecue or a beach party.

SERVES FOUR

- 1 roasting chicken
- 2 lemons
- 1/4 pound chicken livers
- 1/2 cup peanut oil or a mixture of peanut and palm oil
- 1/2 cup scallions, including 3 inches of green part, chopped fine
- 1 clove garlic, minced
- 1 cup cooked rice
- 1 green chile, chopped fine
- 1 teaspoon cayenne pepper
- 1/4 cup thyme or other aromatic herb

Wash the chicken, dry it, and rub the juice of one lemon over it inside and out. Set the chicken aside. In a small frying pan, sauté the chicken livers in 2 tablespoons of the oil. Chop the cooked livers. Mix them with the scallions, garlic, rice, and chile to form the stuffing for the chicken. Stuff the chicken and sew it closed.

Mix the remaining oil, the juice of the remaining lemon, and the cayenne pepper to form the marinade. Coat the chicken with this mixture. Line the bottom of the clay cooker with a bed of thyme; place the chicken on top of it; close the cooker and place it in a 350-degree oven. Cook for 20 to 30 minutes per pound of chicken.

The chicken is served warm and can be accompanied by Gombos à la Senegalaise (page 64), Spicy Rice (page 65), or baked sweet potatoes.

JOLOF RICE
(WEST AFRICA)

This is not the simple rice dish it seems to be. Rather, it is a one-dish meal of rice, chicken, and ham that is served on festive occasions in Sierra Leone and Ghana. The ingredients will vary according to the season and the pocketbook of the host family.

SERVES SIX TO EIGHT

One 1-pound smoked ham hock
4 cups chicken bouillon
4 tablespoons peanut oil
1 medium-sized chicken, cut into pieces
1 pound lean stewing beef
2 medium-sized onions, chopped coarse
1 clove garlic, minced
3 medium-sized ripe tomatoes, peeled, seeded, and chopped coarse
2 tablespoons tomato paste
1 hot green chile, chopped fine
½ teaspoon cayenne pepper
1½ cups long-grain rice
1 small head of green cabbage, cut into pieces
1 medium-sized eggplant, cut into 1-inch dice
1 medium-sized squash, cut into 1-inch dice

Place the ham hock in a stew pot or a large, heavy saucepan with the bouillon and simmer it, covered, for an hour. Meanwhile, in a second pot, heat the peanut oil and brown the chicken and beef. Remove the meat and sauté the onions and garlic for 5 minutes. Add the tomatoes, tomato paste, chile, and cayenne. Stir and cook for an additional 5 minutes.

When the ham hock is cooked (about 1 hour), remove it from the bouillon; discard the skin and bones and return the pieces of ham to the bouillon. Add the bouillon, ham, and beef to the tomato mixture and cook over medium-low heat for 1 hour. Add the chicken and cook for an additional 15 minutes. Add the rice and mix it in well. Cover the pot and simmer for 20 minutes, or until the rice is cooked and the chicken is tender. Let the dish stand for 20 minutes before serving to attain full flavor.

The cabbage, eggplant, and squash may be added with the rice, or they can be steamed separately and served as accompanying vegetables. This is a one-dish meal that looks elegant when served heaped on a platter.

FRANGO PIRI PIRI
(MOZAMBIQUE)

Piri Piri Sauce is a hallmark of the cooking of Mozambique. It adds piquancy to chicken in this recipe and brings life to shrimp in Camarão Grelhado Piri Piri (page 88).

SERVES FOUR

- 2 tablespoons minced hot red chile
- 4 medium cloves garlic, chopped coarse
- 1 cup peanut oil
- ¼ cup freshly squeezed lemon juice
- 1 teaspoon salt
- 1 small frying chicken, cut into pieces

Pulverize the chile, garlic, and ½ cup of the oil in a blender or food processor. Pour the mixture into a shallow bowl and add the remaining oil, the lemon juice, and the salt. Wash the chicken pieces and pat them dry. Drop them into the oil, chile, and lemon marinade. Turn them to coat evenly and allow them to marinate for at least 3 hours. Preheat the oven to the highest broiler setting. Place the chicken pieces on the broiler rack and cook for 10 to 15 minutes, turning the chicken and basting it with the remaining marinade. The chicken is done when it is browned and the juices run clear when the skin is pricked with a fork.

SIK SIK WAT (ETHIOPIA)*

Ethiopia is noted for its spicy food. Pepper and chiles are the name of the game, and they are mixed in different combinations in almost every dish. Although mouth-searing dishes are the norm in Ethiopia, they can easily be adapted to Western palates as this recipe for Sik Sik Wat proves.

SERVES SIX TO EIGHT

- 2 cups onions, chopped fine
- 1/3 cup Niter Kebbeh (see page 57)
- 2 teaspoons minced garlic
- 2 teaspoons ginger root, scraped and chopped fine
- 1/4 teaspoon fenugreek seeds, pulverized with a mortar and pestle or in a bowl with the back of a spoon
- 1/8 teaspoon ground cloves
- 1/8 teaspoon allspice
- 1/8 teaspoon ground nutmeg, preferably freshly grated
- 1/4 cup paprika
- 2 tablespoons Berberé (see page 55)
- 2/3 cup dry red wine
- 1/2 cup water
- 1 large, firm, ripe tomato, chopped coarse and puréed through a food mill or rubbed through a sieve with a spoon

* From *Time/Life Foods of the World: African Cooking*, copyright © 1970 Time-Life Books, Inc.

- 2 teaspoons salt
- 3 pounds boneless beef, preferably chuck, trimmed of excess fat and cut into 1-inch cubes
- Freshly ground black pepper

In a heavy 4- to 5-quart enameled casserole, cook the onions over moderate heat for 5 or 6 minutes, until they are soft and dry. Slide the casserole back and forth over the heat and stir the onions constantly to prevent them from burning; if necessary, reduce the heat or remove the casserole from the stove occasionally to let it cool for a few moments before returning it to the heat.

Stir in the Niter Kebbeh and, when it begins to sputter, add the garlic, ginger root, fenugreek, cloves, allspice, and nutmeg, stirring well after each addition. Add the paprika and the Berberé and stir over low heat for 2 to 3 minutes. Stir in the wine, water, puréed tomato, and salt and bring the liquid to a boil. Add the beef cubes and turn them about with a spoon until they are evenly coated with the sauce. Then reduce the heat to low. Cover the pan partially and simmer the beef for about 1½ hours, or until it shows no resistance when pierced with the point of a small, sharp knife. Sprinkle the Wat with a few grindings of pepper and taste for seasoning. Serve hot in a heated deep platter or bowl.

STUFFED SNAPPER À LA ST. LOUISIENNE DU GUET NDAR (SENEGAL)

Guet Ndar is the area of St. Louis du Senegal where the fishermen live. They mend their nets and go out over the sandbar to battle the Atlantic as they have for generations. They bring home a miraculous catch of large and small fish. When they have a festive occasion and there is enough money to pay for a true celebration, they will prepare a stuffed fish in the St. Louis manner. The preparation is a bit complicated, but the reward is a dish that offers all the sophistication of classic French cuisine but with a Senegalese touch.

SERVES EIGHT

One 4½-pound red snapper, eviscerated, but with the head intact
- ½ cup minced parsley, stems reserved
- 3 bay leaves
- 2 cups water

Salt to taste
- 1 teaspoon white pepper
- ¼ cup minced coriander
- 3 cloves garlic
- 5 scallions
- 3 to 4 slices stale bread, preferably French, soaked in water and squeezed dry
- 6 medium-sized ripe tomatoes, peeled and seeded

Freshly ground white pepper to taste
- 1 teaspoon thyme
- 3 hot, red cherry peppers
- 2 tablespoons peanut oil

Wash the fish inside and out and snip off the fins. With a sharp knife, slit the back skin from the head to the tail. Remove the central bone and the flesh, taking care not to tear the skin. Remove the bones and reserve the flesh; keep it cool.

In a saucepan, prepare a court bouillon by boiling the fish bones, the parsley stems, the bay leaves, 2 cups of water, salt, and the white pepper for 15 minutes.

Mix the coriander, parsley, garlic, and four of the scallions (including some of the green stem) in a food processor or blender until they are chopped fine. Add the flesh from the fish, the bread, two tomatoes, salt, and pepper and mix well.

Check to make sure you have not torn the fish skin. If you have, sew it with gray thread. Cut off the internal fins and stuff the fish skin with the mixture of fish, parsley, spices, and bread. Take care not to overstuff the fish so that it does not burst during cooking. Sew it closed.

In an oven-proof oval dish, slice the reserved scallion and the four remaining tomatoes. Sprinkle with the thyme and salt to taste. Place the fish on this base and set the fish head on a cushion of the cherry peppers. Sprinkle the fish with the oil and cover the dish with a sheet of aluminum foil. Cook the fish in a 350-degree oven for 45 minutes. When the fish is half cooked, baste it with the court bouillon and remove the foil so that it will brown.

Serve the fish with white rice and vegetables.

CAMARÃO GRELHADO PIRI PIRI (MOZAMBIQUE)

Mozambique is noted for its big, beautiful shrimp. They are used in many of the country's dishes. This is a special way to combine grilled shrimp and hot pepper.

SERVES FOUR

1½ pounds uncooked jumbo shrimp
One 1-inch piece of hot red chile, minced
4 medium cloves garlic, chopped coarse
1 cup peanut oil
1 teaspoon salt

Shell and devein the shrimp, leaving the tail shells intact. Wash them under cold water and pat them dry. Combine the minced chile, garlic, and ½ cup of the oil in a blender and mix at high speed until the garlic and chile are pulverized. Add the remaining ½ cup of oil and the salt. Drop the shrimp into the oil and chile mixture and turn them to be sure they are well coated. Allow them to marinate for at least 3 hours, stirring them from time to time.

Preheat the broiler. Remove the shrimp from the marinade and place them on the broiler rack or an outdoor barbecue grill. Cook for about 3 minutes on each side, or until the shrimp are pink and tender. Serve hot, with white rice and lemon butter.

POULET YASSA
(SENEGAL)

Poulet Yassa is one Senegalese dish that has unanimous approval. A specialty of the Casamance region of southern Senegal, this dish can be made as spicy as you like with the addition of more pepper and chile. It is a perfect introduction to West African cuisine.

SERVES SIX

Juice of 3 lemons
3 large onions, sliced
Salt and freshly ground black pepper to taste
1 (or more) hot red chile (Guinea pepper type), cut into small pieces
5 tablespoons peanut oil
1 medium-sized chicken, cut into pieces
½ cup water

Prepare a marinade of the lemon juice, onions, salt, pepper, chile, and 4 tablespoons of the peanut oil. Place the chicken pieces in the marinade and allow them to sit for at least 2 hours. Be sure they are well coated with the marinade. Preheat the broiler to the highest setting. Remove the chicken pieces and reserve the marinade. Place the chicken pieces on the broiler rack and grill them briefly, just until they are lightly browned on both sides. Drain the onions from the marinade and sauté them in the remaining oil. Cook them slowly until tender, then add the reserved marinade. When the liquid is thoroughly heated, add the chicken pieces. Add the water and allow the Yassa to simmer over low heat until the chicken is cooked. Serve hot, over white rice. Yassa can also be made with fish substituted for the chicken.

BARBECUED PEANUT CHICKEN (WEST AFRICA)

Peanuts, chicken, and pepper all come together in this recipe to create a new twist. This grilled chicken offers a spicy alternative to the usual summer barbecue fare.

SERVES SIX

¼ cup peanut oil
2 teaspoons cayenne pepper
1 medium-sized frying chicken, cut into pieces
1 cup creamy peanut butter
1 cup catsup

Heat the oil in a saucepan until it is hot. Add the cayenne pepper and stir. Brush the chicken pieces with the spicy oil mixture. Then mix the remaining spicy oil with the peanut butter and the catsup to form a thick basting sauce. Broil or grill the chicken, basting often with the sauce. The chicken should take about 45 minutes to 1 hour to cook.

MOROCCAN KIDNEYS IN SAUCE (MOROCCO)

Lamb kidneys are tender, and they are tasty in this Moroccan dish, which mixes them with cumin, cinnamon, and paprika.

SERVES SIX TO EIGHT

4 pounds lamb kidneys
2 cups water
2 cups vinegar or lemon juice
2 teaspoons paprika
1½ teaspoons cumin
½ teaspoon cinnamon
8 tablespoons butter (1 stick)

Clean the kidneys and prepare them for cooking by removing any skin and soaking them in a mixture of half water and half lemon juice or vinegar for half an hour. Turn them frequently while they are soaking. Remove them and rinse several times with fresh water. Cut them into 1-inch cubes and allow them to drain. Place the kidneys in a frying pan with a bit of salt and add the spices and butter. Cover them with water and cook, covered, over medium heat. When the kidneys feel firm, they are done. It should take about 20 minutes. Boil down the sauce until it is thick. Check the seasoning and serve hot, over white rice.

POULET M'HAMMER
(MOROCCO)

M'Hammer chicken is prepared in many ways in Morocco. This variation calls for paprika and pepper and results in a fried chicken that would leave the colonel green with envy.

SERVES FOUR TO SIX

½ teaspoon mild paprika
¼ teaspoon ground ginger
½ teaspoon freshly ground black pepper
¼ teaspoon cumin
1 small clove garlic
1 small onion
Salt to taste
2 pinches saffron
One 3-pound chicken, cut into pieces
5 tablespoons butter
2 tablespoons peanut oil
1 cup water
1 small bunch parsley and coriander tied together
1 teaspoon flour

Mix the salt with the spices and spread on the chicken pieces. Peel and mince the garlic and onion. Heat 1 tablespoon of butter in a saucepan and lightly brown the onion and garlic in it. Add 1 tablespoon of the oil and lightly brown the chicken pieces, turning them so that they are well flavored with the spices. After a few minutes, add 1 cup of water and the bunch of parsley and coriander. Cook, covered, over medium heat for 45 minutes, turning the chicken frequently. Add more water if necessary.

When the chicken is cooked, remove it and the parsley-coriander bouquet from the sauce. Add the flour blended with a bit of water to thicken the sauce and bring it to a boil. Stir it, let it boil down, and remove it from the heat.

Fifteen minutes before serving, heat the remaining 4 tablespoons of butter and the remaining 1 tablespoon of oil in a frying pan and carefully brown the chicken so it is crusty and well browned all over. Reheat the chicken sauce, add 2 tablespoons of the frying fat, and stir rapidly. Pour the sauce over the chicken and serve immediately.

TAJINE MSIR ZITUN
(MOROCCO)

Tajines are heavy conical clay cooking pots. They are sold in markets throughout Morocco and are available glazed or unglazed in a variety of sizes, colors, and designs. They have also given their name to a type of Moroccan cooking. This tajine, which can be made without a tajine, in a heavy skillet, is an adaptation of the traditional dish and has chicken, olives, and lemons as its main ingredients.

SERVES FOUR TO SIX

4 tablespoons olive oil
1 medium-sized chicken, cut into pieces
1 onion, minced
2 teaspoons paprika
1 teaspoon ground ginger
¼ teaspoon turmeric
1 teaspoon salt
Freshly ground black pepper
2 lemons, cut lengthwise into quarters and seeded
1 cup water
20 small green olives

In a tajine or a heavy skillet, warm the oil over high heat. Brown the chicken pieces in the hot oil, turning them often and regulating the heat so they brown evenly without burning. Transfer the chicken to a platter. Pour off all but a small amount of the fat from the skillet. Add the onion and cook for 10 minutes, stirring frequently until it is soft and brown. Do not let it burn. Stir in the paprika, ginger, turmeric, salt, and pepper. Add the lemon quarters, the chicken, and any liquid that has accumulated with it. Pour in the water. Bring the mixture to a boil over high heat, then reduce the heat and allow it to cook, covered, over low heat until the chicken is tender (about 30 minutes). Add the olives and cook for an additional 5 minutes until they are tender. Serve the tajine hot, with its sauce.

COUSCOUS DE POULET (MOROCCO)

Couscous is perhaps the national dish of North Africa: Morocco and Tunisia both claim to be the country of its origin. The rich stew of chick-peas, turnips, carrots, tomatoes, and other vegetables served with chicken over a bed of semolina is a dish that is simple to make and yet presents a festive appearance. This is a recipe for quick couscous that eliminates steps from the traditional Moroccan recipe but allows for a presentation and a taste that equal the original.

SERVES SIX

- 1 medium-sized chicken, cut into pieces
- 2 large onions, cut into eighths
- 2 tomatoes (or 1½ cups cherry tomatoes), chopped coarse
- 2 zucchini, sliced
- 1 yellow squash, diced
- 3 small purple turnips, diced
- One (8-ounce) can chick-peas (Goya chick-peas are very good)

⅓ teaspoon of salt and 1 teaspoon freshly ground black pepper to taste

Place the chicken pieces in a large pot and cover with water. Season with ⅓ teaspoon of salt and 1 teaspoon of freshly ground black pepper. Place the pot on medium heat and, when the water begins to boil, reduce the heat and allow the chicken to cook thoroughly, about 30 minutes, over low heat.

Place the onions, tomatoes, squash, and turnips in a 5-quart saucepan. Add the chick-peas and their liquid and 2 cups of water. Season with salt and pepper and cook for 30 minutes or until the vegetables are tender.

Drain the chicken, reserving the broth, and place it on a large platter. Cover the chicken with the vegetable mixture. Combine equal amounts of chicken broth and vegetable juice to make a sauce, which can be passed separately. Serve buttered couscous on the side.*

To present the couscous elegantly, serve it along with any of the North African salads, pita bread, and small dishes of Harissa (page 60) and ground cumin on the side. The couscous itself is not a spicy dish, but guests can add enough Harissa and cumin to make it as piquant as they wish.

* Couscous is the heart of semolina. Hand-rolled in Morocco and North Africa, it is available prerolled and precooked in the United States. To cook, follow the package directions.

MECHOUI
(SENEGAL)

This spit-roasted baby lamb dish comes to Senegal from North Africa. In Black Africa, as in the North, Mechoui is a festive dish that is saved for grand occasions. Started before the arrival of the guests, the meat is finished and literally done to a turn before the assembled guests. It is served with great ceremony and is usually the centerpiece of the culinary presentation. Although spit-roasting is impossible in many urban apartments, for a grand occasion an approximation of the Mechoui can easily be done in the oven.

SERVES TWENTY

One 10-pound baron of lamb
Juice of 2 lemons
3 large cloves garlic
2 tablespoons Dijon-style mustard
Salt and pepper to taste
Thyme, bay leaf, and parsley to taste
½ cup peanut oil
2 hot red chiles (Guinea pepper type), seeded and minced

Wash the lamb thoroughly and rub it with the juice of one lemon inside and out. Mince the garlic cloves and mix them with 1 tablespoon of mustard and salt and pepper to taste. Coat the inside of the lamb with this mixture. Combine the thyme, bay leaf, and parsley and place them inside the lamb. Sew it up.

Meanwhile, heat the oven to 450 degrees; when warm, place the lamb in the oven and sear it. Then lower the heat to 325 degrees and continue to cook the lamb. Make a marinade of the remaining mustard, the lemon juice, the peanut oil, the two hot chiles, and salt and pepper to taste. Use this mixture to baste the lamb as it cooks. Roast the meat for approximately 10 minutes per pound if you like it rare and 12 to 15 minutes if you prefer it medium. Well-done meat will take 20 minutes per pound. These temperatures are only approximate and should be verified with a meat thermometer. Lamb is rare at 140 degrees, medium at 150 degrees, and well done at 160 degrees.

In Morocco and Senegal, Mechoui is eaten with the fingers of the right hand. Serve your Mechoui with a green salad or any of the North African salads and with couscous seasoned with the lamb drippings.

STUFFED PEPPERS À L'AFRICAINE (ALL AFRICA)

Stuffed peppers seem to be a universal dish. Each continent has used the capsicum containers to hold a variety of ingredients. The creative cook adds minced lamb or rice in Greece, tomatoes and chopped beef in the United States, raw beef and hot pepper in Ethiopia, and potatoes and spices in a vegetarian Indian version. Here's an African variety using ground beef and lots of hot pepper.

SERVES EIGHT

- 1 slice stale white bread
- 3 medium-sized onions, peeled and chopped
- 2 tablespoons minced parsley
- 1½ pounds ground beef
- 1 teaspoon cayenne pepper
- 1 teaspoon Harissa (see page 60)
- 3 or more cups peanut oil
- 16 medium green bell peppers (you may also use Italian peppers or hot or mild green chiles)
- 4 eggs

Grate the bread into fine crumbs. Mix the onions, parsley, and bread crumbs with the beef. Season the mixture with the cayenne pepper and the Harissa. Place 2 tablespoons of the olive oil in a skillet and cook the mixture, stirring frequently to prevent sticking. Remove the mixture from the heat, drain it of any fat, and allow it to cool. Meanwhile, slit the peppers and delicately core and seed them, leaving the shell intact. Beat the eggs and add them to the stuffing mixture, taking care that they are well mixed in. Stuff the peppers. Heat the oil to 350 to 375 degrees in a heavy saucepan or a deep fat fryer and fry the peppers until they are crisp. Drain on paper towels and serve warm. The peppers can be accompanied by a Spicy Tomato Sauce (page 42), or a Pili Pili Sauce (page 58) or served alone.

Hot Stuff in Latin America and the Caribbean

COLUMBUS'S MISTAKE was the pepper lover's good fortune, for in his search for the Spice Islands, he stumbled across a continent full of chiles. Capsicum peppers are native to the New World. Cayenne peppers, hot chiles in myriad varieties, and bell peppers are all indigenous to Latin America, and the people of this region have developed their cuisines using capsicums as everything from spice to garnish.

To me, akee, peas and rice, salt fish, mangoes, papayas, and rum summed up the cooking of the Caribbean. I knew nothing of cooking further south, except that Brazilians loved beans, Argentines had good beef, and Mexicans ate chiles with everything. How wrong I was.

The food of Latin America and the Caribbean is as varied as its history. Many cultures have contributed to it, and many hands have stirred the pots. All have had a respect for the native capsicum pepper, and its effective use becomes one of the hallmarks of good Caribbean cooking.

Today peppers poke their red noses up through Martinique's Sauce Chien, a spicy onion, lemon, and pepper mixture that adds a tangy bite to almost any dish. Haitian chefs perform voodoo in creating Sauce Ti-Malice, a concoction of garlic, onions, shallots, hot chile, and lime juice that would make boiled shoe leather taste heavenly.

In Puerto Rico, a drive out of San Juan to Loiza Aldea, the African heart of the island, is a joy for those who relish the mixing of Spanish and African cuisines. There, Bacalaitos, deep-fried codfish fritters, are a specialty. Liberally doused with spicy hot sauce and washed down with coconut water, they are an ideal introduction to the hot food of the Caribbean.

A trip to an open market in any of the islands is sure to reveal the degree to which peppers and chiles are revered. Tiny red bird peppers, larger red and green lantern-shaped peppers, mild green and red chiles, and fiery hot red-orange bird peppers are only some of the varieties to be discovered. Their intensity ranges from mildly biting to smoke-coming-out-of-the-ears WOW. Islanders have also turned their peppery bounty into hot sauces, pepper wines, and innumerable condiments.

Guadeloupe is an earthly paradise for lovers of spicy food. The blend of Caribbean foodstuffs, African seasoning, and French culinary techniques has created a cuisine that is the *summum* of Caribbean cooking. Peppers abound in the markets, and each one has its own name. A small, wrinkled one is rudely known as Bonda Man Jacques (Madame Jacques's behind); a small, eggplant-colored one is called Piment Negresse. But pepper is more than strange names. Guadeloupe is a nation of serious pepper lovers, and small hot peppers are a major ingredient in the island's cooking. They are also occasionally served on the side, whole, with lime, so that the diner can add spice to any dish at will.

On Guadeloupe the great cooks are women, and every August they parade through the streets during La Fête des Cuisinieres, carrying baskets decorated with food and miniature cooking utensils.

Guadeloupe, however, is meeting culinary competition as inventive cooks from other islands produce traditional dishes with new variations and create new dishes that take advantage of the region's natural bounty—the abundant tropical seafood and the ubiquitous capsicum.

South of the border, down Mexico way, chiles spice up many dishes and turn up in some unexpected places. Even breakfast eggs take on a tangy bite as Huevos Rancheros. But they are only the start. Nachos and Bean Dip are piquant appetizers and Pato in Mole Verde, Bacalao Veracruzano, and Higadillos Mexicanos con Jerez offer tasty alternatives to roast duck, codfish, and broiled chicken livers respectively. Anyone who thinks a Margarita is the only way to sample Mexico's tequila have not tasted Sangrita, a tomato, orange, and lime juice mixture seasoned with onion salt and, of course, chile, which can accompany the straight beverage. Hot sauce Mexican style, Salsa Picante, spices up everything and soon becomes a required staple in the refrigerator.

In Brazil, hot stuff takes another turn in the African-inspired recipes from Salvador de Bahia in the Northeast. There, dishes like Salada de Quiabo, Moqueca de Peixe, and Acarajé tell the history of the country better than any text. Brazilians are pepper lovers all. Even the national dish, Feijoada Completa, is not complete without Molho Apimentado, a sauce made from the juices of stewed meat, the liquid from cooked beans, and Brazil's own tiny incendiary malagueta peppers.

The Spanish-speaking areas of the continent are no slouches either when it comes to hot stuff. Coriander and garlic mix with hot chiles and other ingredients to form Chile's Pebre. Chimichurri, a combination of oil, vinegar, onions, garlic, thyme, parsley, oregano, and chiles, adds spice to Argentine barbecues or churrascas. And the Peruvians pull out all stops with their Aji Molido con Aceite a sauce that calls for one cup of dried hot chiles.

Before proceeding with any recipes calling for hot chiles, refer to the Chile Caveats in the front of the book.

PEPPER POT SOUP
(ANTIGUA)

My friend Sandra Taylor is a lawyer who has worked for the U.S. Department of State. In her travels she has lived in various parts of the Caribbean and has visited others as well. One of her favorite places is Antigua. She returns every year for race week and revels in the unique combination of sea, ships, and things nautical. Sandra is also an excellent cook, and one of the recipes she brought back from an Antiguan sojourn is this Pepper Pot Soup.

SERVES EIGHT

1 pound eggplant, cut into ½-inch dice
½ pound spinach, shredded
½ pound Indian kale, shredded
12 okra pods, cut into ½-inch pieces
1 pound yams, peeled and cut into 1-inch dice
1 pound pumpkin, peeled and cut into 1-inch dice
1 scallion, cut into 1-inch pieces
2 small hot chiles, cut into quarters
2 onions, chopped coarse
3 small yellow squash, cut into 1-inch dice
½ pound salt beef
½ pound pig feet
8 cups water
4 cloves
3 cups coconut milk
1 small clove garlic, minced
2 teaspoons minced chives
½ teaspoon thyme
2 cups fresh green peas
4 tablespoons tomato paste
Salt and freshly ground black pepper to taste

Place all the vegetables except the peas in a large stew pot with the meat and the water. Boil until the meat is tender (about 1 hour). Add the coconut milk and the cloves, garlic, chives, and thyme. After the liquid has resumed boiling, add the peas and the tomato paste. Simmer the mixture for about 1 hour or until thick. Adjust the seasoning and serve hot.

SPICY PUMPKIN SOUP
(BARBADOS)

Pumpkins mean more in the Caribbean than pumpkin pie and Halloween. Large pieces of cooking pumpkin are found in markets nestled among the greens and the tomatoes. They are used in stews and to create wonderful hearty soups like spicy pumpkin soup.

SERVES FOUR TO SIX

- 1/3 cup dried split peas
- 4 cups chicken stock
- 1 1/2 cups chopped pumpkin
- 1 medium-sized onion, chopped coarse
- 1 slice bacon, fried and crumbled
- 1 hot chile (Guinea pepper type), minced
- Salt and freshly ground black pepper to taste
- 1/4 teaspoon powdered allspice
- 1/2 cup cooked ham, diced into small bits

Soak the split peas overnight according to package directions. The next day, rinse the split peas and place them in a large soup kettle. Add the stock and all the other ingredients except 1/4 cup of the ham. Simmer until the pumpkin and the split peas are tender, about 1 1/2 hours. Pass the soup through a food mill until the mixture is a smooth, thick liquid. Serve hot, garnished with chopped parsley and the remaining diced ham.

CALALOU
(GUADELOUPE)

Calalou is a hearty soup of greens and herbs. It is eaten throughout the Caribbean and seems to be spelled a different way on each island. Naturally, each island has its own variations for the ingredients. In the French Antilles, they eat a Calalou made with ham or crab, which is usually served with Chiquetaille de Morue *(page 103)**.*

SERVES FOUR

1 pound okra
1 pound fresh spinach
1 medium-sized onion, chopped coarse
1 bouquet garni made of scallions, thyme (fresh if possible), and parsley
Salt and freshly ground black pepper to taste
6½ cups water
½ pound cooked ham cut into ¼-inch dice
1 clove garlic, minced
Juice of 3 limes

Clean the okra and tail and tip them. Clean the spinach, rinsing well to get rid of the grit and removing the thick central stems. Chop the okra and the spinach and place them in a large saucepan. Add the onion, the bouquet garni, salt and black pepper, and the water. Bring the ingredients to a boil, reduce heat, and cook, covered, over a medium flame for 40 minutes. Put the mixture through a food mill until it is smooth. Replace the purée in the saucepan and add the ham, minced garlic, and lime juice. Continue to cook for an additional 15 minutes. DO NOT ALLOW THE SOUP TO COME TO A BOIL OR IT WILL LOSE ITS TEXTURE. Serve hot, accompanied by Chiquetaille de Morue (page 103).

SALTED FISH (CARIBBEAN)

Salted fish is an ingredient in many Caribbean dishes. Cod is the salted fish most often found on the American market. It is easy to reconstitute and prepare.

Soak the salted fish overnight in cold water. Drain the fish, place it in a saucepan, and cover with fresh cold water. Bring the water to a boil and simmer the fish for 15 minutes, or until it is tender. Skin and flake the fish.

If you are in a hurry and overnight soaking is impossible, you can place the salted fish in a saucepan, cover it with fresh cold water, bring it quickly to a boil, and drain it immediately.

CHIQUETAILLE DE MORUE (MARTINIQUE)

Chiquetaille de Morue is the traditional accompaniment to Calalou (page 101) in the French Antilles. This flaked salted codfish dish is a cousin to Trinidad's Buljol (page 110), with a Creole touch. It is also an excellent warm-weather appetizer when served with hot buttered French bread. Add a glass of chilled dry rosé wine, close your eyes, and you're sitting in Chez Lolotte overlooking the swaying masts of the marina in Pointe du Bout, Martinique.

SERVES SIX

1 pound salted codfish
1 cup white wine vinegar
2 medium-sized onions, minced
1 chile (Guinea pepper type), minced

Prepare the salted cod according to the directions on page 102, but leave the fish whole. Roast the fish briefly over a charcoal grill or broil it under the broiler for 5 minutes on each side. When cooked, shred the fish into fine bits. (Chiqueter means to shred in French.) Marinate the fish in the vinegar for 1 hour, then drain it thoroughly. Finally, add the onions and the chile. Mix well and serve. Although Chiquetaille de Morue is the traditional accompaniment to Calalou, it can also be eaten as a main course.

CALALOU AUX CRABES (GUADELOUPE)

A spicier version of Calalou is made with fresh crabs. To make this dish in the traditional manner, you will need a baton lélé, *which is a three-branched stick of dried wood that is used as a whisk. Instead of a* baton lélé, *which you probably will not have (unless you are an inveterate collector of exotic cooking utensils), you may use a wire whisk, but Guadeloupean cooks will tell you that your Calalou aux Crabes will not taste the same.*

SERVES SIX

4 medium-sized crabs
3 tablespoons peanut oil
5 chives or 3 scallions, with the green tops included, minced
3 cloves garlic, chopped
1 branch fresh thyme
½ pound slab bacon, cut into ¼-inch dice
1 pound fresh spinach, cleaned, with stems removed
1 pound okra, topped, tailed, and cut into rounds
6 cups water
Salt and pepper to taste
1 hot chile (Guinea pepper type), minced
Juice of 3 limes

Clean the crabs well, remove their shells, and cut them in half leaving the claws attached. Brown them in the oil with the minced chives or scallions, 1 teaspoon of the garlic, and the thyme.

In a separate pan, brown the diced bacon. Wilt the spinach in the bacon fat. Add the okra. Cover with 6 cups of water and add salt and pepper to taste. Cook for 20 minutes, stirring constantly with the *baton lélé*. When done, pour the mixture over the crabs and cook for an additional 20 minutes over low heat.

When the Calalou aux Crabes is ready to serve, add the remaining garlic, the whole chile, and the lime juice. Serve hot, accompanied by Chiquetaille de Morue (page 103).

SOPA DE MAIS (MEXICO)

Corn is used in Mexican dishes from tortillas to salads. It is the main ingredient in corn soup.

SERVES SIX

4 cups fresh corn kernels, cut off the cob
1 cup chicken stock
¼ cup butter
5 scallions, including some of the green part, minced
3½ cups milk
Salt and freshly ground black pepper to taste
3 mild green chiles, minced
Sour cream, tortilla chips, and parsley for garnish

Place the corn kernels and chicken stock in a food processor and blend them until they are a smooth purée. Melt the butter in a large saucepan. Add the scallions and cook them until they are wilted. Add the corn and chicken stock purée and simmer the mixture for about 5 minutes or until the soup has thickened. Add the milk, salt, and pepper and cook for an additional 15 minutes.

Meanwhile, divide the minced chiles into six individual serving bowls. Pour the soup into the bowls and garnish each serving with a dollop of sour cream, a dash of crumbled tortilla chips, and a bit of chopped parsley. Serve at once.

SCABECHI (ARUBA)

Aruba, located only fifteen miles off the coast of South America, is the "A" of the A.B.C. islands. Although Aruba is a Dutch island, its food owes more to international influence than to that of the Netherlands. Scabechi, a cooked pickled fish dish, dates back to the days before refrigeration, when food had to be preserved by other methods.

🌶🌶🌶 SERVES FOUR TO SIX

2 pounds mackerel, kingfish, or any firm-fleshed white fish
3 tablespoons unsalted butter
6 small onions, diced
2 tablespoons peanut oil
1½ cups water
½ cup white wine vinegar
4 small carrots, sliced very thin lengthwise
4 hot peppers, cut in eighths
3 bay leaves
2 teaspoons salt
12 black peppercorns
2 cloves garlic, crushed
1 tablespoon capers
7 or more pimento-stuffed olives, sliced

Fry the mackerel in the butter until it is golden brown. Place the fish in a deep earthenware bowl. In a saucepan, make a marinade by sautéeing the onions in the oil until soft and tender. Add the remaining ingredients and bring the mixture to a boil. Pour the marinade over the fish. Cover the bowl with plastic wrap and let it stand in the refrigerator for 24 hours. Mix well and serve. The Scabechi may be served cold as an appetizer or reheated and served warm as a fish course.

ACHARDS
(MARTINIQUE)

This appetizer salad from Martinique combines many tropical vegetables, saffron, and, naturally, hot chile to make a marinated vegetable first course.

🌶🌶 YIELD = 2 CUPS

1 pound vegetables, including hearts of palm, cabbage, cauliflower, carrots, and string beans

¼ cup olive oil
1 medium-sized onion, sliced into rings
1 clove garlic, chopped
1 hot red chile (habañero type), chopped fine
2 or 3 pinches of saffron

Wash the vegetables and cut them into bite-sized pieces. Place each vegetable in a separate container of lightly salted water and chill for 24 hours in the refrigerator. When the vegetables are ready, heat the oil and in it cook the onion, garlic, chile, and saffron until the onion is golden. Meanwhile, remove the vegetables from the refrigerator, drain them well, and arrange them on a platter. Pour the hot oil mixture over the vegetables and place the platter in the refrigerator to marinate overnight. Serve chilled.

GREEN MANGO SOUSKAI (MARTINIQUE)

In Martinique when unripe fruit is seasoned with a pepper marinade and served with cocktails, it is called souskai. These spicy bites are tart, tangy, and the perfect complement to the molasses sweetness of the ti' punch that is the traditional Martiniquais aperitif.

SERVES FOUR

2 firm, unripe mangoes
1 clove garlic, minced
1 hot chile (Guinea pepper type), minced
Juice of 2 limes
1 teaspoon salt

Peel the mangoes and cut them into cubes. Make a marinade of the minced garlic, chile, lime juice, and salt. Place the mango pieces in the marinade for 1 hour. Drain them and serve on toothpicks along with cocktails.

COCONUT SOUSKAI (MARTINIQUE)

Coconut can also be turned into Souskai, but it is eaten in its marinade.

SERVES FOUR

½ ripe coconut, shelled and peeled
1 teaspoon salt
1 clove garlic, minced
1 hot chile (Guinea pepper type), minced
Juice of 2 limes

With a potato peeler, cut the coconut meat into long, thin strips. Prepare a marinade from the salt, garlic, chile, and lime juice. Marinate the coconut strips for 1 hour. Serve the coconut with cocktails, in its marinade. Remind your guests to be careful not to bite down on the pieces of pepper.

ROUGAIL DE MANGUES VERTES (MARTINIQUE)

This paste of green mangoes is served as an appetizer in Martinique.

SERVES SIX TO EIGHT

4 firm, unripe mangoes
1 medium-sized onion
2 scallions
1 teaspoon thyme
½ hot chile (Guinea pepper type), minced
3 tablespoons olive oil
Salt and freshly ground black pepper to taste
1 hard-boiled egg
2 sprigs of parsley

Peel the mangoes and cut them into small pieces. Chop the mangoes, onion, scallions, thyme, and hot chile in a food processor. Drizzle in the olive oil until the mixture becomes a smooth paste. Add salt and black pepper to taste, stirring well so all the ingredients are thoroughly mixed. Decorate the Rougail with slices of hard-boiled egg and the parsley sprigs.

COCONUT CRISPS (BARBADOS)

Sundowner time in the Caribbean is when friends gather to watch the sun go down and to have a drink or two of world-famous Caribbean rum. Legend has it that from some parts of the island, if you look closely, you can see a green flash just as the sun is setting. People have been known to spend years watching for the green flash and all they have to report for their vigilance is a growing fondness for rum and a thorough knowledge of the various Caribbean cocktail tidbits. Coconut crisps are one such tidbit that can easily be duplicated in the United States. You may not see the green flash, but you can savor the piquant nibble. And after a few rum drinks, who knows? You may even see a green flash of your own.

SERVES EIGHT TO TEN

1 ripe coconut, shelled and peeled
Chile powder
Salt

After the coconut has been shelled and the brown rind has been pared off, cut the coconut pieces into long, thin strips with a potato peeler. Place the pieces on a cookie sheet and sprinkle them lightly with chile powder. Brown them lightly under the broiler for a few minutes. When ready, remove them, sprinkle lightly with salt, and serve warm with cocktails.

CURRY CRISPS
(BARBADOS)

When you add curry powder instead of chile powder to Coconut Crisps . . . voilà *. . . Curry Crisps.*

BULJOL
(TRINIDAD)

Here is a salted fish salad that is served as an appetizer throughout the Caribbean. The salt fish is mixed with freshly squeezed lime juice, onion, grated cucumber, and hot pepper to make a savory warm weather salad. I first tasted Buljol at the Brown Sugar restaurant in Barbados. The sea tang of the salt fish mixed with the bite of the onion and hot chile to create a taste that will always mean Barbados to me—although the dish originated in Trinidad.

SERVES FOUR

1½ pounds salted codfish
Juice of 4 limes
1 large onion, sliced into rings
½ medium-sized cucumber, peeled
1 small hot chile, minced
2 tablespoons olive oil (optional)

Wash the salt fish according to the directions on page 102. Squeeze the lime juice over the salt fish. Remove the skin and any bones and flake the fish with a fork. Rinse off the lime juice with cold water. Discard the water. Add the onion rings to the salt fish. Grate the cucumber on the coarse end of the grater and add it to the fish and onion mixture. Finally, add the minced chile. Mix well and serve with crackers.

You may choose to pour olive oil over the Buljol; in that case, it is traditionally accompanied by roasted breadfruit.

SALTED FISH BALLS
(BARBADOS)

Salted codfish is one of the staples of Caribbean cuisine. Used in everything from Martinique's Chiquetaille de Morue (page 103) to Jamaica's Ackee and Salt Fish, this easy-to-store, easy-to-prepare fish adds protein to many Caribbean dishes. Here, it forms the basis of fish balls that are served as appetizers along with cocktails.

SERVES FOUR TO SIX

¾ cup salted codfish, prepared and flaked
2 eggs, well beaten
½ cup milk
1 small onion, minced
½ small chile (Guinea pepper type), minced
Salt and freshly ground pepper to taste
1 tablespoon dry bread crumbs
2 cups vegetable oil for deep frying

Prepare the codfish according to the directions on page 102. Mix the fish, eggs, milk, onion, chile, spices, and bread crumbs. Roll the mixture into marble-sized balls. In a heavy saucepan, heat the oil to 350 to 375 degrees. Deep fry the fish balls, a few at a time, until they are browned on all sides. Drain them on a paper towel and keep them warm in the oven. Serve warm on toothpicks and cocktails.

NACHOS
(MEXICO)

Appetizers in Mexico are wonderful—a small bowl of guacamole redolent of coriander greets guests at almost any restaurant, fried pork rinds and various sauces are available, and savory little nibbles called nachos are always a delight.

HOT STUFF

❧❧❧ SERVES SIX

Six 6-inch corn tortillas*
½ cup peanut oil for frying
3 pickled jalapeño peppers
½ cup refried beans (you may use canned but homemade (page 000) are better)
¼ cup grated Monterey Jack cheese

Cut the tortillas into quarters. Heat the oil in a heavy frying pan until it is between 350 and 375 degrees; fry the tortilla pieces until they are crisp. Drain them on paper towels. Stem and seed the peppers, paying attention to the directions for handling peppers on page 29. Cut the peppers into small, thin strips. You should have about six strips per pepper.

Spread each tortilla chip with 1 teaspoon of the refried beans. Place ½ teaspoon of the grated Monterey Jack on top of the beans and decorate the nacho with a jalapeño pepper strip. Place the finished nachos on a cookie tin. Place them under the broiler and cook until the cheese melts. Serve them warm to accompany drinks or at the start of a Mexican meal. You will have 24 appetizers.

QUICK VERSION
Follow the above directions but use purchased tortilla chips and canned refried beans to which you have added a dash of the brine from the jalapeño peppers.

They will be a bit spicier but almost as good as those made from scratch.

* Corn tortillas can be found in the dairy cases of some supermarkets or obtained from mail order houses selling Latin American ingredients (see the end of the book). If frozen, they should be thawed and separated before cutting.

REFRIED BEANS

❧ YIELD = ABOUT 2 CUPS

½ pound dried pinto beans
3 strips of bacon, diced

¼ cup minced cooked ham
1 small onion, minced
1 teaspoon minced garlic

Following the package directions, soak the beans in water overnight. The following day, add enough fresh water to cover the beans and simmer them for 2 hours or until tender. Drain the beans, reserving the liquid, and mash them with a potato masher.

While the beans are cooking, fry the bacon, ham, onion, and garlic. Add the bean paste and fry, stirring, until everything is well mixed. Moisten the mixture with 1 or more tablespoons of the reserved liquid if necessary and serve warm.

GUACAMOLE (MEXICO)

This avocado dip is the ubiquitous Mexican appetizer. It has been made in so many variations and served at so many house parties and inferior restaurants that the taste of a good spicy guacamole redolent of coriander is a surprise to many. Simple to make, yet sophisticated, this appetizer dip is the perfect accompaniment to tequila drinks and the classic starter for many Mexican meals.

SERVES SIX TO EIGHT

3 medium-sized ripe avocados
1 medium-sized tomato, peeled, seeded, and chopped
1 small red onion, chopped
2 pickled jalapeño peppers, stemmed, seeded, and minced
4 sprigs of fresh coriander, minced
1 tablespoon freshly squeezed lemon juice
Salt and freshly ground black pepper to taste

Cut the avocados in half lengthwise; peel off the skin and reserve the pits. Place the avocado meat in a bowl and mash it with a fork until it is a thick paste. Add the other ingredients and mix well to distribute them evenly. Taste for seasoning and place in small bowls. Serve immediately.

If you must make the guacamole in advance, bury the avocado pits in the guacamole. They contain a substance that will help retard discoloration of the avocado. Try, though, to serve the guacamole immediately to avoid this problem. Guacamole is traditionally served with tortilla chips (below), but it can also be used as a dip with raw vegetable pieces.

TORTILLA CHIPS
(MEXICO)

The Mexican equivalent of potato chips, these are found on the tables in cocktail bars and accompany many Mexican appetizers. Although they can be purchased in most supermarkets, the homemade version has a taste all its own.

SERVES EIGHT TO TEN

1 dozen corn tortillas*
Oil for frying (peanut oil or vegetable oil is best)
Salt to taste

Cut each tortilla into eight wedges. (If you like a larger chip, cut into quarters.) In a heavy frying pan or deep fryer, heat the oil to between 350 and 375 degrees. Fry the tortilla pieces, a few at a time, until they are golden and crisp. Remove them from the oil and dry them on paper towels. When all are fried, place them in a brown paper bag with the salt. Shake lightly to be sure the chips are thoroughly salted. Serve with Guacamole (page 113) or other Mexican dips.

* See note page 112.

BEAN DIP
(MEXICO)

I was first served this dip at a friend's cocktail party. The blandness of the beans combined with the bite of the jalapeño peppers surprised and pleased me. I was equally pleased when I learned that the recipe was simple to make, requiring only canned beans, fresh jalapeño chiles, and Monterey Jack cheese.

❧❧❧ SERVES SIX

One pound refried beans, either homemade (page 112) or canned
3 pickled jalapeño peppers, seeded and minced
¾ cup grated Monterey Jack cheese

Mash the beans and jalapeño chiles with the back of a fork. If the mixture is too thick, add a bit of water, or—if you don't mind the heat—a drop or two of the liquid from the pickled jalapeño chiles. Mix well and place in three smal! oven-proof bowls. Sprinkle the top of each bowl with one-third of the cheese (¼ cup per bowl). Heat the bowls as needed in a 350-degree oven. Serve warm with tortilla chips (page 114).

CERBICHE
(MEXICO)

This raw marinated fish dish is now found throughout Latin America. Its home, however, is Mexico. As an appetizer, it is the perfect introduction to more piquant dishes. The lime juice "cooks" the fish, and the tang of the lime brings out its sea taste. The jalapeño pepper brightens up the blandness of the fish and rounds out the taste of the dish. Cerbiche is accompanied by small sections of corn on the cob in some areas of South America and by large kernels of unpopped but grilled popcorn in others.

❧❧❧ SERVES FOUR TO SIX

⅓ pound raw small shrimp, cleaned and deveined
⅓ pound raw bay scallops

⅓ pound raw haddock fillets
Juice of 9 limes, about 1½ cups
2 pickled jalapeño peppers, minced
1 small onion, minced
1 large ripe tomato, peeled, seeded, and chopped coarse
6 tablespoons olive oil
2 tablespoons white wine vinegar
2 sprigs of coriander
Salt and freshly ground black pepper to taste

Rinse the shrimp, scallops, and haddock thoroughly in cold water. Pat dry and verify that the shrimp have been deveined and the scallops cleaned. Shred the haddock. Place the seafood in a non-reactive glass or pottery bowl and cover it with the lime juice. Cover the bowl with plastic wrap and refrigerate for 5 hours. Remove the wrap occasionally to stir the fish with a wooden utensil to be sure it is well covered with the lime juice.

Combine the jalapeño peppers, onion, tomato, oil, vinegar, coriander, salt, and pepper. When the seafood has marinated for 5 hours, add the pepper mixture and mix well. Cover with plastic wrap and refrigerate for an additional 3 hours. When it is ready, allow the Cerbiche to sit at room temperature for 15 minutes before serving. You may wish to garnish it with 2-inch sections of corn on the cob and lime wedges. Alternately, you may mound the Cerbiche on lettuce leaves in cocktail glasses and garnish it with lime wedges and sprigs of coriander.

SALADA DE QUIABO
(BRAZIL)

Okra, a typical African vegetable, is used in a New World way in this salad. The "slime" from the okra that is offensive to those who do not care for the vegetable here becomes part of the salad dressing, and the dash of hot pepper adds bite and spice.

SERVES FOUR

1½ pounds small, firm okra, topped and tailed
¼ cup of your favorite vinaigrette sauce

1 tablespoon onion, minced
1 small clove garlic, minced
3 small malagueta peppers, minced

Place the okra in boiling water for no more than 5 minutes. (If you leave it in the water, longer, it will become extremely slimy.) Meanwhile, prepare your favorite vinaigrette sauce and add the minced onion, garlic, and malagueta peppers. Mix well. Drain the okra, place it in a salad bowl, and serve it warm, topped with the vinaigrette.

GUYANESE CARROT SALAD (GUYANA)

My colleague June Bobb makes this cooked carrot salad for her family. It is a quick and easy dish that can be prepared as much as two days ahead. The dressing serves as a marinade, and marinating improves the flavor of the salad.

SERVES SIX TO EIGHT

1 pound cooked carrots, sliced
1 medium-sized onion, sliced into rings
2 cups blanched cauliflower florets
1 clove garlic, chopped
½ medium-sized green bell pepper, chopped coarse
½ medium-sized red bell pepper, chopped coarse
½ 10¾ oz. can Campbell's tomato soup undiluted
½ cup sugar
⅓ cup peanut oil
⅓ cup or more red wine vinegar
Salt and freshly ground black pepper to taste

Place all the vegetables in a salad bowl. Mix the tomato soup, sugar, peanut oil, and vinegar together to form the dressing. Taste the dressing and add more vinegar if necessary. Adjust the seasoning by adding salt and black pepper to taste. Pour the dressing over the vegetables and mix them well to be sure all are well coated. Cover the bowl with plastic wrap and store it in the refrigerator for a minimum of 24 hours and a maximum of 48 hours. Serve chilled.

ENSALADA DE MAIS (MEXICO)

Most visitors to Mexico have been warned not to eat any vegetables. They stick to a strict meat-only diet and miss much that is enjoyable in Mexican food. With a little bit of adventure, and a good deal of common sense, they could enjoy dishes like Ensalada de Mais, a corn salad made with fresh corn, green pepper, pimento, and hot chiles.

SERVES FOUR TO SIX

- 2 medium-sized onions, chopped
- 1 large green pepper, chopped
- 1 pickled jalapeño pepper, minced
- ¼ cup pimento, chopped
- 2 tablespoons sugar
- Salt and freshly ground black pepper to taste
- ½ teaspoon dry mustard
- ½ cup cider vinegar
- ½ cup water
- 3 cups fresh corn kernels cut off the cob

Place all the ingredients except the corn in a saucepan and bring to a boil over medium to high heat. Cover the saucepan, lower the heat, and simmer for 15 minutes, stirring from time to time. Add the corn and raise the heat. When the ingredients begin to boil for the second time, lower the heat and simmer until the corn is cooked and tender. Drain the salad. You may serve it warm or chill in the refrigerator and serve it cold. Present the salad on a bed of lettuce leaves garnished with strips of pimento and jalapeño pepper.

AVOCADO MAYONNAISE
(GUADELOUPE)

No, this is not a recipe for an avocado with mayonnaise. It is a whipped avocado condiment that can be used instead of mayonnaise.

YIELD = 1½ CUPS

1 medium-sized, ripe avocado
1 hot chile (habañero type), minced
2 teaspoons parsley, minced
2 cloves garlic, minced
3 scallions, minced
Salt and freshly ground black pepper to taste
1 cup olive oil
2 tablespoons freshly squeezed lemon juice

Peel and mash the avocado. In a food processor, mince the chile, parsley, garlic, and scallions. Add the minced ingredients to the mashed avocado and adjust the seasoning, adding salt and black pepper to taste. Add the oil, drop by drop, as though making mayonnaise, while constantly whipping the avocado mixture. Beat in the lemon juice. Avocado mayonnaise is excellent on toast.

FAROFA AMARELA
(BRAZIL)

Farofa is manioc flour toasted to a crispy crunch. It accompanies many Brazilian dishes, and in Brazil a farofa dispenser is frequently found on restaurant tables next to the salt, pepper, and hot sauce. I've met Brazilians who hated their first taste of pizza simply because they assumed the garlic dispenser at the pizzeria was filled with farofa. Farofa is sprinkled on almost all Brazilian dishes from beans to Moqueca de Peixe (page 135). It lends a crispy texture and can become habit forming. Farofa Amarela is traditionally served with Bahian dishes.

YIELD = 1 CUP

1 cup manioc meal
2 tablespons dendê oil (Dendê oil is palm oil)

In a heavy skillet, toast the manioc meal in the dendê oil. Stir constantly to be sure the meal is thoroughly coated and has turned a brilliant yellow. Serve warm to accompany Brazilian dishes. Sprinkle it over beans, eggs, soups, stews . . . whatever.

FAROFA
(BRAZIL)

There are many variations to Farofa, such as the Farofa Amarela (page 119) that is served with Bahian dishes. Cooks add chopped hard-boiled egg, olive slices, parsley, and other ingredients to personalize their Farofa. This simple recipe calls for onion and cooked bacon bits.

YIELD = 1½ CUPS

2 tablespoons butter
1 small onion, chopped coarse
1⅓ cups manioc meal
¼ cup bacon pieces, fried and diced
Salt and freshly ground black pepper to taste

Melt the butter in a heavy frying pan over medium heat. Add the onion and cook until it is soft. Slowly stir in the manioc meal and continue to stir until it becomes golden. Add the bacon pieces, salt, and pepper. Stir well and remove from the heat. Farofa can be served hot or at room temperature.

PEPPER SAUCE
(ST. VINCENT)

Pepper Sauce is the ubiquitous Caribbean seasoning. In restaurants it is served in a shaker-topped bottle along with the more mundane salt and pepper. Pepper sauces come in all colors from the fire-engine red Bello found in the Dominican Republic to the turmeric-hued, mustard-seasoned, homemade sauces sold in washed, sterilized pint rum bottles in the Ladies Self-Help Association shop in Bridgetown, Barbados. This St. Vincent recipe is made with mustard. Leave the seeds in the chiles if you want a hotter sauce.

YIELD = 1½ CUPS

- 8 hot chiles (Guinea pepper type)
- 1 medium-sized onion
- 2 cloves garlic
- 1 teaspoon salt
- 3 teaspoons English-style dry mustard
- 1 cup cider vinegar
- 1 tablespoon peanut oil
- ¼ teaspoon turmeric
- ¼ teaspoon saffron
- 4 cloves

Wash the chiles. Place the chiles, onion, and garlic in a food processor and mince them fine. Add the salt. Mix the mustard with enough of the vinegar to form a paste and add it to the mixture. Add the rest of the ingredients and transfer the mixture to a saucepan. Bring it to a boil and continue to cook over medium heat for 20 minutes. When cooked, transfer the pepper sauce to sterilized bottles, following standard canning directions. (You may wish to use pint liquor bottles to maintain an authentic air.) Serve the sauce with absolutely everything from breakfast eggs to steaks.

SAUCE CHIEN (GUADELOUPE)

Sauce Chien (dog sauce) is spicy, warmed with chile, and so good you could eat a dog if it were covered with it. Served to accompany grilled meats and as a general condiment with just about anything, this dish frequently appears on tables in Haiti and the French Antilles. It's so simple to make that it seems sinful to go without.

YIELD = 1 CUP

3 chives
1 medium-sized onion
1 clove garlic
1 hot chile (Guinea pepper type)
Juice of 1 lemon
Salt and freshly ground pepper to taste
1 cup boiling water

Mince the chives, onion, garlic, and chile very fine in a food processor. Add the lemon juice, salt and pepper, and the boiling water. Allow the ingredients to infuse as though preparing tea, let cool, and serve. In Haiti and Martinique each cook has her own variation. These include adding a dash of olive oil, cinnamon, capers, and other aromatic herbs. Try the basic sauce and then improvise for yourself.

CONFIT DE PIMENT (MARTINIQUE)

With chile an integral part of almost every dish, Antillean cooks have found different ways to preserve the chiles of which they are so fond. One method uses vinegar.

YIELD = APPROXIMATELY 1½ QUARTS

½ pound string beans
½ pound carrots
1 pound small hot red and green chiles (Guinea pepper type)
1½ pounds shallots, peeled and chopped coarse
4¼ cups white wine vinegar

2 tablespoons black peppercorns
1 tablespoon or more salt

Clean the beans and carrots and slice them into bite-sized pieces. Wash the chiles carefully. Place the beans, carrots, whole chiles, and shallots in a large glass jar. Boil the vinegar with the peppercorns and the salt and pour it over the vegetable and chile mixture while it is still very hot. Allow the mixture to cool completely before placing the top on the jar. This Confit de Piment is much hotter than Piment-Confit, its cousin from Guadeloupe (below).

PIMENT-CONFIT
(GUADELOUPE)

This condiment of fresh vegetables is marinated in hot chile-flavored vinegar. Milder than its Martiniquais cousin, it nevertheless packs a wallop.

YIELD = 4 CUPS

10 hot chiles (Guinea pepper type), cut in half lengthwise
1 cup carrot sticks
1 cup string beans, tailed
1 cup cauliflower florets
10 small shallots, peeled
10 black peppercorns, cracked
2½ cups or more red wine vinegar or sherry vinegar

Place the chiles in a large jar. Blanch the vegetables in boiling water, drain them well, and add them to the jar. Add the shallots and peppercorns. Cover the vegetables with the vinegar. (Add more vinegar if the vegetables are not covered.) Allow the vegetables to marinate for at least 24 hours before serving. Serve chilled to accompany everything. Eat the hot chiles at your own risk; they will sear your tongue.

MOLHO BAIANO
(BRAZIL)

This Bahian sauce is eaten with all variety of dishes. It contains some of the ingredients that are hallmarks of Bahian cooking and make it the most famous regional cuisine of Brazil.

YIELD = ⅓ TO ½ CUP

¼ cup dried smoked shrimp*
3 or 4 dried malagueta peppers
1 teaspoon salt
¼ cup palm oil (dendê type)

Roast the dried shrimp on a baking sheet in a 350-degree oven for 5 minutes on each side. In a wooden mortar and pestle crush the malagueta peppers. Add the shrimp and continue to crush the pepper and shrimp mixture until it becomes a paste. Add the salt to taste. Transfer the mixture to a heavy saucepan. Add the oil and bring the mixture to a boil over medium heat. Serve in a small bowl to accompany grilled meats and other Bahian dishes.

* See note, page 72.

MOLHO NAGO
(BRAZIL)

Nago is a Bahian term for descendants of the Yoruba peoples of Nigeria. Derived from the ritual cooking in the temples of the Afro-Brazilian Candomblé religion, Nago cooking uses elements that betray its west African origins—okra, malagueta peppers, and dried shrimp. This sauce is traditionally served with stews, and a tablespoon or two of the liquid from the stew is added to the sauce before it is served.

YIELD = 1 CUP

3 or 4 malagueta peppers
½ teaspoon salt

¼ cup dried smoked shrimp*, ground
¼ cup freshly squeezed lemon juice
5 or 6 okra pods, topped, tailed, cut into rounds, and cooked

Place the malagueta peppers, salt, and shrimp in a food processor and grind them until they are pulverized. Add the lemon juice and the okra. If serving with a stew, add one or two tablespoons of the stewing liquid to the sauce before serving it in a sauce boat.

* See note, page 72.

MOLHO DE PIMENTA E LIMÃO (BRAZIL)

This is a special sauce that is served to accompany dishes like Moqueca de Peixe (page 135). It also goes well with grilled and roasted meats.

YIELD = ½ CUP

1 teaspoon salt
3 or 4 dried malagueta peppers, minced
1 small onion, minced
1 clove garlic, minced
Juice of 3 lemons

Place the salt and the minced peppers in a small clay bowl. Add the minced onion and the minced garlic. Mix the ingredients until you have a paste. Add enough lemon juice to the paste for it to become liquid. Mix the ingredients together well and serve.

PEBRE (CHILE)

As do most other countries in South America, Chile has its own hot sauce, Pebre. The fresh coriander used in Pebre is replaced by fresh parsley in Argentina's Chimichurri (page 126). Both are accompaniments for meats; Pebre also harmonizes with bean and fish dishes.

🌶🌶🌶 YIELD = 1¼ CUPS

- 2 tablespoons olive oil
- 1 tablespoon red wine vinegar
- ⅓ cup water
- ½ cup fresh coriander, minced
- 1 small onion, minced
- 1 tablespoon Aji Molido con Aceite (page 127)
- ½ teaspoon minced garlic

Place all the ingredients in a small glass bowl. Whisk well to mix thoroughly. Taste and adjust seasonings. Allow the sauce to stand for 3 hours at room temperature to attain full flavor. Serve with Chilean dishes.

CHIMICHURRI
(ARGENTINA)

Argentina is the home of the gaucho and of the churrasca, the Argentine barbecue. Beef is king, and roasts and grills are served accompanied by Chimichurri, a spicy parsley sauce.

🌶🌶🌶 YIELD = 1½ CUPS

- ½ cup olive oil
- 4 tablespoons red wine vinegar
- ½ cup minced onion
- 1 teaspoon minced garlic
- ¼ cup fresh minced parsley
- 1 teaspoon dried oregano
- ½ teaspoon dried thyme
- 1 teaspoon crushed dried hot chiles

Place all the ingredients in a small glass bowl. Whisk well to mix thoroughly. Taste and adjust seasonings. Allow the sauce to stand for 3 or so hours at room temperature to attain full flavor. Serve with roasts and grilled meats.

AJI MOLIDO CON ACEITE
(PERU)

Aji is the Peruvian term for the fiery hot chiles that form the basis of many of the traditional dishes of that country. The chiles are ground and mixed with olive oil to form a paste that keeps well and is a good way to preserve a bumper crops of chiles. The hot Japanese Hontaka chile, also known simply as japonés, is recommended, although you may use any dried chile. The difference will be in the piquancy of the paste.

YIELD = 2 CUPS

1 cup dried Hontaka chiles
2 cups boiling water
5 tablespoons olive oil
1 teaspoon minced garlic
Salt and freshly ground black pepper to taste
1 cup chicken stock

Pick over the chiles, discarding any that have discolorations or soft spots. Then break the chile pods in half and remove the seeds and the ribs. Place the chiles in a nonreactive bowl and pour the boiling water over them. Soak the chiles in the water for 2 hours. Remove the chiles, drain them, and discard the soaking water. Place the chiles, olive oil, garlic, salt, black pepper, and chicken stock in a food processor and purée them until they form a smooth paste. Store the chile paste in a bowl or plastic bags. It will keep for 2 or more weeks if refrigerated. It can also be frozen. In that case, thaw and drain of excess water before using. This paste can be substituted for fresh chiles in many Caribbean and Latin American dishes.

SAUCE TI-MALICE
(HAITI)

In Haitian folktales, Bouki and Ti-Malice are two of the main characters. Bouki is the gullible one who takes everything at face value. Ti-Malice, his friend, is crafty and a tease. Bouki and Ti-Malice both love grilled meat. Ti-Malice eats grilled meat every day for lunch; Bouki, enjoying his friend's company and also loving meat, appears every day at lunch time. Although Ti-Malice is fond of Bouki, he tires of his daily visits. He decides to fix a sauce that will break him of this habit. He prepares a sauce of fiery hot pepper and pours it all over the meat. Imagine his surprise when Bouki, tasting the sauce, takes an additional piece and runs through the town yelling, "Me zammi, vini goute sauce Ti-Malice." (My friends, come and taste Ti-Malice sauce.) Sauce Ti-Malice is served with grilled meats, but it also accompanies Griots de Porc (pages 143–44) and many other Haitian dishes.

YIELD = 1 CUP

2 large onions, minced
2 shallots, minced
6 tablespoons freshly squeezed lime juice
2 cloves garlic, minced
4 teaspoons hot chile (red and green), minced
Salt and freshly ground black pepper to taste
3 tablespoons olive oil

Mix the onions and shallots with the lime juice and allow them to marinate for 1 hour at room temperature. Pour the mixture into a small saucepan and add the remaining ingredients. Bring to a boil over medium heat, stirring occasionally. Remove from the heat and let cool. Serve cold with grilled meats and with Griots de Porc, and your friends will also spread the word, "Me zammi, vini goute sauce Ti-Malice."

AJILIMOJILI
(PUERTO RICO)

Roast suckling pig is a festive dish anywhere in the world. When served with Ajilimojili, as in Puerto Rico, it's a special treat.

YIELD = 1½ CUPS

3 hot chiles (Guinea pepper type), seeded
3 red bell peppers, seeded
4 black peppercorns
4 cloves garlic
2 teaspoons salt
6 tablespoons freshly squeezed lime juice
6 tablespoons olive oil

Pulverize the chiles, bell peppers, peppercorns, garlic, and salt in a food processor. When they are a smooth paste, place them in a glass bowl and whisk in the lime juice and olive oil. Mix well; taste to verify seasoning and serve with roast suckling pig.

MOLHO DE PIMENTA MALAGUETA
(BRAZIL)

This sauce, Afro-Bahian in origin, is now the Brazilian hot sauce. It is found on restaurant tables from Salvador to São Paulo. A dash adds spice to any dish.

YIELD = 1 CUP

1 cup malagueta peppers, minced
¼ cup red wine vinegar
2 tablespoons olive oil

In a small jar, mix the ingredients. Shake well. Seal and let sit for 24 hours. Serve as a condiment with Bahian dishes.

SALSA PICANTE
(MEXICO)

Salsa Picante (hot sauce) goes with everything. Add a dash to a soup, a drop to Guacamole, a temperate splash to Sangrita; it even goes into Huevos Rancheros. This liquid fire is the hot stuff that Mexican dreams are made of.

YIELD = 1½ CUPS

4 medium-sized ripe tomatoes, peeled, seeded, and chopped
8 scallions, including some of the green part, minced
5 pickled jalapeño peppers, minced
4 sprigs of fresh coriander, minced
Salt and freshly ground black pepper to taste

Mix all the ingredients in a food processor until they form a thick sauce. Add more jalapeño pepper if you wish a hotter sauce. Chill and serve.

PEPPER WINE
(BARBADOS)

In downtown Bridgetown, Barbados, there is a wonderful store called the Ladies Self-Help Association. The store is the retail arm of a charitable organization of church women. It sells knick-knacks, antique and simply elderly, glass and porcelain items, flowers, crocheted doilies (in case your Victorian furniture needs anti-macassars), plants, and condiments made by the members of the organization. It was here that I first saw a bottled labeled "pepper wine." I tried it and was amazed at the zest a dash of pepper wine can bring to soups and stews. It's simple to make and will keep virtually forever if topped periodically with sherry.

YIELD = 1½ CUPS

¼ cup bird peppers
1¼ cups dry sherry

Sterilize a stoppered bottle by washing it thoroughly with scalding water. Fill it half full of bird peppers. Pour the sherry over the peppers, put the stopper in the bottle, and allow it to stand for several days. Use the Pepper Wine to add flavor to soups, stews, salad dressings, or on any dish that needs a dash of peppery taste. As the sherry diminishes, top the bottle with more sherry.

PLANTANUTRI
(PUERTO RICO)

First-time visitors to the Caribbean are frequently startled by their first taste of what they take to be potato chips. They're not potato chips but plantain chips. The versatile banana fries into crisp chips that have a sweeter taste than their potato cousins. These chips are perfect snacks and make great cocktail nibbles.

SERVES SIX

3 large plantains
Peanut oil for frying
Salt to taste

Peel the plantains and slice them crosswise into thin rounds. Place the rounds in iced water for half an hour. Heat the oil for frying to 350 to 375 degrees in a heavy saucepan or deep fat fryer. Add the plantain slices a few at a time and fry them until they are crisp. Remove them from the oil with a slotted spoon and drain on paper towels. Place the chips in a paper bag and add salt. Shake to salt them evenly. Serve with drinks or as a vegetable dish with main courses.

COUVE A MINERA
(BRAZIL)

This dish is traditionally made with kale, but collard greens, broccoli leaves, and even cabbage may be substituted. It is a "must" accompaniment for Feijoada (pages 141–43) or any dish from the Minas region of Brazil.

SERVES TEN

5 pounds kale
½ cup bacon fat
1 medium-sized onion, minced
1 clove garlic, minced
Salt to taste

Wash and pick over the kale. Take time to check each leaf thoroughly. Discard any that are brown or that have discolored spots. Cut off the tough center ribs. Bunch the leaves together, roll them tightly, and cut them into very thin strips. Wash them again and drain them.

In a frying pan heat the bacon fat and sauté the onion and garlic. Add the kale strips, turning them frequently so they cook rapidly and thoroughly. Cook for about 6 minutes or until the greens are tender. Serve warm, along with the Feijoada.

BAKED TOMATOES (BARBADOS)

The Atlantis Hotel on Barbados' surf-weathered east coast is the home of a fascinating Bajan tradition, Sunday brunch. Brunch at the Atlantis is a two-table spread of all the local delicacies a gourmet or gourmand could possibly want to eat. Peas and rice nestle next to pudding and souse (in case you missed it at its traditional Saturday serving). Baked ham, coucou, and christophene (chayote) join the lineup. These tomatoes, stuffed with a spicy sweet potato and chicken mixture, are a favorite of many brunch guests.

SERVES SIX

6 large, ripe, firm tomatoes
2 cups mashed sweet potato

2 cups cooked chicken, boned and diced
1 tablespoon onion, minced
2 teaspoons hot chile, minced
Salt and freshly ground black pepper to taste
2 tablespoons bread crumbs
2 tablespoons butter

Wash and dry the tomatoes. Cut off the tops and remove the pulp, leaving a shell about 1/4 inch thick. In a bowl, mix the tomato pulp with the sweet potato, chicken, onion, chile, salt, and pepper. Fill the tomato shells with the mixture. Sprinkle bread crumbs over each tomato, top with a dab of butter, and place them in a lightly greased baking dish. Bake the tomatoes in a 350-degree oven for 25 minutes. Serve hot, on a bed of white or saffron rice.

SOPA SECA
(MEXICO)

This "dry soup" is usually served as a separate course in a classic Mexican meal, but it also makes a wonderful side dish to accompany any meat.

SERVES FOUR TO SIX

3 tablespoons peanut oil
2 medium-sized onions, chopped
1 clove garlic, minced
1 cup uncooked long-grain rice
2 red bell peppers, chopped
Salt and freshly ground black pepper to taste
1/4 teaspoon cayenne pepper
2 cups boiling chicken stock
1/4 cup fresh peas
2 large carrots, diced
1 medium-sized tomato, peeled, seeded, and chopped coarse

Heat the peanut oil in a heavy frying pan. Add the onions, garlic, rice, and red pepper and cook, stirring occasionally, until the onion is transparent and the rice is opaque. Add salt and black pepper to taste, the cayenne pepper, chicken stock, peas, carrots, and tomato. Cook for 20 minutes or until the chicken broth has been absorbed. Stir well to be sure the vegetables are distributed through the rice and serve immediately, either as a separate course as is traditional in Mexico or as a side dish.

ARROZ VERDE
(MEXICO)

Green rice makes an unusual accompaniment to any dish. It gets its color from green peppers, parsley, and coriander.

SERVES EIGHT

4 green bell peppers
4 cups fresh chicken stock
¾ cup chopped fresh parsley
¼ cup chopped fresh coriander
2 medium-sized onions, chopped
½ clove garlic, minced
Salt and freshly ground black pepper to taste
¼ cup olive oil
2 cups raw long-grain rice

Peel and seed the bell peppers according to the directions on page 28. Cut the peeled peppers into chunks and combine with half a cup of the chicken stock, the parsley, coriander, onions, garlic, salt, and pepper in the container of a food processor. Process until they are a smooth purée. You may have to process them in small batches, but be sure that they all have the same consistency.

Then place the oil in an oven-proof casserole over medium heat. When the oil is warm, add the rice and stir until all the rice grains are coated with oil. Add the vegetable purée and simmer the mixture for 5 minutes.

Meanwhile, place the remaining chicken stock in a saucepan and bring it to a boil, pour it over the rice and vegetable mixture in the casserole, and bring it back to a boil. Cover the casserole and reduce the heat to low. Simmer the casserole for 20 minutes or until the rice is tender.

MOQUECA DE PEIXE
(BRAZIL)

The cooking of Bahia, Brazil, is a direct descendant of West African cooking. This cuisine, based on the extensive use of palm oil—called dendê—coconut milk, and tiny hot malagueta peppers, was brought by the slaves who found many familiar foodstuffs in the New World. Many of the popular Bahian dishes are based on the ritual foods served to the gods of the Candomblé religion, which was also brought from Africa. All combine the tropical abundance of Brazil's forests and seas with Portuguese tastes and African culinary know-how.

SERVES FOUR

3 sprigs coriander
1 medium-sized tomato
½ green bell pepper
½ large onion
3 tablespoons peanut oil
Salt to taste
2 pounds fish fillets (cod, scrod, haddock, or any firm-fleshed white fish)
1 tablespoon freshly squeezed lemon juice
½ cup coconut milk
2 tablespoons dendê oil

In a blender or food processor, chop the coriander, tomato, bell pepper, and onion until they form a coarse paste. Place the mixture in a heavy frying pan with 1 tablespoon of the peanut oil. Add salt to taste and cook the mixture over medium heat for 15 minutes. Stir frequently to prevent sticking. Add the fish fillets and continue to cook for an additional 15 minutes. Add the lemon juice, coconut milk, remaining peanut oil, and the dendê. Stir the sauce, but try not to break up the fish fillets. Serve the Moqueca hot, over white rice.

PEPPERY HENS
(CAYMAN ISLANDS)

Although the Cayman Islands are perhaps best known for their turtles, this dish combines rock cornish game hens with pepper, and curry powder. Islanders also use this method for cooking game birds such as quail, teal, and baldpate, which abound on the island in the fall.

SERVES FOUR

4 medium-sized onions, peeled
½ cup white wine vinegar
4 rock cornish game hens
2 tablespoons freshly ground black pepper
2 tablespoons curry powder
4 tablespoons unsalted butter

Place the onions in a saucepan, cover them with water, and boil until they are soft. Drain and soak them in the vinegar for 2 hours. Clean the game hens and stuff each with an onion. Mix the pepper and curry powder. Melt the butter and brush it over each bird. Dip the game hens in the pepper and curry mixture to coat them. Preheat the broiler to a high setting and grill the game hens until they are tender and brown. You may need to baste them with additional butter to prevent them from becoming too dry. When they are done, sprinkle them with the remaining pepper and curry mixture. Serve hot with plantain chips (Plantanutri, page 131).

CURRIED CHICKEN SALAD

Warm climates frequently call for cold dishes. The curry in this chicken salad adds a spicy tang to the conventional dish. The salad can be served with any of the spicy chutneys found in this book.

SERVES SIX

- 1 medium-sized chicken, cooked, boned, and cut in cubes
- 1 small onion, chopped
- 3 sticks of celery, chopped
- 1 medium-sized green bell pepper, chopped
- ½ red bell pepper, chopped
- ½ cup mayonnaise
- 1 tablespoon medium hot curry powder
- Salt and freshly ground black pepper to taste
- 1 medium cucumber
- 1 pink grapefruit

Mix together the chicken, onion, celery, and bell pepper. Mix the mayonnaise with the curry powder until the powder is absorbed and the mayonnaise becomes a mustardly yellow. Then combine the chicken mixture with the mayonnaise. There should be just enough mayonnaise to bind the ingredients together; use less if you have too much and add a bit more if your salad does not hold together. Add salt and black pepper to taste. Cover the salad with plastic wrap and refrigerate it for at least 1 hour. While the salad is in the refrigerator, dice the cucumber and segment the grapefruit, making sure that the membrane is fully removed from the grapefruit segments. Before serving, mix in the grapefruit segments and the diced cucumber. Serve chilled, on a platter garnished with chopped parsley.

GRILLED PORK CHOPS WITH CREOLE MARINADE
(GUADELOUPE)

Lime, olive oil, and spices form the marinade that gives a piquant taste to these grilled pork chops. The marinade brings out the sweetness of the pork and gives it a flavor that harmonizes well with the Sauce Chien that is served with this dish.

SERVES FOUR

4 center-cut loin pork chops
2 tablespoons olive oil
Juice of 2 limes
2 cloves garlic, minced
½ hot chile (Guinea pepper type), minced
2 teaspoons quatre épices
Salt and freshly ground black pepper to taste
Sauce Chien (page 121)

Wash and trim excess fat from the chops. Pat them dry with paper towels. Prepare a marinade from the olive oil, the lime juice, the minced garlic, minced chile, quatre épices, and salt and pepper to taste. Place the chops in the marinade, turning to be sure they are well coated, and allow them to sit for about 1 hour. Meanwhile, prepare the Sauce Chien that will accompany the chops. Heat the broiler to its highest setting. (This recipe can also be prepared outdoors on a grill.) Remove the chops from the marinade and grill them for about 10 minutes on each side. When the chops are done, place them on a platform and cover them with the sauce. Serve hot, with white rice and fried plantains.

COLOMBO DE MOUTON
(GUADELOUPE)

What is called curry in the English-speaking islands is called Colombo in the French Antilles. Colombo takes its name from the capital of Sri Lanka. Colombo powder can be purchased in markets in Martinique and Guadeloupe, and its taste is slightly different from that of the curry powders of the English-speaking islands. It can be duplicated in your kitchen for greater authenticity.

SERVES SIX

2 pounds stewing lamb cut into 1-inch dice
2 medium-sized onions, chopped coarse
3 tablespoons olive oil
1 cup water
3 tablespoons Poudre de Colombo (page 140)
Salt and freshly ground black pepper to taste
1 bouquet garni made up of 2 teaspoons thyme, 1 scallion, and 3 sprigs of parsley
1 medium-sized zucchini, peeled and cut into rounds
1 small eggplant, peeled and diced
1 medium-sized chayote, peeled and diced
2 medium-sized white potatoes, peeled and cut into quarters
2 cloves garlic, crushed
1 hot chile (Guinea pepper type), prickled with a fork

In a heavy saucepan, cook the lamb and the onions in the oil until the onions are soft and the lamb is browned on all sides. Pour in the water and the Poudre de Colombo. Mix well and add salt and black pepper to taste. Continue to cook over medium heat. When the mixture begins to boil, add the bouquet garni, the zucchini, eggplant, chayote, potatoes, garlic, and chile. Cover the saucepan and simmer the stew over low heat for 1 hour. When cooked, stir and taste to verify seasonings. Then serve over white rice. In the French Antilles, this is a Sunday or feast day dish. The lamb is frequently replaced by goat or wild game.

POUDRE DE COLOMBO (GUADELOUPE)

YIELD = ⅓ CUP

1 tablespoon ground coriander
1 tablespoon cumin
1 tablespoon turmeric
1 tablespoon black peppercorns
1 thumb-size piece of fresh ginger, peeled, scraped, and grated
½ to 2 hot chiles (Guinea pepper type), depending on their intensity and your love of pepper, minced fine

Grind the coriander, cumin, turmeric, and peppercorns together in a spice grinder. Add the spice mixture to the grated ginger and the minced hot chile. Mix well and use in recipes such as Colombo de Mouton (page 138).

BACALAO VERACRUZANO (MEXICO)

Even Mexico is not immune to the lure of salted codfish, so popular in Latin America. One way of preparing it is Veracruz style, with bell pepper, pimento, and, naturally, hot chiles.

SERVES SIX

2 pounds dried salted codfish
1 bouquet garni made of 2 cloves, 5 peppercorns, and 1 bay leaf
3 cloves garlic
¾ cup olive oil
3 large onions, chopped coarse
5 large tomatoes, peeled, seeded, and chopped
1 hot chile, minced
1 medium-sized green bell pepper, chopped

2 pimentos, diced
1 cup pitted black olives, chopped
Salt and freshly ground black pepper to taste

Follow the directions for preparing salted fish (page 102), but do not flake the fish. Instead, cover the cod with cold water and boil it with the bouquet garni and two of the garlic cloves. Lower the heat and simmer the cod for 1 hour. Drain the fish; strain and reserve ½ cup of the stock. Slice the remaining garlic clove. In a frying pan, heat ½ cup of the olive oil and sauté the slivered garlic. When the garlic is browned, remove it from the oil and discard it. Add the codfish to the oil and heat it through. In another saucepan, heat the remaining ¼ cup of olive oil and cook the chopped onion until soft. Add the tomatoes and simmer the mixture for 15 minutes. Add the reserved stock and all the remaining ingredients. Season the sauce to taste and pour it over the fish. Serve warm, accompanied by white rice.

FEIJOADA COMPLETA
(BRAZIL)

Feijoada Completa is Brazil's national dish. In Rio, and other parts of the country, people gather in restaurants and homes on Saturday afternoons to enjoy this complete meal made up of smoked meats, black beans, Couve a Minera (shredded kale greens), and rice. Additional side dishes include sliced oranges, which offer a sweet contrast to the beans and smoked meat; Farofa which provides texture; and Molho de Pimenta e Limão, which provides an extra bite. The whole is usually washed down with liberal amounts of Bramha Chopp, the Brazilian beer, though a dry rosé wine or a chilled light red wine would also go well. Feijoada has even become popular in Paris, where the Brazilian community can revel in a Saturday Feijoada Chez Guy, a restaurant in the Saint Germain des Près area. There, Brazilian musicians gather to sing, luncheon patrons join in with rattling beer cans filled with pebbles and tambourines, and lunch rocks and rollicks until late in the afternoon.

SERVES TEN

1 pound pork shoulder
1 pound corned spareribs, if available
1 pound pigs' feet
1 pound or more carne seca (Brazilian jerked beef; dried beef, or jerked beef may be substituted)
½ pound chouriço (Portuguese sausage)
1 pound smoked pork shoulder
1 pound lean bacon, in one piece, with the rind removed
1 pound lean beef chuck in one piece
4 cups dried black beans (try to get the small Brazilian type that is slightly larger than a lentil)
2 medium-sized onions, chopped
2 cloves garlic, crushed
1 stalk of celery, minced
1 bouquet garni made of 3 bay leaves, 3 sprigs of parsley, and 1 teaspoon dried thyme
1 teaspoon freshly ground black pepper
3½ quarts water

The evening before, rinse the salted meats in cold water and leave to soak overnight. The next morning, change the water and leave to soak until you are ready to begin cooking.

Place all the meats, the beans, onions, garlic, celery, bouquet garni, and pepper in a large, heavy pot. Cover with water and bring slowly to a boil. When the water has begun to boil, lower the heat and simmer for 2 hours. Remove each piece of meat as soon as it is done. Continue to cook the beans for an additional hour until the liquid has become thick and creamy. Place the beans in a heavy saucepan; cube the meats and add them to the saucepan. Bring the ingredients to a boil and simmer for 10 minutes. Remove from the heat and serve.

Mound the meats and beans in the center of a large platter. Place white rice around the edges of the platter. Serve the garnishes in separate dishes. Garnishes must include sliced oranges,

Farofa (page 120), Couve a Minera (page 131), Molho de Pimenta e Limão (page 125), and Molho Apimentado (below).

To add a truly Brazilian touch to your Feijoada, create an authentic atmosphere. Purchase or tape records by Brazilian musicians such as Gilberto Gil, Maria Betania, Elis Regina, or any other Brazilian singers and composers, serve Brazilian beer, and enjoy.

MOLHO APIMENTADO
(BRAZIL)

This sauce is served exclusively with Feijoada (page 142). It includes some of the liquid from the cooked beans and meats.

YIELD = 1½ CUPS

2 small onions, chopped
2 medium-sized firm, ripe tomatoes, chopped
1 green bell pepper, chopped
¾ cup distilled white vinegar
2 or 3 malagueta peppers, minced
4 tablespoons liquid from the Feijoada
Salt and freshly ground black pepper to taste

Mix all the ingredients in a small nonreactive bowl. Stir well and taste to adjust the seasoning. Serve to accompany Feijoada.

GRIOTS DE PORC
(HAITI)

I first tasted Griots de Porc at Le Rond Point restaurant in Port-au-Prince, Haiti. I recall the surprising taste of the pork cubes marinated in onion and garlic, orange and lemon juice. The hot chile added just the right amount of bite.

SERVES SIX

3 pound pork shoulder, cut into 2-inch cubes
1 large onion, minced

- 3 shallots, chopped
- ½ teaspoon dried thyme
- ¾ cup freshly squeezed orange juice
- ¼ cup freshly squeezed lemon juice
- 1 hot chile (Guinea pepper type), minced
- 2 cloves garlic, minced
- Salt and freshly ground black pepper to taste
- 6 tablespoons peanut oil

Marinate the pork overnight in a mixture of all the ingredients except the peanut oil. When ready to prepare, place the pork and the marinade in a heavy casserole and cover the meat with water. Cover the casserole and simmer the pork over medium heat until it is tender, about 1½ hours. Drain the pork thoroughly. In a heavy frying pan, sauté the pork in the oil until the pieces are crunchy on the outside. Serve warm with rice, Sauce Ti-Malice (page 128), and Fried Plantain (page 147).

BACALAITOS
(PUERTO RICO)

These codfish fritters are the fast food of Puerto Rico. At any time, but particularly in the summer when the Fiestas Padronales de San Juan are held in Loiza Aldea, people drive the short way from San Juan to Loiza, the city that is the keeper of the island's African traditions. There, they hear bombas, couplets sung to the beat of drums, watch dances, and feast on Bacalaitos washed down with fresh coconut water and rum. It is a feast for all the senses. You may not be able to have the bombas, but you can enjoy Bacalaitos, and even if you cannot obtain fresh coconut water, you can take consolation in the rum.

YIELD = APPROXIMATELY 24 BACALAITOS

- ½ pound salted codfish
- 2 cups flour
- ½ teaspoon baking powder
- 2 cloves garlic, minced

1 hot chile (Guinea pepper type), minced
Salt and freshly ground black pepper to taste
2 cups water
Peanut oil for frying

Prepare the codfish according to the directions on page 000. Mix the flour and baking powder and add the codfish, garlic, chile, salt and pepper, and water. Stir well to be sure the ingredients are well blended. In a heavy pot, heat the oil to 350 to 375 degrees. Drop the Bacalaitos by teaspoonfuls into the oil. Fry them until they are browned and crispy. Drain on paper towels and serve warm. Bacalaitos are a perfect snack to serve with cocktails or as an appetizer. They can also be served covered with a spicy tomato sauce: Salsa por Bacalaitos (below).

SALSA POR BACALAITOS
(PUERTO RICO)

This spicy sauce is occasionally poured over Bacalaitos. Personally, I prefer it served along side as a dipping sauce.

YIELD = 1½ CUPS

2 medium-sized onions, chopped
¼ cup olive oil
½ to 1 hot chile, minced, according to taste
1 sprig of parsley, minced
2 tomatoes, peeled, seeded, and puréed
½ cup water

Fry the onions in the olive oil until they are tender and golden. Add the minced chile and the parsley and continue to cook, for an additional 3 minutes, taking care that the ingredients do not burn. Add the tomato purée and the water and bring the sauce to a boil. Reduce the heat and simmer the sauce for 5 minutes. Serve in a small bowl as a dipping sauce or poured over the Bacalaitos.

CURRIED GOAT (JAMAICA)

Curried Goat is the national dish of Jamaica. Served at open-air gatherings throughout the island and in the homes of homesick Jamaicans around the world, the dish conjures up a symphony of Caribbean tastes. The sweetness of the goat meat, with its slight, underlying gamey tang, the bite of the onion and the pepper, and the subtle flavor of the curry powder combine to make a dish that is at once festive and homey. Lamb is frequently substituted for goat.

SERVES FOUR TO SIX

2 pounds goat or lamb, cut into cubes
1 clove garlic, minced
2 tomatoes, peeled, seeded, and chopped coarse
2 onions, chopped
1 scallion, chopped
2 hot chiles (Guinea pepper type), minced
3 tablespoons curry powder
Salt and freshly ground black pepper to taste
2 tablespoons butter
¼ cup peanut oil
2½ cups water

Place the meat in a large bowl and add the garlic, tomatoes, onions, scallion, chiles, curry powder, salt, and pepper. Mix well together and marinate for half an hour. Then remove the meat and, in a large frying pan, brown it in the butter and the oil. Add the marinade and the water. Cover and cook over medium heat for 1¼ hours or until the meat is tender. Taste for seasoning and serve over white rice.

FRICASEED CHICKEN
(JAMAICA)

Chicken is one of the most reliable dishes to order in many areas of the Caribbean. It is served grilled, barbecued, boiled, broiled, sautéed, and in many other ways, such as this piquant Jamaican fricasee.

SERVES SIX

One 4-pound chicken, cut into serving pieces
Juice of 1 lime
2 large onions, chopped
2 tomatoes, peeled, seeded, and chopped coarse
1 scallion, including some of the green part, minced
1 clove garlic, crushed
1 sprig of fresh thyme, or 2 teaspoons dried
Salt and freshly ground black pepper to taste
2 tablespoons butter
½ cup peanut oil
2½ cups water

Wash the chicken pieces thoroughly and rub them with the lime juice. Place the chicken in a large bowl, add the onions, tomatoes, scallion, garlic, thyme, salt, and pepper, and mix well. Marinate the chicken for half an hour, then remove it. Heat the butter and the peanut oil in a large frying pan, add the chicken, and fry it until it is lightly browned on all sides. Reduce the heat and add the marinade and the water. Cover and simmer over medium to low heat for 1 hour or until the chicken is tender. Serve with Peas and Rice (page 148) and Fried Plantain (below).

FRIED PLANTAIN
(PUERTO RICO)

Plaintains are members of the banana family. Larger than the banana with which we are familiar, they cannot be eaten raw. They are cooked in many different ways (see Aloco, page 60, and Stuffed Plantains, page 156). In this recipe, which frequently accompanies Caribbean dishes, they are fried.

SERVES FOUR TO SIX

2 pounds ripe plantains
2 cups vegetable oil for frying
1 tablespoon sugar

Peel the plantains and slice them lengthwise. Heat the oil in a heavy frying pan and fry the plantain slices for 5 minutes on each side, or until they are brown and crisp on the outside but soft on the inside. Sprinkle sugar over the slices and serve hot.

PEAS AND RICE (TRINIDAD)

It's peas and rice in some parts of the Caribbeon, rice and peas in others, and morros y cristianos in still others. Whatever the name, this dish is a staple everywhere in the Caribbean. Each island has its own way of preparing it. This version, from Trinidad, uses not only the expected peas and rice but also onion, red bell pepper, and hot chile.

SERVES SIX TO EIGHT

½ pound salt pork
2 cups pigeon peas
4 cups cold water
2 tablespons vegetable oil
1 small onion, minced
½ red bell pepper, chopped coarse
1 small hot red chile (bird pepper type)
2 medium-sized tomatoes, chopped coarse
1 teaspoon minced parsley
1 teaspoon minced fresh thyme, or ½ teaspoon dried
1 cup white rice

Soak the salt pork overnight in water to cover. Then cut it into ½-inch dice. Wash and pick over the pigeon peas, discarding any stones or grit. Soak the peas in cold water to cover for half an hour. Cook the peas and salt pork in 2 cups of the water for 1½ hours. Heat the vegetable oil in a frying pan and brown the onion, pepper, chile, tomatoes, parsley, and thyme for 5 minutes or until the onion is translucent. When the peas and pork are almost ready, add the rice, the browned vegetables and spices, and the remaining water and cook for 15 minutes or until the rice is done. Serve warm to accompany Caribbean dishes.

HUEVOS RANCHEROS
(MEXICO)

Huevos Rancheros are on the menu at almost all Mexican hotels and restaurants. I first tried them at the spa at San José Purua one summer. There, in the dining room of a magnificent Spanish colonial-style building surrounded by mountains, I savored every bite of the eggs, which were served with a sauce of tomatoes, coriander, garlic, and chiles and sitting on a bed of tortilla and avocado.

SERVES FOUR

2 tablespoons olive oil
1 small onion, minced
1 clove garlic, minced
4 large tomatoes, peeled, seeded, and chopped coarse
2 hot green chiles, minced
3 sprigs fresh coriander, minced
Salt and freshly ground black pepper to taste
1 cup vegetable oil for frying
4 corn tortillas*
2 tablespoons butter
8 eggs
1 small ripe avocado, peeled and sliced

* See note page 112.

Heat the olive oil in a small frying pan. Sauté the onion and garlic until they are lightly browned. Add the tomatoes, chiles, coriander, salt, and pepper. Stir well and simmer for 5 minutes until the sauce is thick.

Meanwhile, heat the vegetable oil in a second small frying pan. Fry the tortillas, one at a time, until they are slightly crisp and brown. Keep them warm. Drain the oil and add the butter. Melt the butter and fry the eggs to the desired doneness.

To serve, place a tortilla on each plate, top with two eggs and some of the sauce, and garnish with the avocado slices.

PATO EN MOLE VERDE
(MEXICO)

Everyone has heard of Mexico's famous chocolate chicken or turkey. Not as well known but just as delicious is duckling in green mole. This dish consists of a duckling served with a sauce made of bread, olive oil, almonds, pumpkin seeds, Mexican green tomatoes (tomatillos), green chiles, coriander, and chicken broth.

SERVES EIGHT TO TEN

One 5–6-pound duckling
1 clove garlic, crushed
Salt and freshly ground black pepper to taste
3 tablespoons butter
3 tablespoons olive oil
1 slice white bread
½ cup raw pumpkin seeds (pepitas)
¼ cup blanched, slivered almonds
1 (10-ounce) can Mexican green tomatoes (tomatillos) *
6 mild green chiles, peeled, seeded, and chopped
3 tablespoons chopped fresh coriander
1½ cups chicken broth
Salt and freshly ground black pepper to taste

* These have a particular taste, and if you cannot find them do not attempt the dish. They can, however, be obtained by mail order from sources listed at the end of the book.

Singe any pinfeathers off the duckling, then wash it, inside and out, and clean it thoroughly. Rub the duckling with garlic, salt, and pepper. Heat the butter in a dutch oven until it is lightly browned. Brown the duckling in the butter, turning it several times. Prick the duckling with the tines of a fork to release the fat. Cover the dutch oven and reduce the heat to low. Cook the duckling without liquid for 30 to 40 minutes until it is done through.

Meanwhile, prepare the sauce. Heat 2 tablespoons of the olive oil in a frying pan. Fry the bread slice until it is browned on both sides. Drain it on a paper towel. Add the remaining tablespoon of oil to the frying pan and brown the pumpkin seeds and almonds. Drain them on paper towels. Drain the canned tomatillos. Place the tomatillos, fried bread (torn into pieces), pepitas, almonds, green chiles, coriander, ½ cup of the chicken broth, and salt and pepper to taste in a food processor and reduce to a purée. Heat a frying pan over moderate heat and pour in the purée. Add the remaining chicken broth and stir well. Simmer the sauce for 10 minutes. Carve the duckling and serve it topped with the sauce and accompanied, if you wish, by white rice.

CHILES RELLENOS
(MEXICO)

This is a Mexican variation on the stuffed pepper that appears in so many parts of the world.

SERVES EIGHT

2 medium-sized onions, chopped
1 clove garlic, minced
2 tablespoons peanut oil
½ pound ground beef
½ pound ground pork
1 cup fresh tomatoes, chopped
Salt and freshly ground black pepper to taste
¼ cup blanched, sliced almonds

¼ cup raisins
8 medium-sized mild chiles, suitable for stuffing (you may substitute Italian peppers)
½ cup flour
4 eggs, separated
3 cups vegetable oil for frying

In a frying pan, sauté the onions and garlic in the peanut oil until the onions are transparent. Add the ground meats and cook until the meat is browned and crumbly. Add the tomatoes, salt, pepper, almonds, and raisins. simmer the mixture for 5 minutes or so.

Prepare the chiles, slitting them around the stem and removing the seeds but leaving the skin intact. Stuff the chiles with the meat and tomato mixture. Roll them well in flour. Make an egg batter by beating the egg whites until stiff and then adding the beaten egg yolks. Heat the oil in a heavy saucepan to between 350 and 375 degrees. Dip the chiles in the egg batter and fry them in the fat until they are golden brown on all sides. Remove the chiles from the oil and drain them on paper towels. Serve warm. You may wish to accompany the chiles with a hot sauce such as Salsa Picante (page 130), or for an international flavor, experiment by using any of the African or Asian hot sauces to enhance the dish. A side dish of white or saffron rice should also be served.

HIGADILLOS MEXICANOS CON JEREZ (MEXICO)

Riñones al jerez (kidneys with sherry) is a typical Spanish dish. In Mexico, however, chiles heat up a similar dish made with chicken livers.

SERVES FOUR

1 pound chicken livers
¼ cup flour
Salt and freshly ground black pepper to taste

6 tablespoons butter
1 small onion, minced
1 teaspoon minced fresh green hot chile
½ cup mushrooms, sliced
⅓ cup dry sherry (Fino or Amontillado type)

Clean the chicken livers. Mix the flour with salt and pepper and coat the chicken livers with the flour mixture. Heat the butter in a frying pan over medium heat and sauté the livers until they are browned on all sides. Add the onion, chile, and mushrooms and cook until the mushrooms are tender. Pour in the sherry and simmer the chicken livers over low heat for 5 minutes. Serve warm, with Sopa Seca (page 133) or white rice.

PICADINHO
(BRAZIL)

This simple dish is a Brazilian favorite. It can be made blander by eliminating the malagueta pepper, but I prefer the extra bite.

SERVES SIX

4 strips streaky bacon, chopped
1½ pound rump steak, cut into ½-inch cubes
1 medium-sized onion, chopped
2 medium-sized tomatoes, peeled, seeded, and chopped
2 malagueta peppers, seeded and minced
Salt and freshly ground black pepper to taste
½ cup water

Render the bacon in a frying pan. Leaving the bacon bits in the pan, add the steak, onion, tomatoes, peppers, salt, and pepper to the fat from the bacon and sauté until the meat is well browned. Add the water and simmer over low heat until the liquid is reduced. Serve the Picadinho with white rice and Farofa (page 120). In Rio, the dish is frequently accompanied by fresh green peas.

CARURU
(BRAZIL)

Caruru is an Afro-Bahian dish that came to Brazil's Northeast with the slaves from West Africa. It is derived from the ritual caruru that is traditionally served to the ibeji (twins) of the Yoruba. In the Yoruba culture, twins are sacred, to be feared and venerated. The Afro-Bahian religion has adapted this belief to worship of the twin saints Cosme and Damian. On their saint's day in Salvador de Bahia and throughout the Northeast, families of twins celebrate by serving a Caruru. In the traditional Caruru, each piece of okra must be cut a ritual number of times; for home enjoyment, this arduous task can be omitted. Caruru is traditionally served with Molho de Pimenta e Limão (page 125) and white rice.

SERVES SIX TO EIGHT

2 pounds fresh okra, topped and tailed
Juice of 2 lemons
1 medium-sized onion, minced
1 clove garlic, minced
4 sprigs fresh coriander, minced
2 tablespoons dendê oil
3 tablespoons dried shrimp, pulverized
1 pound raw fresh shrimp, cleaned and deveined
⅓ cup roasted peanuts, shelled, peeled, and pulverized
Salt and freshly ground black pepper to taste
¾ cup water
Molho de Pimenta Malagueta (page 129) to taste

Cut the okra into small pieces and soak it in the lemon juice to which a pinch of salt has been added. In a frying pan, brown the onion, garlic, and coriander in the dendê oil. In a food processor, pulverize the dried shrimp, the fresh shrimp, and the peanuts. Add these, along with the okra and salt and pepper to taste, to the contents of the frying pan. Pour in the water and cook the Caruru for half an hour. When ready, add a few drops of Molho de Pimenta Malagueta to taste. Serve with white rice, Farofa Amarela (page 119), and Molho de Pimenta e Limão (page 125).

HUACHINANGO YUCATECO (MEXICO)

In the Yucatan, this dish was originally baked in a banana leaf. This version, however, can be baked in the oven, using aluminum foil instead of the traditional banana leaf.

SERVES SIX

One 5-pound red snapper, cleaned but with the head on
Juice of 2 limes
Salt and freshly ground black pepper to taste
3 tablespoons olive oil
1 small onion, minced
1 guero chile, minced
5 sprigs of fresh coriander, chopped
½ cup freshly squeezed orange juice
1 lime, cut in wedges

Rinse the fish in cold water and dry it. Be sure it has been well cleaned. Rub the fish all over with the lime juice and place it in an 18-inch-square piece of aluminum foil. Sprinkle the fish with salt and pepper.

Heat the olive oil in a frying pan and sauté the onion, chile, and half of the coriander until the onion is transparent and the chile is soft. Be careful not to brown the vegetables. Spread the vegetables over the fish and pour the orange juice over it. Close the aluminum foil around the fish to make a tightly sealed package. Place the fish in a baking dish and bake it in a 350-degree oven for half an hour.

Serve the fish warm, garnished with lime wedges and the remaining coriander. The Huachinango can also be accompanied by white rice.

STUFFED PLANTAINS (ANTIGUA)

Plantains are the big brothers of the banana family. They are ripe when their skins blacken and they feel soft. Plantains are always eaten cooked, and plantain chips, plantain fritters, and, of course, stuffed plantains are among the staples of the Caribbean. This variation on the stuffed plantain theme comes from Antigua, where Chef Harry plays new variations on old Caribbean culinary themes at his Green Parrot restaurant.

SERVES SIX

- 6 slices of bacon
- 3 large, ripe plantains
- 1 pound ground beef
- 2 medium-sized onions, chopped
- 1 clove garlic, minced
- 1 green bell pepper, chopped
- 1 hot chile (Guinea pepper type), minced
- 2 medium-sized, firm, ripe tomatoes, chopped
- ½ teaspoon oregano
- Salt and freshly ground black pepper to taste
- 2 cups peanut oil
- 2 eggs, beaten

Fry the bacon until it is crisp and remove it from the fat to drain on a paper towel. Cut each plantain into four sections lengthwise and shape them into hollow tubes. Fasten the ends together with toothpicks and sauté them in the bacon fat until they are golden brown. Drain the segments on paper towels.

To make the filling, brown the ground beef in the remaining bacon fat and add the onions, garlic, bell pepper, chile, tomatoes, oregano, salt, pepper, and reserved bacon, crumbled into bits. Cook the mixture until the onion and green pepper are tender, about 20 minutes. Fill each plantain tube with the stuffing.

Heat the peanut oil in a heavy skillet until it is 350 to 375 degrees. Dip the stuffed plantains into the beaten egg and fry them in the hot oil. Turn them once to be sure both sides are browned. Serve hot, with white rice.

ACARAJÉ
(BRAZIL)

These little black-eyed-pea fritters are direct descendants of the African Akkra (see page 37). Delicious as appetizers, they are also typical Bahian snacks in Brazil. There, they are cooked on the streets by Bahian women who wear the traditional wide-skirted costumes.

YIELD = ABOUT 15 FRITTERS

1 pound dried black-eyed peas
1 large onion, minced
Salt to taste
2 cups dendê oil

Soak the black-eyed peas in water overnight. The next day, peel the peas by rubbing off the outer skin. Grind the peas in a blender until they form a firm paste. Add the onion and salt to taste. Heat the dendê oil in a cast-iron pot. When the oil is very hot, drop in the bean paste one spoonful at a time. When fried to a golden brown, about 10 minutes, place the fritters on absorbent paper to drain. Serve plain or with Acarajé Sauce (below).

ACARAJÉ SAUCE
(BRAZIL)

Acarajé are round or oval black-eyed-pea fritters. Served as a ritual dish in the Candomblé religion, they have become the favorite street snack of Bahia. In the streets throughout the city of Salvador de Bahia, it is possible to see Bahian women dressed in traditional costume (multiple starched petticoats, brightly colored skirts with colors that identify their gods or orixas in the Candomblé religion, intricate lacework blouses, turbans, and heavy ropes of glass bead necklaces) stirring the heavy black pots of oil in which they fry acarajé. Known as Baianas da Tabuleiro (Bahian women with trays), they are symbols of all that is wonderful in Brazilian cooking. After the acarajés are cooked, the Baianas deftly slit them open and fill them with Acarajé Sauce.

YIELD = SAUCE FOR 15 FRITTERS

- 3 or 4 preserved malagueta peppers
- ¼ pound dried smoked shrimp, ground
- 1 small onion, chopped
- ½ teaspoon salt
- ½ teaspoon powdered ginger
- 2 tablespoons palm oil (dendê type)

Grind the peppers, dried shrimp, onion, salt, and ginger together in a food processor until they form a smooth paste. Place them in a heavy saucepan with the dendê oil and cook over medium heat for 10 minutes. Serve on split acarajé.

SANGRITA (MEXICO)

I had my first taste of Sangrita at Ixtapan de la Sal, a spa outside Mexico City that has been known for its mineral baths since the time of the Aztecs. After a strenuous morning of exercising and being pampered and an afternoon of more pampering, the hour came when the tequila was on the house. At first, I learned to drink it the traditional way, with salt and lime, but I noticed that some people were drinking their tequila with what looked like tomato juice. I inquired and was told that it was not tomato juice but Sangrita, a traditional accompaniment to tequila. I tried it and found that it was delicious. A sip of Sangrita followed by a sip of tequila produced results that were somewhat like a tequila Bloody Mary. The tomato juice was sweetened with orange juice, and the ubiquitous Mexican chile added enough bite to keep the drink tangy.

YIELD = 3 CUPS

2 cups tomato juice
¼ cup freshly squeezed orange juice
6 tablespoons freshly squeezed lime juice
1 small onion, minced
1 teaspoon hot chile, seeded and minced
Salt to taste

Pour the tomato juice, orange juice, and lime juice into a small pitcher. Stir the juices to blend well and place the pitcher in the refrigerator. Just before serving, add the minced onion, the chile, and salt to taste and stir well.

Sangrita is served in tumblers to accompany shot glasses of tequila. Take a sip from one glass and then a sip from the other.

FRUIT CURRY
(TRINIDAD AND TOBAGO)

Curry came to Trinidad and Tobago with the Indian immigrants of the late nineteenth and early twentieth centuries. This fruit variation combines tropical fruit with curry powder and raisins.

SERVES FOUR

4 tablespoons unsalted butter
2 medium-sized onions, sliced thin
1 small hot green chile, seeded and minced
2 tablespoons curry powder
1 teaspoon milk
2 slices pineapple, peeled and cut into pieces
2 small, firm, ripe bananas, peeled and cut into pieces
1 medium-sized apple, cored and chopped coarse

1 tablespoon freshly squeezed lime juice
2½ cups coconut water
1 tablespoon coconut cream
¼ cup freshly grated coconut
½ teaspoon powdered ginger
¼ cup raisins
Salt and freshly ground black pepper

Heat the butter in a heavy saucepan and in it sauté the onion until lightly browned. Add the chile pieces and brown them as well. Stir in the curry powder and milk and cook over high heat, stirring constantly, for 5 minutes. Mix the pineapple, papaya, banana, and apple pieces and pour the lime juice over them. Add the fruit and the coconut water to the onion and curry mixture. Cook an additional 10 minutes. Finally, add the coconut cream, grated coconut, ginger, raisins, salt, and pepper to taste. Stir to mix well, then cook over low heat for 1 hour. When cooked, adjust seasoning and serve hot, over white rice.

This dish can also be made with nontropical fruits such as pears, peaches, and necetarines. Omit the coconut water if you prefer a drier curry.

QUINDINS
(BRAZIL)

The Brazilian sweet tooth owes a great deal to the Moorish influence of Portugal. Achingly sweet pastries accompany the spicy hot dishes that are usually served as main courses. These Quindins, similar to coconut macaroons, are less sweet than many.

YIELD = 12 QUINDINS

¾ cup light brown sugar
1 tablespoon unsalted butter, softened
1 cup freshly grated coconut
5 egg yolks
1 egg white stiffly beaten
Freshly ground white pepper to taste

Preheat the oven to 350 degrees. Place the sugar, butter, and coconut in a bowl. Beat in the egg yolks one at a time, stirring well. Fold in the beaten egg white. Add the white pepper. Grease one dozen muffin molds and divide the mixture into them. Set the muffin molds in a baking pan filled with 1 inch of boiling water to form a bainmarie. Bake in the preheated oven for 35 minutes or until the Quindins are firm and golden. Let them cool and remove them from the muffin molds. They will look like large macaroons with a jellylike top. They're wonderful served with tea, or, of course, as dessert after a Brazilian meal.

◂§ Hot Stuff in Asia

THIS IS THE AREA where it all started. Many of the spices we use today were first found in the islands that are known today as the Moluccas. Markets in Hong Kong and Singapore abound with finely woven baskets of shiny, waxy green chiles and small fiery red ones. In India, chiles are added to foods until the dishes are literally mouth-searingly hot for the unwary and unaccustomed. Throughout Asia, from Vietnam to China's Szechwan province, from Taiwan to Sri Lanka, pepper is the punctuation within the meal, the exclamation point that makes the diner pause and savor. It looms large in my own gustatory memories of Asia.

Hong Kong, which means Fragrant Harbor in Chinese, smells of jasmine tea. The tea came hot and steaming in a cloth-lined bamboo basket a few minutes after I had checked into my room at the Excelsior Hotel overlooking the Causeway Bay Typhoon Shelter. The fragrance of the jasmine mingled inextricably with the view from the windows. Outside junks, yachts, and sampans bobbed up and down in the water, forming an almost picture-postcard-perfect view of Hong Kong Harbor and mainland Kowloon.

But jasmine tea was only my first taste of the Fragrant Harbor. This island city is a gourmet's paradise, and anyone interested in cooking will be fascinated by Hong Kong's markets.

They hold the secret of the British Crown Colony's culinary success. Ingredients are the freshest possible and come from far and wide. Fish swim in glass tanks or plastic buckets. Bamboo shoots, bok choy, watercress, chives, green peppers, long, thin green chiles, ginger, and a cornucopia of vegetables are piled up and shining with dew. But the appeal of Hong Kong's market is more than visual; it is also in the mingling of subtle aromas and in the cacophony of the hawkers' cries, the agitated haggling of customers, and the shrill cackling of chickens.

Sampling all of the available bounty would require an orgy of eating, and there are an astonishing number of restaurants waiting to serve. I was fortunate enough to be guided through the mysteries of Chinese cuisine by one of Hong Kong's leading gourmets, Willie Mark.

Mark is an international culinary caliph and has been lauded as Hong Kong's ultimate authority on the best places to dine. He explained the culinary styles of Canton, Peking, Shanghai, Szechwan, Fukien, Swatow, and the far northern regions of Mongolia, all of which can be found in Hong Kong. Even though I was interested mainly in the cuisines of the Szechwan and Hunan regions, where pepper is a major ingredient, he reminded me that it would be a good idea to sample as many of the styles as possible to get a broad idea of the whole of Chinese cuisine. Pepper and chiles, he assured me, were used in innovative ways in the other cuisines as well.

Then, with a thoroughness that is typical of gourmets worldwide, and with the precision that is the mark of the perfect Chinese host, he planned a meal that was a banquet of nine courses and a culinary tour of China's regions.

Hong Kong, however, is only the tip of Asia's culinary iceberg. Singapore, a melting pot of Asian cuisines and cultures, also calls, with dishes like Chile Crab. Hawkers' stands are pristine clean and offer all manner of food for the adventurous. Chicken, beef, and lamb satés are served with piquant sauces of peanuts and spices. Restaurants offer everything from Indian vegetarian dishes to Mongolian barbecue. India, home of Tellicherry, the world's best black pepper, is another stop in the search for Asian hot stuff. There yogurt salads are an innovative way of cooling the heat of the Indian curries. Delicately spiced Moghul dishes from the North bring another variation. Madras in the south, offers fish dishes spiced with ginger, chile, and fiery hot sauces. The Spice Islands to the south are where the pepper rush started. There sambals, or condiments, offer the inventive cook a wide array of peppery dishes. Korea's cooking does not insist on pepper, but occasionally a red nose will point up from a crock of Kim'chi to indicate that chiles are indeed present.

Before proceeding with any recipes calling for hot chiles, refer to the Chile Caveats in the front of the book.

TINOLANG MANOK (MALAYSIA)

This recipe for gingered chicken soup surprises the diner because of the pieces of papaya that are used as a finishing touch.

SERVES FOUR

2 pounds skinless and boneless chicken breast cut into ½-inch cubes
Salt and freshly ground white pepper to taste
1 tablespoon freshly squeezed lime juice
2 tablespoons peanut oil
2 medium-sized onions, minced
2 cloves garlic, minced
One 2-inch piece fresh ginger, minced
3 cups water
1 small, firm papaya, peeled, seeded, and cut into ½-inch dice

Season the chicken with salt, pepper, and lime juice. Place it in a bowl and set aside. Meanwhile, heat the peanut oil in a heavy frying pan and sauté the onions and garlic until the onions are golden. Add the chicken and the ginger and cook, stirring constantly, until the chicken lightens. Place the sautéed ingredients in a saucepan and add the water. Bring the ingredients to a boil, then lower the heat and cook for 20 minutes or until the chicken is tender. When ready, add the papaya and cook for an additional 5 minutes. Adjust the seasonings and serve hot.

MINTED YOGURT SOUP
(TURKEY)

One of Turkey's many yogurt soups, this one hot, depends on mint and white pepper for its zest.

SERVES SIX TO EIGHT

7 tablespoons butter
3 medium-sized onions, minced
2 pints plain yogurt
1 egg
1 tablespoon flour
4 cups chicken broth
1 cup chopped fresh mint
1 teaspoon freshly ground white pepper
Chopped chives for garnish

In a skillet, melt 3 tablespoons of the butter and brown the onions lightly. Set them aside. Place the yogurt in a large soup pot over very low heat. Gradually stir in the egg and flour. Add the chicken broth 1 cup at a time, stirring the mixture until it comes to a boil. Add the reserved onions and let the mixture simmer. When ready to serve, sauté the mint in the remaining butter and add it to the soup along with the salt and pepper. Stir well to be sure all ingredients are mixed and serve the soup in individual bowls, garnished with chopped chives.

MIDDLE EASTERN TOMATO YOGURT SOUP (TURKEY)

The hint of curry powder and a small dash of red pepper make this cold soup a distinctive dish.

SERVES FOUR TO SIX

1½ cups plain yogurt
1 tablespoon extra virgin olive oil
¼ cup freshly squeezed lemon juice
1½ teaspoons curry powder
¼ teaspoon basil
¼ teaspoon thyme
4½ cups tomato juice
Salt and freshly ground black pepper to taste
Dash of cayenne pepper
Chopped chives for garnish

Place the yogurt in a large glass or earthenware bowl and whisk it until it is smooth. Add the olive oil, lemon juice, curry, basil, and thyme, continuing to whisk. Gradually add the tomato juice, still whisking to be sure all the ingredients are well blended. Season with salt, pepper, and cayenne. Cover and refrigerate for at least 1 hour. When ready to serve, place in individual bowls and garnish with chopped chives.

MINT CORIANDER DIP (INDIA)

This dip is served with fresh poppadoms at many Indian restaurants. You break off a bit of the poppadom, which may have been made extra spicy with chile, and dip it into the mint, coriander, and yogurt mixture. The dip also makes a raita (yogurt salad) that can accompany any curry and is delicious with Western roasts or grilled meats.*

SERVES FOUR

1 cup plain yogurt
2½ tablespoons cold water
3 scallions, including some of the green top, minced
1 teaspoon ginger, minced
1 fresh jalapeño chile, seeded and minced
¼ cup fresh mint leaves, chopped
½ cup fresh coriander, minced

Place all the ingredients in a food processor or blender and mix until you have a rich sauce with the consistency of light cream. (You may need to add more yogurt.) Pour the dip into a small bowl and refrigerate it for at least an hour before serving. Serve cold, with poppadoms, as an appetizer or an hors d'oeuvre.

* Poppadoms are crisp, flat wafers made from chick-peas flour that are staples on any Indian table. Plain or spiced with black pepper or chile powder, they are eaten as an appetizer or as an accompaniment to curry dishes. Poppadoms are complicated to prepare at home, but they can be obtained from the stores specializing in Indian ingredients that are listed at the end of the book.

SPICY PLANTAIN CHIPS (SINGAPORE)

This savory variation on plantain chips is an Asian cocktail treat.

SERVES FOUR

2 large green plantains
1½ teaspoons Asian chile powder
1 teaspoon powdered turmeric
Salt and freshly ground black pepper to taste
2 tablespoons cold water
2 cups peanut oil

Peel the plaintains and cut them into very thin rounds. Soak them in cold salted water for a few minutes. Meanwhile, make a paste by mixing the chile powder, turmeric, salt, pepper, and water. Coat the plantain slices with this paste.

Heat the oil in a heavy cast-iron saucepan to 375 degrees. Drop in the plantain slices a few at a time and fry until golden brown and crisp. Drain on paper towels and serve.

Plantain chips can be served warm or stored in an airtight container and used at any time.

RAITA
(INDIA)

These mixtures of yogurt and vegetables are perfect for tempering the heat of India's spicy dishes. The coolness of the yogurt is a perfect foil for the fresh taste of cucumber in the first recipe, while diced tomatoes, cucumbers, and chile add color and zest in the second. Raitas also make perfect savory snacks for those who do not like sweet fruity yogurts. Radishes, green and red bell peppers, and other vegetables and spices may be added to create new variations.

SCALLION-CORIANDER RAITA

SERVES FOUR AS AN ACCOMPANIMENT

- 1 cup plain yogurt
- 1½ tablespoons fresh coriander, minced
- 2 scallions, including 3 inches of the green part, minced
- ½ teaspoon cumin

Mix the yogurt, coriander, scallions, and cumin thoroughly in a small bowl. Cover the bowl and refrigerate for 1 hour before serving to allow the flavors to mingle. Serve chilled, to accompany Indian dishes.

CUCUMBER-TOMATO RAITA

SERVES FOUR

1 cup plain yogurt
1 small, ripe tomato, chopped
½ cucumber, peeled and cut into matchstick strips
1 scallion, including 3 inches of the green part, minced
½ teaspoon chile powder
½ green chile, seeded and diced

Mix all the ingredients thoroughly in a small bowl. Cool in the refrigerator for at least 1 hour before serving to allow the flavors to mingle. Serve chilled.

KATCHUMBER SALAD (INDIA)

This chopped vegetable salad is easten not as a side salad in the Western manner but as condiment along with the chutneys and raitas during an Indian meal.

SERVES SIX

2 medium-sized green bell peppers, cored, seeded, and chopped coarse
2 medium-sized firm, ripe tomatoes, chopped coarse
1 medium-sized onion, chopped coarse
1 tablespoon fresh coriander, minced
2 tablespoons freshly squeezed lemon juice
Freshly ground black pepper to taste

Place the vegetables in a nonreactive glass or china bowl; add the coriander and lemon juice and mix thoroughly. Cover with plastic wrap and chill in the refrigerator for at least 1 hour. Add a few grindings of black pepper before serving.

SPICED SUMMER FRUIT SALAD (MALAYSIA)

In Southeast Asia, the love of chile extends even to desserts. This recipe is inspired by Rujak—a tropical summer fruit salad. Instead of the exotic tropical fruits called for in the traditional recipe, this version uses ingredients that are available year-round. The Asian chile powder adds a surprising piquancy but does not mask the delicate flavors of the fruit.

SERVES SIX TO EIGHT

- 1 medium-sized firm mango, peeled and cut into ½-inch dice
- 2 medium-sized crisp Granny Smith apples, peeled, cored, and cut into ½-inch dice
- ½ fresh pineapple, cut into ½-inch dice
- 1 large pink grapefruit, peeled and divided into segments, with the membrane removed
- 1 large orange, peeled and divided into segments
- ½ teaspoon Asian chile powder (this type has no cumin)
- ¼ cup natural raw sugar or dark brown sugar
- 1 tablespoon orange water (Be sure that the orange water you purchase is suitable for internal use.)
- Salt to taste

Place the fruit in a nonreactive glass or ceramic bowl. Let the fruit stand so the juices will mingle. Meanwhile, in a small bowl, mix the chile powder, sugar, orange water, and salt. Add to the fruit and mix it well with the juices that have drained. Cover the bowl with plastic wrap and refrigerate it for at least half an hour to allow the flavor to develop. Serve chilled.

VINEGARED GREEN CHILES (SINGAPORE)

Served as a condiment in Singapore's Chinese restaurants, this simple pickle is a testament to that country's love of hot stuff. Eaten with a slight sprinkling of soy sauce, they go with everything from breakfast jook (rice gruel) to supper noodles.

YIELD = 1 CUP

10 fresh green chiles, sliced crosswise
½ cup white cider vinegar
½ cup boiling water

Place the chiles in a 2-cup screw-top jar. Mix the vinegar and boiling water and pour it over the chiles. Allow them to cool, cover the jar, and let it sit in a cool, dark place for 4 days before serving. It will keep unrefrigerated for 2 weeks and longer in the refrigerator.

CHILE SAMBAL (MALAYSIA)

In Malaysian cooking, a wide variety of sambals are served as complements to traditional dishes. They range from relatively mild carrot and cucumber sambals to this fiery hot chile sambal.

SERVES FOUR

8 fresh red chiles
1 shallot
1 clove garlic
¾ teaspoon brown sugar
2 teaspoons lemon juice
Salt and freshly ground black pepper to taste

Place the chiles in boiling water for 10 minutes; remove and drain them. Remove the seeds and ribs from the chiles (see

Chile Caveats on page 29). Peel the shallot and the garlic. Place the chiles, shallot, and garlic in a blender or food processor and grind them into a thick paste. Add the sugar, lemon juice, salt, and pepper. Mix again. Place the mixture in a small bowl and refrigerate it for 1 hour. Serve cold. This condiment will not keep well and should be eaten the day it is prepared.

MINT CHUTNEY (INDIA)

In the United States, we tend to think of Major Grey's as the definitive chutney. In India, however, chutneys may be wet or dry, jellylike in consistency, or simply a mixture of ingredients that enhance a meal. This mint chutney not only goes with traditional Indian dishes, it is also an excellent accompaniment to Western dishes like roast lamb. It beats the cloying taste of mint jelly by a mile.

YIELD = ¾ CUP

2 teaspoons fresh mint leaves, minced
2 teaspoons tamarind juice*
½ cup plain yogurt
½ clove garlic, minced
½ teaspoon cayenne pepper
Salt to taste

Bruise the mint leaves and mix them with the tamarind juice and the yogurt. Add the garlic, cayenne, and salt. Mix well and place in the refrigerator for 1 hour. Serve cool.

* Tamarind juice is available from Oriental spice shops listed at end of book.

KIMCH' I (KOREA)

This sauerkraut is a staple of the Korean cuisine and appears on almost all tables at every meal. The savory, sometimes salty, salad goes well with many spicy dishes. Kimch' i has one draw-

back. To the uninitiated it has a strong odor that many consider unpleasant, but a few bites will usually convince the unbeliever. Ingredients can be adjusted to individual taste, and no two kimch' is are alike. Almost every Korean household has a crock of kimch' i hidden away or mellowing in the yard. For this reason, it was a frequent source of jokes on television's late, lamented M.A.S.H. on which suspected bomb sites often revealed kimch' i crocks.

YIELD = ABOUT 7 CUPS

6 cups vegetables, cut up (Chinese cabbage, celery, onions, cauliflower, turnips, carrots, cucumbers, rutabagas, or other hard vegetables in any combination)
2 scallions, including 3 inches of the green part, minced
3 tablespoons salt
2 cloves garlic, minced
1 thumb-size piece fresh ginger, minced
1 teaspoon crushed dried red chiles
1 cup water

Place the vegetable mixture in a large nonreactive bowl and sprinkle it with half the salt. Let it stand for 15 minutes. Rinse the vegetables and drain them well. Add the remaining salt to the mixture and place it in a crock. Cover the crock loosely and let the vegetable mixture marinate at room temperature for approximately 4 days, depending on the room temperature. (The warmer the room, the shorter the time.) Chill the kimch' i well before serving.

THREE INDIAN CHUTNEYS

Chutneys are the typical Indian accompaniment to curries. Originally a way to preserve fruits in the fierce Indian sun, chutney has developed into a way of life. A gala curry dinner is all the more elegant when it is accompanied by homemade chutneys, which are surprisingly easy to make. The recipes that follow are for small amounts of chutney. They should be eaten immediately because they will last in the refrigerator for only one week. For larger batches, you must follow proper canning procedures to inhibit growth of bacteria.

APRICOT-PLUM CHUTNEY (INDIA)

YIELD = 2 CUPS

1½ cups dried apricots
Water to cover
2 medium-sized Santa Rosa plums
1 clove garlic, minced
1 bird chile pepper
1 thumb-size piece of fresh ginger
¼ teaspoon salt
½ cup distilled white vinegar
½ cup sugar

In a medium-sized bowl, soak the apricots in water to cover for 1 hour. When ready, drain the apricots, reserving ¼ cup of the soaking liquid. Place the drained apricots, the plums, garlic, pepper, ginger, and salt in a food processor or blender and chop until you have a smooth paste. Place the mixture in a small saucepan and add the reserved soaking water, the vinegar, and sugar. Stir to mix well. Bring the mixture to a boil over high heat, then reduce the heat and allow the mixture to simmer for 30 minutes, stirring constantly. When the chutney has thickened and taken on a jellylike consistency, remove it from the heat and spoon it into scalded glass jars.

NECTARINE-MINT CHUTNEY (INDIA)

🙞🙞 YIELD = 2 CUPS

1 bunch fresh mint (approximately ten 3-inch-long sprigs)
2 large, firm nectarines
1 small bird pepper
½ cup red wine vinegar
½ cup sugar
1 quarter-sized piece of fresh ginger, minced
1 clove garlic, minced
½ teaspoon salt

Place all the ingredients in a food processor and chop them fine. Place the mixture in a nonreactive saucepan. Bring to a boil over high heat, then reduce the heat and simmer for 30 minutes, stirring constantly. When the chutney has thickened and taken on a jellylike consistency, remove it from the heat and spoon it into scalded glass jars.

CRANBERRY CHUTNEY (INDIA)

I first made this chutney when I had cranberries in the freezer but no cranberry sauce to accompany a roast chicken. Although cranberries are not an Indian fruit, the method of preparation is traditional. The cranberry chutney has since become a family favorite and is now served as a peppery alternative to the traditional sauce at Thanksgiving, with chicken and other roasts, and, of course, with curries.

🙞🙞🙞 YIELD = 1 CUP

1½ cups fresh cranberries (These may be kept frozen for up to 6 months and can be used without defrosting in this recipe.)

- 1 small piece of fresh ginger, scraped and minced
- 5 bird peppers preserved in vinegar
- ½ cup freshly squeezed lemon juice or raspberry vinegar
- ½ cup dark brown sugar

Chop the cranberries, ginger, and peppers in a food processor or blender. (If using a blender, you may have to add some of the lemon juice to moisten the berries.) Place the mixture in a small saucepan. Add the lemon juice and sugar, stirring well to be sure the ingredients are evenly distributed and there are no clumps of pepper. Place the saucepan over medium heat and bring to a boil, stirring constantly to avoid sticking. Then reduce the heat to low and continue to cook, stirring occasionally, until the chutney thickens, about 25 minutes. Pour the chutney into scalded glass jars.

ONION RELISH (INDIA)

Onion Relish frequently turns up on tables at Indian restaurants. It is super hot but provides an excellent foil for grilled meats and tandoori dishes.

YIELD = 1 CUP

- 3 medium-sized onions, chopped
- 1 hot green chile, seeded and chopped coarse
- 1 teaspoon cayenne pepper
- 2 teaspoons freshly squeezed lemon juice
- Salt to taste

Place the onions in a small nonreactive bowl and add the chile and cayenne. Add the lemon juice and mix well. Add salt to taste and mix again. Serve at room temperature.

COCONUT SAMBAL
(INDIA)

This is a specialty of southern India, where tastes are similar to those of Southeast Asia. The food is ultra hot, and condiments accompany all meals. This sambal mixes the mild taste of coconut with the bite of fresh hot chiles.

YIELD = 1½ CUPS

1 cup freshly grated coconut
5 shallots, peeled
2 hot green chiles
1½ teaspoons lemon zest
One ½-inch piece of fresh ginger, scraped and minced
1 clove garlic, minced
Salt to taste

Place all the ingredients in a food processor or blender and mix until they are a fine paste. When done, place in a small bowl and serve to accompany grilled meats or chicken.

ONION SAMBAL
(SINGAPORE)

This mild sambal is a traditional Indian dish that has been taken to heart by the spice-loving Singaporeans and is frequently found on tables with Malaysian food as well.

YIELD = 1½ CUPS

2 large onions, sliced thin
1 teaspoon salt
Freshly ground black pepper
2 tablespoons freshly squeezed lemon juice
2 teaspoons Asian chile powder or cayenne pepper

Mix the onions and salt in a glass bowl, cover with plastic wrap, and refrigerate for 2 hours. When ready, remove the onions and squeeze them to remove the liquid. Discard the liquid and place the onions in a small serving bowl. Add a few grindings of black pepper, the lemon juice, and the Asian chile powder. Mix well and serve.

SATÉ SAUCE (SINGAPORE)

Saté is traditionally served with an accompanying peanut sauce. This sauce is only remotely related to its African cousins and is redolent of chile and coconut milk. The creamy consistency of the sauce as well as its spicy bite go well with the grilled meat.

🌶🌶🌶🌶 **YIELD = 2 CUPS**

7 dried chiles (bird pepper type), soaked
7 shallots
1 clove garlic
4 macadamia nuts
2 teaspoons minced lemon zest
2 tablespoons peanut oil
1 cup coconut milk (page 67)
¼ cup freshly squeezed lemon juice
1 teaspoon dark brown sugar
½ cup crunchy peanut butter
Salt to taste

Place the drained soaked chiles, the shallots, garlic, macadamia nuts, and lemon zest in a food processor and mix until they are a fine paste. Heat the oil an a heavy saucepan and gently fry the paste for 5 minutes. Add the coconut milk and bring the mixture to a boil, stirring constantly. Add the lemon juice, dark brown sugar, peanut butter, and salt. Simmer the mixture for 3 to 5 minutes, then pour into a small bowl. You may wish to serve the sauce thinned slightly with a bit of hot water. The Saté Sauce is served at room temperature to accompany Saté (page 191).

SAUCE FOR SATÉ BABI (SINGAPORE)

The Nonya are descendants of the Chinese men who first migrated to the Malay Straits and their Malaysian wives. Their cooking is a mixture of Chinese and Malaysian cuisines. In Saté Babi, a traditional Chinese meat—pork—is cooked in a traditional Malaysian saté. It requires a special sauce, which mixes crushed pineapple with the traditional Saté Sauce.

YIELD = 2 CUPS

Saté Sauce in the quantity given in the previous recipe
¾ cup fresh pineapple, chopped fine

Prepare the Saté Sauce as directed on page 178. While the sauce is cooking, dice the pineapple into very small pieces and mix it with the sauce. Serve as Saté Sauce to accompany Saté Babi (page 192).

CUCUMBER SALAD (SINGAPORE)

This salad is my own variation of the one that is traditionally served with saté. It is a marinated onion and cucumber mixture in a sweet and sour vinegar.

SERVES SIX

2 medium-sized cucumbers, peeled, seeded, and sliced thin
2 medium-sized onions, sliced thin
¾ cup red wine vinegar
¼ to ½ cup water
2 tablespoons sugar

Place the cucumbers and onions in a glass or other nonreactive bowl. Mix the vinegar, water, and sugar together and pour them over the onion and cucumber mixture. Place a dish directly on top of the salad and weight it with a heavy object. Refrigerate the cucumber mixture (with the weight) and allow it to marinate for 2 hours. Serve cool to accompany Saté (page 191) or Saté Babi (page 192).

SPICY BEAN CURD (CHINA)

Bean curd is an Asian art. Monks in some areas of the continent never eat meat but have developed the fine art of transforming bean curd into various dishes that have the consistency and, what is more astonishing, the taste of many meat dishes. Bean curd, or tofu as it is called in Japan, has the wonderful property of taking on the flavor of the sauces with which it is cooked. In this recipe, hot chiles form the basis of the sauce, and the resulting dish is a pepper lover's delight.

SERVES FOUR

Four 3-inch-square pieces of bean curd
- 4 dried hot chiles
- 2 tablespoons bean paste (If this is unavailable you may add an equal amount of additional soy sauce.)
- 4 tablespoons soy sauce
- 2 teaspoons sugar
- 1 cup chicken broth
- ¼ cup vegetable oil
- 2 scallions, including 3 inches of the green tops, chopped
- 1 clove garlic, minced
- ½ pound ground beef (optional)
- 3 teaspoons cornstarch
- 3 teaspoons cold water

Place the bean curd in lightly salted hot water for a few minutes. Remove and drain on paper towels. Cut the bean curd into ½-

inch cubes. Remove the seeds and ribs from the chiles and crumble the chiles. In a bowl, mix the bean paste, soy sauce, sugar, and chicken broth. Heat the oil in a wok and add the chiles, scallions, and garlic. Stir fry until the garlic is golden. (At this point you may wish to add ½ pound of ground beef to make a more substantial dish. If so, cook the beef until it is browned before proceeding.) Add the bean curd to the wok and mix it with the other ingredients, stirring cautiously to avoid breaking the cubes. Add the bean paste, soy sauce, sugar, and chicken broth mixture, cover the wok, and bring the ingredients slowly to a boil. Cook for an additional 3 minutes. Mix the cornstarch with an equal amount of cold water and add it to the ingredients in the wok. Stir until the sauce thickens. Serve hot.

SABZI
(INDIA)

The best vegetable curry I ever ate was, ironically, not in India or Pakistan, not even in Asia, in fact. It was in a small lodge on the outskirts of Masai Mara in Kenya. This recipe closely approximates that savory mixture of vegetables and spices.

SERVES SIX TO EIGHT

- 1 medium-sized onion, chopped
- 4 tablespoons peanut oil
- 2¼ cups water
- ½ pound fresh broccoli cut into florets
- ½ pound fresh cauliflower cut into florets
- 1 pound carrots cut into 1-inch pieces
- ½ teaspoon cayenne pepper
- ½ teaspoon ground coriander
- Salt to taste
- One 1-inch piece of fresh ginger, scraped and minced
- 2 cloves garlic, minced
- 2 medium-sized tomatoes, peeled, seeded, and chopped coarse

In a large frying pan, brown the onion in the peanut oil. Add ¼ cup of the water, the vegetables, spices, and coarsely chopped tomato. Cook over medium heat for 5 to 7 minutes, stirring constantly. Add the remaining water, cover the pan, and simmer the curry for 15 minutes or until the water has almost completely evaporated and the vegetables are tender. Serve hot, with white or saffron rice.

EGGPLANT IN YOGURT (INDIA)

Deep-purple-hued eggplants are frequently found in India's markets. They are cooked in a savory yogurt mixture and served as a vegetable accompaniment to many curries and other dishes.

SERVES FOUR

½ pound eggplant
3 tablespoons vegetable oil
1 cup plain yogurt
½ teaspoon salt
½ teaspoon freshly ground black pepper
¼ teaspoon cumin
Dash of cayenne pepper

Cut the eggplant crosswise into thin slices. Sauté the eggplant in the vegetable oil until it is soft and brown. Remove the eggplant from the heat. In a bowl, mix the yogurt and the spices; add the eggplant, stirring carefully to avoid breaking up the slices. Serve warm.

SPICY POTATOES (SINGAPORE)

This mixture is found not only in the Far East; it has also traveled to Trinidad in the Caribbean, where it frequently serves as a filling for that island's ubiquitous roti, in which a whole wheat crepe called a paratha is wrapped around the mixture.

SERVES SIX

1 pound Idaho potatoes
2 tablespoons vegetable oil
½ teaspoon brown mustard seed
1 large Bermuda onion, chopped
½ teaspoon powdered turmeric
½ teaspoon cumin
1 teaspoon hot Asian chile powder (it does not contain the cumin that American versions do)
Salt and freshly ground black pepper to taste

Boil the potatoes until they are cooked but still firm. Peel the potatoes, cut them into ½-inch cubes, and set aside. Heat the oil and fry the mustard seed until it begins to pop. Add the onion and fry for 5 minutes, stirring occasionally. Take care that it does not stick or burn. Add the remaining spices and continue to cook for a few minutes, stirring constantly. Finally, add the potatoes and continue to fry for 5 minutes, stirring occasionally. Remove the spicy potatoes from the heat and serve hot to accompany curries and other Indian dishes. Or you may wish to wrap the spicy potato mixture in a paratha for a Trinidadian-style roti.

JOOK
(SINGAPORE/CHINA)

Jook is a rice gruel that is fed to babies in China. It is also served as a breakfast food in many parts of the Far East. It can be transformed from simple food to luncheon extravaganza by the addition of a variety of garnishes.

SERVES FOUR

2 cups short-grain rice
2 large skinless and boneless chicken breasts, cut into ½-inch cubes
½ cup raw peanuts, skinned
Chicken stock to cover the rice and chicken breasts by 4 inches

- 1 tablespoon vegetable oil
- 4 cloves garlic, peeled and sliced thin
- 5 strips of bacon, cut into ½-inch pieces
- 3 scallions, chopped
- 2 fresh red chiles, seeded and chopped
- Vinegared Green Chiles (page 171)
- Fresh coriander leaves, chopped for garnish
- Freshly ground white pepper to taste

Wash the rice thoroughly and place it in a deep, heavy saucepan. Add the chicken and the raw peanuts. Cover with the chicken stock and bring to a boil. Cover, lower the heat, and simmer on the lowest heat for 1½ hours, or until the chicken is well cooked and the rice has turned into a mushy porridge. (You may find that you have to add additional chicken stock or water so that the Jook does not dry out.)

While the porridge is cooking, prepare the garnishes. Heat the vegetable oil in a frying pan and fry the garlic until it is browned. Remove the garlic, drain, and set aside. Cook the bacon in the frying pan in which the garlic was fried. When the bacon is crispy, remove it and drain on paper towels. Place all the garnishes in separate small dishes so that the diners may add them to their Jook according to their taste.

When the porridge is done, serve it in individual bowls sprinkled with white pepper.

VEGETARIAN STUFFED PEPPERS (INDIA)

Sangita, a student of mine at Queens College, lives in a vegetarian household. She gave me the recipe for this unusual variation on the stuffed pepper theme made from potatoes and hot chiles.

SERVES FOUR

- 4 medium-sized green bell peppers
- 4 medium-sized Idaho potatoes

2 tablespoons heavy cream
2 tablespoons red bell pepper, minced
Salt and freshly ground black pepper to taste
½ hot green chile, minced

Core and seed the green peppers, leaving them whole, and set them aside. Boil the potatoes until they are tender, about 30 minutes. Drain, peel, and purée them in a food processor or food mill, adding the heavy cream to make them smooth. Mix in the red bell pepper, the salt and pepper, and the hot chile, stirring well to distribute them evenly throughout the potato mixture. Stuff the bell pepper shells with the potato mixure. Grind a few sprinklings of black pepper on the top of each pepper. Place them in a baking dish and bake in a 350-degree oven for 20 to 30 minutes. Serve hot.

BHINDI BHAJI
(INDIA)

Although okra is best known in the United States for its use in Caribbean, Cajun, Creole, and black American cooking, it is also a frequently used Indian vegetable. Fresh okra can be unpleasantly slimy for some when it is boiled. Cooked in the Indian manner, however, it acquires a subtle and pleasing taste. The okra should be small in size, fresh, and crisp.

SERVES FOUR

4 tablespoons butter
1 medium-sized onion, sliced thin
1 clove garlic, peeled and sliced
½ teaspoon powdered coriander
½ teaspoon turmeric
¼ teaspoon freshly ground black pepper
¾ pound fresh okra
½ teaspoon Garam Masala (page 186)

Melt the butter in a heavy frying pan. Add the onion and the garlic and cook until they are soft and the onion is transparent.

Add the spices (except the Garam Masala) and cook for an additional 3 minutes. Top and tail the okra and slice it crosswise into ½-inch pieces. Add the okra to the frying pan and stir to coat it with the spices. Cook over low heat for 5 to 10 minutes until the okra is tender but still firm. Stir in the Garam Masala, taking care to mix it well, and serve hot.

GARAM MASALA

Garam Masala is a blend of dried spices used in Indian cooking. It is the stuff that in its homogenized form becomes curry powder. In India, though, there are as many blends of Garam Masala as there are cooks. This is one variation you can prepare at home. It will keep for up to five months in an airtight jar so you may wish to enlarge the proportions.

YIELD = ABOUT 1 CUP

¾ cup whole green cardamom pods
Four 3-inch pieces of stick cinnamon
¼ cup whole cloves
¼ cup cumin
½ cup coriander seeds
½ cup whole black peppercorns

Preheat the oven to 475 degrees. Remove the seeds from the cardamom pods; discard the pods. Place the cardamom seeds and the other ingredients in a shallow baking pan. Bake for 10 minutes. Remove the spices; crush the cinnamon and place all the ingredients in a spice grinder. Grind until they are a fine powder.

If this seems like too much work, you may order ready-made Garam Masala from the stores specializing in Indian ingredients listed at the end of the book.

LENTIL CURRY
(INDIA)

Lentils, or Dal as they are called in India, are a part of every Indian meal. Used in an accompanying soup or as a vegetable dish, they add variety and protein to the menu. This dish is a vegetarian specialty.

SERVES SIX TO EIGHT

1 pound red lentils
3 cups cold water
½ teaspoon turmeric
1 tablespoon butter
2 hot red chiles, seeded and minced
½ teaspoon cumin
4 cloves garlic, minced
2 teaspoons fresh ginger, minced
2 medium-sized tomatoes, peeled, seeded, and chopped coarse
2 sprigs fresh coriander, minced

Wash and clean the lentils according to package directions. (If you are using lentils from an Indian store or a produce market, take particular care because they tend to be grittier than those packaged for supermarkets.) Boil the lentils in the water for 45 minutes with the minced onion and the turmeric. Drain well.

In a frying pan, heat the butter and fry the sliced onion until it is lightly browned. Add the chiles, cumin, garlic, and ginger. Fry well, but take care not to burn the ingredients. When done, add the boiled and drained lentils to the mixture. Allow the mixture to cook for 5 minutes. Finally, add the tomatoes and coriander. Cook for 5 minutes more. You may serve the lentil curry on its own as a vegetarian dish with rice or to accompany another curry.

RICE INDIAN STYLE
(INDIA)

Rice, the staff of life in many parts of the world, is a "must" accompaniment with almost all Indian dishes. This is an interesting variation on the more common saffron or white rice.

SERVES FOUR TO SIX

1 cup long-grain rice
1 tablespoon butter
2 medium-sized onions, minced
12 cardamom pods
Four 2-inch pieces of stick cinnamon, crushed
7 black peppercorns
12 cloves
1 teaspoon sugar
2½ cups water
1 teaspoon salt

Wash the rice thoroughly, rinsing it twice to remove excess starch. Heat the butter in a large saucepan and fry the onions until they are golden. Crush the spices in a spice mill or with a mortar and pestle and add them to the onions along with the sugar. Fry the mixture until it is golden brown, taking care that it does not burn. Pour in the water, add the salt, and bring to a boil. When the water has boiled, add the rice, cover, and cook until the water evaporates. Remove the pot from the heat immediately and place it in a warm oven to dry out thoroughly. Fluff the rice with a fork and serve warm, to accompany curries.

NASI GORENG
(SINGAPORE)

This is a Malaysian version of fried rice. Served to accompany many dishes, or on its own with the addition of diced beef, it is a good way to make use of leftover rice.

🙚🙚🙚 SERVES FOUR

4 tablespoons peanut oil
7 shallots, chopped
1 tablespoon dark raisins
1 egg
2 hot red chiles
2 cloves garlic, minced
½ pound good quality beef, cut into ½-inch cubes
5 to 6 cups cold cooked rice
2 scallions, sliced thin lengthwise and cut into 2-inch sections for garnish

In a small frying pan heat half of the peanut oil and gently fry half the shallots until they are brown. Remove and place them in a small bowl. They will be a garnish. Fry the raisins in the same oil for 1 minute and set them aside in another small bowl. They, too, will be a garnish. Make a thin omelette from the egg; you may need to add a bit more oil. Allow it to cool and, when cool, shred it; this goes into a third small bowl and will also serve as a garnish.

Grind the remaining shallots, the chiles, and the garlic in a food processor to make a paste. Fry the paste gently for 5 minutes in the remaining 2 tablespoons of oil. Add the beef and stir fry it briefly just until cooked. Separate the grains of rice with a fork and add to the beef mixture. Stir fry it for 3 minutes. Serve the Nasi Goreng on a large platter with the garnishes in side dishes. Decorate the platter with the scallions.

SAVORY TOMATOES (INDIA)

In this dish tomatoes are spiced with the bite of Asian chile powder and the subtle mixture of spices that is the hallmark of Indian cooking.

🙚🙚 SERVES FOUR TO SIX

1 tablespoon peanut oil
One 1-inch piece of stick cinnamon

3 cloves garlic
3 cardamom pods
1 small onion, minced
6 medium-sized ripe tomatoes, diced
2 teaspoons Asian chile powder or cayenne pepper
½ tablespoon coriander
½ tablespoon turmeric
½ cup water
1 tablespoon distilled white vinegar
1 tablespoon dark brown sugar
Salt and freshly ground black pepper to taste

Heat the oil in a heavy saucepan and add the cinnamon, garlic, cardamom, and onion. Fry until the mixture is scented with the spices. Add the tomatoes and the remaining ingredients. Bring the mixture to a boil and cook for 3 minutes.

SPICY BEANS (INDIA)

This recipe brings the bite of chile powder to the crunch of string beans.

SERVES FOUR

1 pound fresh string beans, topped and tailed
1 teaspoon turmeric
2 teaspoons Asian chile powder or cayenne pepper
Salt and freshly ground black pepper to taste
¼ cup or more peanut oil

Blanch the beans briefly in boiling water. Drain and sprinkle them with the turmeric, Asian chile powder, salt, and pepper. Allow them to sit for 15 minutes. In a heavy frying pan, heat the oil, add the seasoned string beans, and stir fry for 2 minutes, turning rapidly. When the beans are crisp, remove them from the heat and serve hot.

SATÉ
(SINGAPORE)

Singapore is noted for its food hawkers' stands. Immaculately clean, these booths are invitations to gluttony. From behind a counter, chefs prepare chile crab, fried and spicy noodles, and a wide variety of the ubiquitous Singaporean nibble, saté. Saté Babi (page 192) is a Nonya, Straits Chinese, invention using pork, but saté is traditionally made with lamb, beef, or chicken, all meats that can be eaten by the country's Islamic population as well. Grilled over charcoal braziers and dipped into a variety of sauces, these skewers of meat accompanied by their traditional marinated onions and cucumbers make a perfect barbecue.

SERVES FOUR TO SIX

60 long, thin bamboo skewers
1 tablespoon coriander seeds
1 teaspoon cumin
10 shallots
2 cloves garlic
2 teaspoons minced lemon zest
One ½-inch piece of fresh ginger
Salt to taste
1 teaspoon turmeric
2 teaspoons dark brown sugar
2 pounds boned chicken breast, leg of lamb, or steak cut into ¾-inch cubes
¼ cup freshly squeezed lemon juice
4 tablespoons peanut oil

Soak the skewers in water for half an hour to be sure they do not burn during the cooking. In a small, heavy, dry frying pan, heat the coriander seeds and cumin over medium heat until they are warmed through. Remove them from the pan and grind them in a spice mill until you have a fine powder. Place the shallots, garlic, lemon zest, and ginger in a food processor or blender and grind them to a fine paste. Mix the paste with the ground spices and the salt, turmeric, sugar, and lemon juice. Add the meat to the paste and marinate it for approximately 8 hours. When marinated, place the chunks of meat on the prepared bamboo skewers. Brush the meat with the oil and grill the saté over charcoal or in a broiler until it is browned. Serve hot, with Saté Sauce (page 000) and chile sauce. You may wish to make a variety of satés and sauces and let your guests choose. If so, add a dish of the traditional Cucumber Salad (page 179).

SATÉ BABI
(SINGAPORE)

Although Saté (or satay) is a snack specialty throughout Southeast Asia, Saté Babi or pork saté is typical of Singapore. There, the Nonya, Straits-born Chinese, have adapted the Chinese love for pork to create a dish that is a welcome addition to any saté spread.

SERVES FOUR

25 thin bamboo skewers
1 pound boneless pork loin
1 stalk lemon grass (citronella) *
1 medium-sized onion
2 teaspoons coriander seeds
½ teaspoon turmeric
2 teaspoons light brown sugar
Salt to taste
4 teaspoons peanut oil

Soak the bamboo skewers in water for half an hour so they will not burn during the cooking. While soaking the skewers, cut the pork into small pieces. Saté is not shish kebab; the pieces must be small enough to eat off the skewer, approximately ¾ inch square.

* Lemon grass can be obtained from some of the stores specializing in Asian ingredients listed at the end of the book.

Slice the lemon grass, place it in a food processor with the onion, and grind them into a paste. Heat the coriander seeds and pulverize them in a spice mill. Mix the coriander powder with the onion–lemon grass paste, the turmeric, sugar, salt, and 1 tablespoon of the oil. Place the pork pieces in this marinade and allow them to stand for at least 2 hours. When ready to serve, heat the broiler to its highest setting or make sure that the charcoal is well heated and covered with a gray ash. Place the saté pieces on the skewers, four or five pieces to a skewer, and grill them for 20 to 30 minutes or until well cooked. Serve the saté with pieces of raw onion or Cucumber Salad (page 179) and Sauce for Saté Babi (page 179).

The skewers of saté can be served as appetizers, with cocktails, or, taking care that you have enough for everyone, as a main course. If serving saté as a main dish, make some of each type (see previous recipe) enabling your guests to choose the variety that they prefer.

CHILE CRAB
(SINGAPORE)

For me, as for many others, Chile Crab is a dish that will always mean Singapore. I remember the tang of the salt air in the seaside restaurant where I first saw them, the bright red of the crab shells, and the delight in sucking out all of the little bits of meat.

SERVES FOUR

3 live 1-pound crabs
Lemon juice
One 1-inch piece of fresh ginger, scraped and minced
4 hot red chiles
3 tablespoons peanut oil
1 tablespoon salted soybeans, pulverized
2 teaspoons sugar
¾ cup water
2 medium-sized tomatoes, peeled, seeded, and chopped fine

It sounds barbarous, but cut the crabs in half lengthwise and remove the back shells. (The squeamish can stun the crabs by freezing them for 10 minutes or go immediately to the Quick Chile Crab recipe below.) Remove and discard any gray matter. Take off the claws and crack them with a mallet or the side of a heavy Chinese cleaver. Cut the crab body into six pieces leaving the legs attached. Wash the crabs thoroughly with a mixture of lemon juice and water and drain them on paper towels.

Place the ginger and the chiles in a food processor and grind them to a fine paste. Fry the paste in the oil in a heavy frying pan for 3 minutes. Add the soybeans and cook for an additional minute, stirring the mixture constantly to be sure the ingredients are well mixed. Add the crab pieces and stir fry over high heat until they turn bright red. Lower the heat and add the sugar, water, and tomatoes. Cover the frying pan and allow the Chile Crab to simmer for 5 minutes, stirring occasionally. Serve it with rice or as part of a gala Singaporean buffet along with satés (page 191) of beef, chicken, and lamb and several sambals. Your guests should feel free to eat the Chile Crab with their fingers and suck the crabmeat out of the claws and legs. Provide fingerbowls and plenty of napkins.

QUICK CHILE CRAB
(SINGAPORE)

This is a fast way to enjoy Singapore's Chile Crab. You don't get the pleasure of sucking the crabmeat from the shells, but then again you don't have to go through the pain of cutting up the live crab. To make Quick Chile Crab, simply prepare according to the directions above, substituting fresh lump crabmeat for the whole crabs used in the traditional recipe.

COZIDO DE PEIXE
(MACAO)

The Portuguese who live in Macao have brought with them not only the pastel-colored baroque churches of their homeland but also some of their culinary traditions. One such dish uses local fish along with the ubiquitous Asian chile to create a Portuguese-style fish stew in the Asian manner.

SERVES FOUR

6 ripe, firm tomatoes, peeled, seeded, and chopped coarse
2 medium-sized onions, sliced
6 fresh green medium-hot chiles, sliced
1 tablespoon tomato paste
1 cup water
1 tablespoon freshly squeezed lime juice
Salt and freshly ground black pepper to taste
2 ounces (½ stick) butter
1 pound halibut or swordfish steaks

Place all the ingredients except the fish in a heavy flame-proof earthenware casserole. Bring to a boil and simmer for 5 minutes. Add the fish and continue to cook for about 15 minutes. When the fish is tender and the sauce has thickened slightly, serve the Cozido with white rice.

SAMBAL UDANG
(SINGAPORE)

Large shrimp can be used in this dish to replace the prawns called for in the traditional recipe. If you live in an area where prawns are readily available, use them. (Note that prawns are not simply large shrimp, they are the bright pink species usually found in Europe. They are called langoustines in France and scampi in Italy.)

🌶🌶🌶🌶 SERVES FOUR

1 pound raw prawns, or use jumbo or colossal shrimp
15 dried red chiles
10 shallots
3 cloves garlic
One 1-inch piece of fresh ginger, scraped and minced
½ teaspoon dried shrimp paste
2 tablespoons vegetable oil
1 large onion, sliced thin
2 medium-sized tomatoes, peeled, seeded, and quartered
1 teaspoon sugar
Salt to taste
½ cup freshly squeezed lemon juice

Peel and devein the prawns or shrimp and set them aside. Soak the chiles and then grind them along with the shallots, garlic, ginger, and shrimp paste in a food processor to make a fine paste. Heat the oil in a heavy cast-iron frying pan and fry the paste for 5 minutes. Add the prawns or shrimp and continue to fry, stirring constantly, until they change color. Add the remaining ingredients and simmer the mixture uncovered for an additional 5 minutes, until the shrimp are cooked through. Serve with white rice.

SPICY LAMB (CHINA)

Here is another lamb dish from China, this one using chile peppers and sesame seeds. One provides the heat and the other the crunch.

🌶🌶🌶 SERVES FOUR

2 pounds lean leg of lamb, cut into 1-inch cubes
2 dried chiles, seeded and chopped coarse
4 scallions, minced

2 cloves garlic, minced
2 teaspoons fresh ginger, minced
2 egg whites
5 tablespoons cornstarch
2 tablespoons dark soy sauce
2 tablespoons sugar
2 tablespoons sesame oil
2 tablespoons grilled sesame seeds
⅓ cup peanut oil

Place the lamb, the chiles, scallions, garlic, and ginger in a bowl and mix well to cover the lamb. Let the lamb marinate for 15 minutes, then stir the egg whites, and add them to the lamb mixture. Add the cornstarch and mix all the ingredients well to coat the lamb. Combine the soy sauce, sugar, sesame oil, and sesame seeds.

In a wok, heat ¼ cup of the peanut oil to 300 degrees. Cook the lamb in the oil until it is crisp and brown. Remove the lamb from the wok and discard the oil. Then heat the remaining oil in the wok and quickly stir fry the lamb. Add the soy sauce mixture and cook until the liquid has almost evaporated. Serve hot with white rice.

SPICY SESAME CHICKEN (CHINA)

Sesame chicken is a fixture on the menus of many Chinese restaurants. This variation calls for a bit of crushed red chile, which adds zip to the dish.

SERVES FOUR

2 whole chicken breasts
1 egg white
Salt and freshly ground white pepper to taste
2 teaspoons crushed red chile
2 tablespoons grilled sesame seeds
3 tablespoons peanut oil
1 tablespoon sesame oil

Skin the chicken breasts, bone them, and cut lengthwise into six pieces. Season the egg white with the salt, white pepper, and chile. Dip the chicken into the egg white and then coat it with the sesame seeds.

Heat the peanut and sesame oils in a heavy frying pan or wok to 350 degrees. Rapidly deep fry the chicken pieces in the oil, turning them so they are cooked evenly on all sides. Serve hot, with soy sauce or a sweet and sour dipping sauce.

SHAMI KEBABS
(INDIA)

The Mogul legacy of Pakistan and northern India has left the area with a taste for lamb. These lamb and split-pea patties are a typical regional appetizer.

SERVES FOUR

½ cup yellow split peas
1 pound ground lamb
2 tablespoons butter
1 teaspoon Garam Masala (page 186)
½ teaspoon cayenne pepper
Salt to taste
2 eggs, separated
1 small bunch of fresh coriander, minced

Boil the split peas according to package directions. When they are cooked, drain them and mix with the ground lamb. Heat 1 tablespoon of butter in a frying pan and cook the meat and split-pea mixture for 10 minutes, stirring frequently. Add the spices and cook for an additional 2 minutes. When the lamb is cooked through, put the mixture through a meat grinder or food processor to make a fine paste. Add the egg yolks and coriander to the mixture. Reserve the egg whites. Shape the mixture into flat, round patties; it should make ten to twelve patties. Heat the remaining butter in a no-stick frying pan, dip each patty into well-beaten egg white, and fry until well browned on each side. Serve the Shami Kebabs hot as a side dish. You may find that you enjoy them with a little Mint Coriander Dip (page 166) on the side.

LAMB TIKKA
(INDIA)

Here is another Mogul dish from northern India. Lamb cubes are marinated in a yogurt and spice mixture and grilled over charcoal. The dish is served as an appetizer or snack and can become a main course with the addition of rice, condiments, onion relish, and chutneys.

SERVES FOUR TO SIX

1 cup plain yogurt
2 large onions, cut into cubes
1 teaspoon cayenne pepper
½ teaspoon coriander
½ teaspoon Garam Masala (page 186)
2 tablespoons freshly squeezed lime juice
2 pounds leg of lamb, cut into 1-inch cubes

In a medium-sized bowl, mix all the ingredients except the lamb. Add the lamb, making sure it is well coated with marinade. Cover the bowl with plastic wrap and allow the lamb to marinate in the refrigerator for at least 6 hours. When ready to cook, place the lamb pieces on skewers, alternating them with the onion cubes. Heat the broiler to its highest setting and place the skewers on the broiler rack. Cook for approximately 10 minutes, turning frequently. Alternately, the Lamb Tikka can be cooked over charcoal. In that case, place the skewers on the grill over a medium-hot fire and cook for 10 minutes, turning frequently. Serve either as appetizers or with rice and condiments as a complete meal.

SHRIMP CURRY
(INDIA)

Here is an ideal summer dish combining the delicacy of shrimp with the taste of fresh, ripe tomatoes and a dash of cayenne pepper.

SERVES FOUR TO SIX

½ cup peanut oil
1 pound shrimp, cleaned, peeled, and deveined
1 onion, chopped
1 clove garlic, minced
One 1-inch piece of fresh ginger, scraped and minced
1 teaspoon cayenne pepper
½ teaspoon turmeric
Salt to taste
2 large ripe tomatoes, peeled, seeded, and chopped coarse
2 cups water

Heat the peanut oil in a large frying pan and lightly sauté the shrimp for 3 to 5 minutes, turning frequently. Remove the shrimp and set aside. Brown the onion in the same oil and when browned add the garlic and spices. Stir well so all the ingredients are thoroughly mixed. Add the tomatoes and cook for an additional 5 minutes. Pour in 2 cups of water and bring the mixture to a boil. Then add the sautéed shrimp and lower the heat. Cook for an additional 10 minutes and serve hot, with white rice or Rice Indian Style (page 188).

MONGOLIAN LAMB
(CHINA)

Although many people think of China as a country with a homogeneous civilization, this is not really so. Many races make up the people of China; the Mongols are one of them. Many of China's barbecued foods took form around Mongol campfires as the legendary horsemen made camp for the evening. Among the Mongols were Islamic groups who followed the dietary laws of Islam. Pork, a mainstay of southern Chinese cooking, was anathema and replaced in many dishes by lamb. Here, then, is a recipe for Mongolian Lamb, a grill-it-yourself dish that lets everyone join in the cooking.

SERVES SIX

3 pounds lean leg of lamb
2 cups dark soy sauce
2 cups dry sherry
1 teaspoon sesame oil
Salt and freshly ground black pepper to taste
1 teaspoon cayenne pepper
2 cloves garlic, minced
5 scallions, including 3 inches of the green tops, cut lengthwise into strips

Slice the lamb into paper-thin slices using a very sharp knife or Chinese cleaver. (This will be easier to do if you have partially frozen the lamb.) Place the lamb slices in a marinade made from the remaining ingredients. Grease the grill of a small hibachi or charcoal brazier, light it, and wait until you have a low fire with gray, ash-coated coals. When the fire is ready and the meat has marinated thoroughly, at least 15 minutes to half an hour, give your guests bamboo skewers or long fondue forks and allow them to cook their own meat. This barbecue dish also makes a cocktail conversation piece when done with smaller pieces of lamb. As a dinner, it goes well with any vegetable dish, rice, and, although not traditionally Chinese, a salad.

HUNAN LAMB
(CHINA)

Hunan lamb is one of my favorite Chinese dishes. It is found in almost all restaurants specializing in the spicy hot dishes of the Hunan province of China. Some variations cook the lamb with scallions, others with leeks. This variation calls for the lamb to be cooked with broccoli. The sweet and slightly gamey taste of the lamb mixes well with the piquant sauce and the delicate crunch of the broccoli to create a dish that is a special treat.

❧❧❧ **SERVES FOUR TO SIX**

- 2 pounds boneless leg of lamb
- 1½ tablespoons cornstarch
- 1 egg white
- 4 black mushrooms*
- 2 cups broccoli florets
- 4 bamboo shoots,* sliced into strips
- 1½ cups dark soy sauce*
- 2 tablespoons sugar
- 2 tablespoons dry sherry
- ½ teaspoon rice vinegar
- ½ teaspoon sesame oil
- 1½ tablespoons chile paste with garlic*
- ½ tablespoon water
- 2 cups corn oil

Slice the lamb thin. Put it in a small bowl and add 1 tablespoon of the cornstarch and the egg white. Mix well. Soak the black mushrooms for 5 minutes in hot water, then slice them into strips and place them in a bowl with the broccoli and the bamboo shoots. In another bowl, combine the soy sauce, sugar, sherry, vinegar, sesame oil, chile paste, and remaining cornstarch mixed with the water.

Heat the corn oil in a wok, add the lamb slices, and cook for about 1 minute, stirring and turning the meat so it cooks on all sides. Add the broccoli and other vegetables and cook for an additional half minute. Drain the meat and vegetable mixture reserving 1 tablespoon of the cooking oil in the wok. Return the lamb and vegetable mixture to the wok and add the soy sauce mixture. Cook for about half a minute or until the ingredients are well coated with the sauce. Serve hot, with white rice.

* See mail order sources at the back of the book.

VINDALOO CURRY
(INDIA)

This is a curry from southern India. The English word "curry" comes from the Hindu word "tucarri" meaning sauce. Contrary to popular impressions, no self-respecting Indian cook would ever consider making a curry with powder from a jar. Each spice is measured, and mixtures are determined according to the region and the foods to be curried. They are either homemade or purchased from spice stalls in the market. Vindaloo curries from southern India are bitey because they are made with vinegar, which acts as an effective preservative in the warm climate of that area.

SERVES SIX

1 large onion, minced
3 cloves garlic, minced
3 tablespoons butter
3 sprigs of fresh coriander, minced
2 teaspoons turmeric
1 teaspoon cumin
1 teaspoon crushed dried red chiles
1 teaspoon dry mustard
One 1-inch piece fresh ginger root, scraped and minced
Salt and freshly ground black pepper to taste
½ cup or more distilled white vinegar
3 pounds boned chicken breasts, cut into 1-inch cubes

In large frying pan, sauté the onion and garlic in the butter until they are soft and golden but not brown. Grind the herbs and spices in a spice mill. Add them to the onion and garlic, stirring so they neither stick nor burn. Add the vinegar. It should be enough to make a smooth paste. If not, add more vinegar (up to another ¼ cup). Cover the chicken pieces with the paste and marinate them for at least 1 hour. (The longer the chicken pieces marinate, the hotter the curry.) When ready to cook, place the chicken in a large frying pan and add enough water to reconstitute the paste and prevent scorching. Cover and cook over low heat for 1 hour. You may find that you have to add more water during the cooking process. Serve the Vindaloo Curry warm, with Rice Indian Style (page 188) and accompanied by a selection of chutneys and raitas and Katchumber Salad (page 169). You may wish to add freshly grated coconut or roasted peanuts served in separate small dishes to make a gala meal.

CHICKEN TIKKA
(INDIA)

Chicken Tikka is an Indian barbecued dish. The chicken is marinated in red pepper and lemon juice for ten hours and then broiled over charcoal. The dish is easily duplicated in the kitchen broiler.

SERVES FOUR TO SIX

One 2½- to 3-pound chicken cut into serving pieces
1 teaspoon cayenne pepper
1 clove garlic, minced
1 quarter-sized piece of fresh ginger, minced
2 tablespoons freshly squeezed lemon juice

Wash the chicken pieces thoroughly and pat them dry with paper towels. Mix the remaining ingredients to form a marinade. Let the chicken sit in this mixture in the refrigerator for 10 hours or overnight. When ready, remove the chicken from the marinade and grill it over an open fire. Alternately, heat the broiler to the highest setting and place the chicken pieces on the broiler rack. Cook the chicken for 20 to 30 minutes or until done, turning frequently. You may wish to baste the chicken with a mixture of 1 tablespoon of butter and 1 tablespoon of freshly squeezed lemon juice. When the chicken is cooked, serve it hot, garnished with slices of fresh, ripe tomato and onion and a wedge of lemon.

KEEMA CURRY
(INDIA)

This traditional Indian dish is usually made with ground lamb. It is a savory way to give ground meat a new and more exotic lease on life. Served with a variety of homemade chutneys, Rice Indian Style, and Lentil Curry, it becomes a quick, inexpensive, and yet impressive meal.

❧❧ SERVES FOUR TO SIX

2 tablespoons butter
1 large onion, chopped
1 clove garlic, minced
1 teaspoon fresh ginger, minced
5 cloves
5 green cardamom pods, crushed
1 teaspoon cinnamon
½ teaspoon turmeric
½ teaspoon hot Asian chile powder (it does not contain the cumin that American versions do)
1 pound ground lamb or beef
2 teaspoons Garam Masala (page 000)
1 cup green peas, fresh or frozen

In a frying pan, heat the butter and gently fry the onion, garlic, ginger, and cloves and cardamom pods for 4 minutes. Add the cinnamon, turmeric, and chile powder and fry briefly. Break up the meat and add it, stirring until the color changes. Cover the frying pan and cook for 10 minutes. Add the Garam Masala and cook for 5 additional minutes. Finally, add the peas and cook 5 minutes until the meat and peas are thoroughly cooked. Serve hot, either with rice or accompanied by chutneys, raitas, Rice Indian Style (page 188), and Lentil Curry (page 187) for a more gala meal.

ROGAN GOSHT
(INDIA)

This is a lamb dish that is served with a spicy cream and almond sauce. Lamb is one of the centerpieces of the Mogul cooking of northern India and Pakistan. Islamic religious proscriptions forbade the eating of pork and so lamb and chicken became the major meats. The Moguls must have eaten very well indeed if they feasted on dishes such as Rogan Gosht.

SERVES FOUR TO SIX

1 cup plain yogurt
2 medium-sized onions, quartered
1½ tablespoons fresh ginger, chopped
2½ tablespoons slivered blanched almonds
½ tablespoon ground coriander
2 tablespoons ground cardamom
1 or more teaspoons freshly ground black pepper
1 cup heavy cream
2 pounds boneless leg of lamb
3 medium-sized white potatoes

Place the yogurt, onions, ginger, and almonds in a food processor or blender and mince them to make a fine paste. Place the paste, with the coriander, cardamom, pepper, heavy cream, and lamb, in a heavy nonstick frying pan and bring the mixture to a boil over medium heat. Reduce the heat and simmer the Rogan Gosht for 2 hours. Add the potatoes and continue to cook until they are done (about 30 minutes). Stir frequently so the sauce does not stick, but be careful not to break up the potatoes or the meat. Check the seasoning and serve the Rogan Gosht with Rice Indian Style (page 188). If you let the dish stand for a few hours before serving, the sauce will mellow and the flavor will improve.

TEA SPICE
(INDIA)

Even tea takes on a new taste with the addition of spices. Tea spice mixture can be obtained ground in many Indian stores. (I actually purchased my first tea spice from a stall in the open-air market in Mombasa, Kenya.) You can, however, make your own. Tea spice not only picks up the flavor of regular orange pekoe teas, it is also excellent when added to herb teas and wonderful for making mulled cider, with warm fruit juices, or even for making vin chaud.

SERVES TWO

One 3-inch stick of cinnamon
6 to 8 green cardamom pods
6 whole cloves
10 to 12 whole black peppercorns
2 cups liquid

Tie the dry ingredients in a small cheesecloth bag and infuse the spices with the tea or other liquid while bringing it to the boiling point. Reduce the heat and allow the tea, or other liquid, to simmer for 5 minutes so it is thoroughly flavored with the spices. Remove the bag and serve the beverage.

The Western Tradition: Culinary Omnivores

THE WESTERN TRADITION in cooking encompasses the cuisines of western Europe, the United States, and Canada. It is all-accepting and all-adapting. From China it has taken stir frying and from India, curries. Here in the United States, the African culinary tradition has not yet been thoroughly explored, but the indigenous cooking of black Americans has preserved its soul in such dishes as barbecued ribs, collard greens, hot sauces, and hearty spicy stews. And Latin American migrations have made tacos and chile as common in the American Southwest as roast beef and apple pie.

American tastebuds are becoming more and more sensitized to the fiery edge of culinary life. We are a nation in the midst of a growing love affair with hot stuff. In supermarkets and local groceries, in specialty food shops and fresh produce stores it is becoming possible to find fresh chiles and root ginger where it was once impossible even to find fresh corn; coriander, jalapeño jelly, and several kinds of curry powder are sold where it was once difficult to find parsley. We are beginning to go to restaurants where Creole mustard and Louisiana Red Hot Sauce are standard table condiments and where wasabi and pickled ginger can be found alongside the traditional salt.

Tex-Mex, Creole and Cajun, Indian and Mexican, along with the traditional cuisines of Brazil, Ethiopia, Morocco, and other far-off places have found their way to our tables. Chile cook-offs and summer barbecues have been joined by classes in southern Indian cooking and in the spicy foods of the Szechwan and Hunan regions of China. A brunch may find us eating anything from grits and bacon with jalapeño cornbread and homemade chile jelly to a complete Brazilian Feijoada.

Omnivorous as the Western culinary tradition is, it is also inventive. Each dish is adapted slightly to Western tastes. Curries are attenuated and then accented in a new way to create something totally different. Chiles are used not just to spice up dishes but to add zip to vinegars and jellies. The ubiquitous bell pepper is used in everything from stuffed peppers to salads and is even puréed to add taste and color to the soups of nouvelle cuisine.

Peppercorns find their way into almost everything in their black, white, and green forms. A grinding of black pepper even brings new zest to fruit. Green peppercorns, both preserved and freeze-dried, add their piquancy to salads and to such classic nouvelle cuisine dishes as duck with green peppercorns. They can also turn up in traditional dishes such as steak au poivre and a variation on that theme prepared with leg of lamb.

The Western tradition is so vast that many cookbooks have been devoted exclusively to exploring one small segment of it. There are omissions, I am sure. For example, there is no recipe for chicken paprikash, and I have included only two recipes for chile.

The dishes selected are not those that are available in every cookbook. They are a result of my particular tastes and tend to be grilled or roasted or stewed. There are few heavy sauces, and the cooking usually does not require a great deal of pre-preparation. They are dishes that a busy cook can prepare and dishes that will look equally well on a table of scrubbed pine set with spatterware or on a mahagony one set with fine linen. Only two ingredients are required—a love of good food and an affection for hot stuff.

Before proceeding with any recipes calling for hot chiles, refer to the Chile Caveats in the front of the book.

PHILADELPHIA PEPPER POT (UNITED STATES)*

This is a variation on the traditional tripe soup that has made Philadelphia famous. Pepper lovers can add enough dried red chile and freshly ground black pepper to give it a decided bite.

SERVES SIX

1 pound tripe, cut into ½-inch cubes
A meaty veal shank (about 1 pound), sawed into 2 or 3 pieces
2 quarts water
4 to 6 whole black peppercorns
1 teaspoon salt
4 tablespoons butter
1 cup onions, chopped fine
½ cup celery, chopped fine
½ cup green pepper, chopped fine
3 tablespoons flour
2 medium-sized boiling potatoes, peeled and cut into ¼-inch dice
Crushed dried hot red pepper
Freshly ground black pepper

Combine the tripe, veal shank, and water in a heavy 4- to 5-quart casserole. The water should cover the meats by at least 2 inches; if necessary, add more. Bring to a boil over high heat, skimming off the foam and scum as they rise to the surface. Add the peppercorns and salt, reduce the heat to low, and simmer partially covered for 2 hours or until the tripe is tender.

* From *Time/Life Foods of the World/American Cooking: The Eastern Heartland*, copyright © 1971 Time-Life Books, Inc.

With a slotted spoon, transfer the tripe and pieces of veal shank to a platter or cutting board. Remove the veal from the shank, discard the bones, and cut the meat into ½-inch pieces. Strain the cooking liquid through a fine sieve set over a bowl; measure and reserve 6 cups. If there is less, add enough water to make the amount.

In the same 4- to 5-quart casserole, melt the butter over moderate heat. When the foam subsides, add the onions, celery, and green pepper and stir for about 5 minutes. When the vegetables are soft, but not brown, add the flour and mix well. Stirring constantly, pour in the reserved cooking liquid in a slow, thin stream and cook over high heat until the soup thickens slightly, comes to a boil, and is smooth. Add the potatoes, tripe, and veal, reduce the heat to low, cover partially, and simmer for 1 hour.

Taste for seasoning. Add more salt if needed and enough crushed red pepper and freshly ground black pepper to give the soup a distinctly peppery flavor. Serve at once from the casserole or in individual soup plates.

SPICY HAM SPREAD (UNITED STATES)

One of my mother's specialties is a ham spread that is mixed with cayenne. It is delicious on rye crisp crackers or on Italian bread toasted with butter and garlic.

SERVES FOUR TO SIX AS AN APPETIZER

- 1 cup ground cooked ham or pork shoulder
- 1 teaspoon cayenne pepper
- 1 dash Worcestershire sauce
- 2 tablespoons mayonnaise (or enough to hold the ham together for spreading)

Mix all the ingredients in a small bowl. Cover with plastic wrap and allow the flavors to blend in the refrigerator overnight. Serve as a spread with crackers.

PEPPER QUICHE (UNITED STATES)

Pepper Quiche is a good example of what happens when American ingredients meet with European cooking traditions. Here the Quiche Lorraine is transformed by Jalapeño Monterey Jack cheese into something with a taste of the southwest. The ingredients will fill a 9-inch pie shell.

SERVES SIX

½ cup ham, diced
5 strips of bacon, cut into pieces
¼ pound swiss cheese
¼ pound jalapeño Monterey Jack cheese
1 small onion
3 eggs
½ cup heavy cream
Salt and freshly ground black pepper to taste

Prepare a 9-inch pie crust. Precook it so that it is firm, but not completely cooked. Cook the bacon and ham in a medium frying pan until the bacon is crisp and the ham is well done. Reserve 1 tablespoon of the rendered fat.

Meanwhile, grate the cheese and onion in a food processor or by hand. You will have approximately 2 cups of cheese-onion mixture. Reserve ½ cup of the mixture and place the rest in a mixing bowl. Add the drained bacon and ham, the reserved fat, the eggs, and the cream. Mix well so that the ingredients are well distributed. Pour the mixture into the pie crust and sprinkle the top with the reserved cheese and onion mixture. Cook in a 350-degree oven for 30 minutes. The quiche can be served warm or cool with an accompanying green salad as a light luncheon meal.

MARINATED CANNELLI BEANS (ITALY)

These white beans, when marinated with oil, parsley, red bell pepper, and black pepper, make an interesting addition to any antipasto.

SERVES SIX

2 (16-ounce) cans of cannelli beans
1 (4-ounce) can of Italian oil-packed tuna
½ teaspoon dried oregano
¼ cup red bell pepper, minced
¼ cup extra virgin olive oil
Salt and freshly ground black pepper to taste
Parsley, chopped fine, for garnish

Drain the beans and place them in a large bowl or serving dish. Add the remaining ingredients and mix well, taking care not to break the beans. Cover with plastic wrap and refrigerate for at least 1 hour. Garnish with chopped parsley and serve either alone or as part of a larger antipasto.

GRAVLAAX (SWEDEN)

This salmon marinated in dill is emblematic of the subtle uses to which European cooking puts white pepper.

SERVES EIGHT TO TEN

3 pounds center-cut fresh salmon, cleaned and scaled
2 large bunches of fresh dill
¼ cup kosher salt
¼ cup sugar
3 tablespoons cracked white pepper

Cut the salmon in half lengthwise and remove all the bones. Place half the fish, skin side down, in a large glass casserole or earthenware dish. Wash the dill, separate the stalks, and place them on top of the fish. Mix the salt, sugar, and white pepper in a small bowl and sprinkle them liberally over the fish. Place the other half of the fish on top, skin side up. Cover the fish with foil and weight it with a dish holding heavy cans. Place the fish, with the weights, in the refrigerator for 2 days. Twice a day, turn the fish over and baste it with the juices that run off, then return it, and the weights, to the refrigerator.

When ready to serve the Gravlaax, remove the weights and the foil, pick off the dill, and scrape off the seasonings. Reserve the brine for the accompanying Mustard Sauce (below). Pat the fish dry with paper towels. To serve, slice the fish on the diagonal, skin side down. Gravlaax is perfect served with mustard sauce or simply on its own.

MUSTARD SAUCE FOR GRAVLAAX (SWEDEN)

This slightly spicy mustard sauce goes perfectly with Gravlaax.

YIELD = ½ CUP

3 tablespoons Dijon-style mustard
1 teaspoon dry mustard
2 tablespoons sugar
1 tablespoon white wine vinegar
3 tablespoons brine from the Gravlaax

Mix all the ingredients except the brine in a small bowl. Add the brine slowly and whisk the mixture into a thick sauce. Serve with Gravlaax.

HOT CASHEWS (UNITED STATES)

This southwestern nibble uses chile powder and cumin to spice up cashews.

WESTERN TRADITION

SERVES EIGHT

- 2 cups cashew nuts
- 1½ tablespoons butter
- 1 teaspoon salt
- 1 teaspoon powdered red chiles
- ½ teaspoon ground cumin

In a heavy frying pan, sauté the cashew nuts in the butter for about 10 minutes. Stir occasionally to be sure the nuts do not burn. Remove the nuts and drain them well on paper towels. Place the salt, powdered chiles, and cumin in a paper bag. Add the nuts and shake to coat them well. Serve warm, with cocktails.

CHILE ALMONDS (SPAIN)

Almonds are the traditional accompaniment to a cold glass of fino sherry in many parts of Spain. Served blanched and roasted, they have a sweetness that is the perfect foil for a light dusting of powdered chile. These mildly spicy nuts are simple to make and an ideal cocktail snack.

SERVES EIGHT

- 2 cups blanched almonds
- 1½ tablespoons olive oil
- 2 teaspoons powdered pasilla chile
- 2 teaspoons salt

Place the blanched almonds on a cookie tin, drizzle olive oil over them, and bake in a 350-degree oven until they are browned on both sides. Remove the almonds from the oven and drain them well on paper towels. Place the powdered chile in a paper bag with the salt. Add the nuts and shake to be sure they are well coated. Serve warm, with cold glasses of dry cocktail sherry.

MULES
(UNITED STATES)

My mother thinks that these appetizers should be called mules because they have a "mean kick." They are the traditional mix of chicken livers and bacon with the added jolt of a strip of preserved jalapeño chile. Lovers of hot stuff find them so good that you might wish to consider placing several on a skewer shish-kebab style and serving them as a main dish.

SERVES EIGHT AS AN APPETIZER

24 long cocktail toothpicks
12 whole chicken livers or 24 chicken liver pieces
12 strips of bacon cut in half crosswise
2 preserved (pickled) jalapeño chiles cut into 12 strips each
Freshly ground black pepper to taste
24 small button mushrooms

Soak the toothpicks in water for half an hour so that they do not burn during the cooking. Clean the chicken livers and cut them in half if using whole livers. Place one chicken liver half on half a strip of bacon. Add a jalapeño chile strip and black pepper to taste. No salt is needed because the bacon itself is quite salty. Wrap the bacon around the chicken liver and the jalapeño chile strip and fasten it with a cocktail toothpick. Add a small button mushroom to the end of the toothpick. Preheat the broiler to the highest setting. Place the Mules in a broiling pan or on a cookie sheet with sides (the bacon will render its fat as it cooks) and broil, turning once, until the bacon is crisp. Serve hot.

PEPPER DIP
(UNITED STATES)

This mixture of various peppers and minced onion blended with mustard and cream cheese makes a dip that is excellent with crudités and that can also be mixed with oil and vinegar to make a spicy summer salad dressing.

WESTERN TRADITION

SERVES FOUR AS AN APPETIZER

2 teaspoons dried bird chiles
2 teaspoons black peppercorns
2 teaspoons white peppercorns
2 teaspoons freeze-dried green peppercorns
1 teaspoon dry mustard
1 teaspoon minced onion
3 ounce cream cheese, at room temperature

Place the chiles and the peppercorns in a spice mill and grind them to obtain a coarse powder. Add the chile-pepper powder, the mustard, and the minced onion to the cream cheese and mix well with a fork. You may find that you will have to add a teaspoon or so of milk to soften the cheese. When well mixed, place in a serving dish and refrigerate until ready to serve with crudités.

BAKED OYSTERS WITH SPICY PERNOD VINAIGRETTE (UNITED STATES)

New Orleans is the home of a variety of baked oyster dishes: Oysters Rockefeller, Oysters Sardou, and Oysters Roffignac to name a few. This variation bakes the oysters with pernod and then pours on a sauce of bell peppers, crushed chiles, and green peppercorns.

SERVES FOUR AS AN APPETIZER

24 large oysters, shucked, with their liquor and half of each shell reserved
¾ cup pernod
1½ cups chablis
1 tablespoon Pepper Oil (page 221)
1 tablespoon minced chives
¼ cup minced red and green bell pepper

2 tablespoons green peppercorns, drained and minced
½ teaspoon crushed dried red chile
⅓ cup white wine vinegar

Place the oysters on the half shell in a shallow roasting pan and pour approximately 1½ teaspoons of pernod and 1 tablespoon of chablis into each shell. Cover the pan tightly with aluminum foil and bake the oysters in a 350-degree oven for 10 minutes. Combine the remaining ingredients in a saucepan and heat through, stirring to be sure they are well mixed. Place the oysters on a serving dish and pour the hot sauce over them. Serve immediately.

PEPPER SLAW (UNITED STATES)

This Pennsylvania Dutch variation on cole slaw is made with sweet bell peppers, which give it color and flavor. Its sweet-sour distilled vinegar and sugar dressing and the grindings of black pepper on top make it deliciously unusual.

SERVES SIX

1 pound green cabbage
½ cup cold water
¼ cup distilled white vinegar
¼ cup sugar
Salt to taste
½ cup green bell pepper, minced
½ cup red bell pepper, minced
¼ cup carrot, grated
Freshly ground black pepper to taste

Clean the cabbage and shred it into narrow strips. In a large glass or ceramic bowl, mix the water, distilled vinegar, sugar, and salt. Add the shredded cabbage and the other vegetables to the bowl and mix to be sure all the vegetables are well coated with the dressing. Cover the bowl with plastic wrap and let it stand in the refrigerator for 5 hours. When ready to serve, toss again and top with a few grindings of black pepper.

ARUGULA SALAD

With salads as with many foods, presentation is everything. If this salad is served artistically arranged on a white or glass plate, the colors of the ingredients will stand out. It may not actually taste better, but you'll certainly think it does.

SERVES ONE

½ cup cleaned arugula leaves
½ avocado cut into ½-inch chunks
2 slices smoked turkey, julienned
½ green bell pepper, julienned
½ yellow bell pepper, julienned
½ red bell pepper, julienned
2 scallions, including 3 inches of the green top, minced
2 tablespoons freshly squeezed lemon juice
2 teaspoons freshly ground black pepper

Place the arugula leaves on a plate. On top of the arugula, mound the avocado, turkey, and bell pepper pieces. Scatter the scallion bits on the top. Pour the lemon juice over the salad. It will form the dressing. Sprinkle with black pepper and serve immediately.

COLETTE'S SALAD (FRANCE)

Colette Fumpfschilling was a close friend when I was in graduate school in France. Although her name is German, she is very French in her appreciation of excellent food. Her father was a forest ranger in the Lorraine region of France, and the produce she was served at the family table was uncompromisingly fresh. When she moved to Paris to set up housekeeping on her own, the same high standards prevailed. This is a salad she made only when she could obtain fresh, sweet, firm, ripe tomatoes. When you are able to get your hands on such wonders, or when you harvest your own, try Colette's Salad.

SERVES FOUR

3 large, firm, ripe tomatoes, sliced
1 medium-sized green bell pepper, sliced crosswise into rings
1 medium-sized yellow bell pepper, sliced crosswise into rings
1 medium-sized red Bermuda onion, sliced thin
2 small cloves garlic, minced

Arrange the sliced vegetables on a platter alternating tomato, green and yellow pepper, and onion. Scatter the minced garlic evenly over the entire salad. Serve with a simple vinaigrette made from the freshest olive oil and pepper vinegar (below).

PEPPER VINEGAR (UNITED STATES)

This recipe can be prepared from any type of vinegar. I have chosen white wine vinegar, but red wine or distilled vinegars would work equally well. You might even wish to prepare this dressing and offer it as a gift in a decorative cruet.

YIELD = 1 PINT OR MORE

10 or more black and white peppercorns, cracked
One 1-pint bottle white wine vinegar

Crack the peppercorns and steep them in the vinegar for 3 days. When ready to decant the vinegar into a decorative cruet, strain out the cracked peppercorns and place a few whole ones in the bottom of each cruet for decoration.

PEPPER OIL
(UNITED STATES)

This recipe can be prepared from any type of olive oil. I have chosen a light Italian olive oil because its flavor is enhanced by the peppercorns and chiles. A light French, Greek, Portuguese or other olive oil would work equally well. This oil is excellent on meats to be grilled, on pizzas, and, of course, in salad dressings.

YIELD = 1 PINT

1 pint light Italian olive oil
1 tablespoon dried bird chiles
2 teaspoons cracked black peppercorns
2 teaspoons cracked white peppercorns
2 teaspoons freeze-dried green peppercorns

Place all the ingredients in a jar and steep them for 2 weeks to a month. Use the oil to enhance the flavor of any dish. You may wish to add herbs such as tarragon or wild thyme to the mixture for a more complex taste.

SPICY BARBECUE SAUCE
(UNITED STATES)

No one seems to know the origin of the barbecue; some cite the cave men, others the buccaneers of the Caribbean. Clearly, cooking meats over an open fire is not new. This manner of cooking has, however, found a home in the United States. Here, a piquant red basting sauce makes the difference and marks the barbecue as ours. Whether spicy-sweet or mouth-numbingly hot, served on beef or on pork, the sauce makes the barbecue. Here is one recipe to try with barbecue on the outdoor grill or in your oven.

YIELD = APPROXIMATELY 2½ CUPS

1 cup beer
Salt and freshly ground black pepper to taste

1 cup catsup
3 tablespoons Worcestershire sauce
1 tablespoon paprika
1 teaspoon crushed hot red chile
2 teaspoons minced jalapeño peppers
2 teaspoons Dijon-style mustard
1 tablespoon freshly squeezed lemon juice
1 medium-sized onion, minced

Place all the ingredients in a medium-sized saucepan and bring them to a boil over medium heat. Lower the heat and continue to cook the sauce for 5 minutes, striring occasionally. Brush the sauce over ribs, chicken, or steaks to be charcoal broiled.

CREOLE SEASONING (UNITED STATES)

Chefs in Louisiana always have a bit of Creole Seasoning in the kitchen. Recipes vary with individual chefs, but all use it to enhance everything from hamburgers to salads.

YIELD = ABOUT ¼ CUP

1 tablespoon salt
1 tablespoon dried red chile, pulverized
1 tablespoon chile powder
1 teaspoon garlic powder
1 teaspoon onion powder
1 teaspoon freshly ground black pepper
1 teaspoon freshly ground white pepper

Combine all the ingredients and store in a screw-top glass jar at room temperature. The seasoning mixture can be used for almost anything. As you cook with it, you will find that you may wish to make adjustments for your own taste and that particular dishes will require a bit more of one or another ingredient.

HOT PLUM CHUTNEY
(UNITED STATES)

This is one of the chutneys I concocted when I went chutney crazy. It is quite hot and therefore goes best with grilled meats or dishes that are not too spicy. It tastes of the tartness of the Santa Rosa plums and the bite of the bird peppers.

YIELD = 1 CUP

- 6 medium-sized Santa Rosa plums, pitted
- 3 to 5 preserved bird peppers (to taste)
- ⅓ cup golden raisins
- ½ cup red wine vinegar
- ½ cup sugar

Mix the plums, peppers, and raisins in a food processor or blender until they are reduced to a thick purée. Pour the purée into a medium-sized saucepan and the vinegar and sugar. Cook over low heat, stirring occasionally, for about half an hour, or until the mixture has the consistency of jam. Pour the chutney into a screw-top jar that has been sterilized in boiling water. Allow the mixture to cool before serving.

This chutney and those in the Asian section of the book are quick to make and designed to be eaten immediately. If you wish to make large batches, consult a canning cookbook for the correct procedure to prevent growth of bacteria.

CHILE JELLY
(UNITED STATES)*

When made with jalapeño chiles, this becomes Jalapeño Jelly. It is delicious served with grilled meats, fowl, and, for pepper lovers, on hot buttered biscuits at Sunday brunch.

* From *Time/Life Foods of the World/American Cooking: The Great West*, copyright © 1971 Time-Life Books, Inc.

HOT STUFF

❧❧❧

YIELD = 5 CUPS

- ½ pound fresh hot chiles, washed, stemmed, and seeded
- 2 medium-sized sweet bell peppers, washed, stemmed, seeded, and deribbed
- 1½ cups cider vinegar
- 5 cups sugar
- 1 bottle liquid fruit pectin

Put the chiles and the bell peppers through the medium blade of a food grinder, or chop them very fine with a large, sharp knife. You will need about ½ cup of each kind of pepper after chopping.

Combine the chiles, bell peppers, and vinegar in a 1- to 2-quart enameled or stainless steel saucepan and bring to a boil over high heat. Reduce the heat to low, cover tightly, and simmer for 15 minutes.

Line a colander with a double thickness of dampened cheesecloth and set it over a large enameled pot. The bottom of the colander or sieve should be suspended above the bottom of the pot by at least 2 or 3 inches. Pour the chili mixture into the sieve and allow the liquid to drain through. (Do not squeeze the cloth or the finished jelly will be cloudy.)

When all the liquid has drained through, remove the sieve and discard the chiles and the bell peppers. Add the sugar to the strained liquid and, stirring constantly, bring it to a boil over high heat. Still stirring, boil briskly for 1 minute. Then remove the pan from the heat at once and stir in the pectin. Carefully skim off the surface foam with a large spoon. Ladle the amber-colored jelly into hot sterilized jars or jelly glasses following standard directions for home canning. Serve with grilled meats, roasts, or whenever you're in the mood for something hot and sweet.

OKRA AND TOMATOES (UNITED STATES)

This dish surely has African origins because it uses okra and tomatoes, two vegetables often found in the cuisine of that continent. The New World brought to it pork in the form of bacon for seasoning, corn, and, of course, the capsicum chiles that give it its zing.

SERVES FOUR

1 pound fresh okra; choose small, even-sized pods
3 slices bacon, cut into 2-inch pieces
1 medium-sized onion, chopped coarse
Salt and freshly ground black pepper to taste
3 medium-sized tomatoes, peeled, seeded, and chopped coarse
½ cup fresh corn cut off the cob
2 teaspoons hot red chile, minced

Wash the okra and top and tail it. Pat it dry on paper towels. In a heavy saucepan brown the bacon until it is crisp. Drain the bacon on paper towels and reserve it for garnish. Add the okra and the onion to the bacon fat remaining in the saucepan and cook until the onion is transparent. Stir occasionally to be sure the vegetables do not burn. Then add the salt, pepper, tomatoes, corn, and hot chile and simmer for 10 minutes, or until the corn and tomatoes are cooked. Adjust the seasonings if necessary and serve hot, with crumbled bacon as a garnish.

JALAPEÑO MACARONI AND CHEESE (UNITED STATES)

My mother is known among her friends for her excellent macaroni and cheese. It owes its taste to the bite of the extra sharp cheddar that she uses. One day when we were experimenting in the kitchen we decided to see what would happen if we added a tablespoon of minced preserved jalapeño peppers to the macaroni and cheese. The result is a pepper lover's dream.

SERVES SIX

- 1½ cups elbow macaroni
- 2 tablespoons butter
- 2 tablespoons flour
- 2 tablespoons milk
- 1½ cups grated extra sharp cheddar cheese
- 1 tablespoon minced preserved jalapeño peppers, drained
- Salt and freshly ground black pepper to taste
- ¼ cup dry bread crumbs

Cook the macaroni in boiling salted water and boil for 15 minutes or until it is fork tender. Drain, transfer to a buttered casserole, and set aside. In a small saucepan, melt the 2 tablespoons of butter and combine it with the milk and the flour, stirring constantly. Add most of the cheese and stir until it melts. Add the minced jalapeño peppers and stir to be sure that they are well distributed through the sauce. Season to taste and pour the sauce over the macaroni, tossing so that it completely covers the macaroni. (If the sauce is too thick, you may add a bit more milk.) Cover the top of the casserole with the bread crumbs and the rest of the cheese. Place the casserole in a preheated 350-degree oven and bake for 20 minutes. Serve piping hot.

CHILE CORN
(UNITED STATES)

Corn and chile, two southwestern staples, combine in this vegetable dish. The sweetness of the corn and the slight tang of the mildly hot green chiles are an interesting variation on the blander and more traditional succotash.

SERVES FOUR

- 2 tablespoons peanut oil
- 2 cups fresh corn cut off the cob

$1/4$ cup mildly hot green chiles, chopped
1 clove garlic, minced
Salt and freshly ground black pepper to taste
Pinch of sugar

Heat the peanut oil in a frying pan until hot and add the remaining ingredients. Cover the pan and cook the mixture slowly, over low heat, for 20 minutes. If the mixture seems to be too dry, add a few teaspoons of water. Serve with rice.

STRING BEANS WITH GARLIC AND BELL PEPPER
(UNITED STATES)

This dish is a variation on the classic way the French serve string beans, blanched and then sautéed with garlic. The red bell pepper adds color and taste. This vegetable goes well with roasts, grilled meats, or fried dishes.

SERVES FOUR TO SIX

1 pound string beans, choose young ones of uniform size
3 tablespoons butter
1 clove garlic, minced
1 red bell pepper, cored, seeded and cut into julienne strips
Salt and freshly ground black pepper to taste

Top and tail the string beans and place them into a saucepan of boiling water. Blanch the beans by cooking them at a full boil for 3 to 5 minutes or until they are bright green and crisp. Remove the beans and drain them.

Meanwhile, heat the butter in a frying pan, add the minced garlic, the bell pepper and the drained string beans. Toss them well for 2 minutes until they are coated with the butter. Season with salt and freshly ground black pepper and serve.

JALAPEÑO CORN STICKS (UNITED STATES)

In my parents' house on Martha's Vineyard, there's a beautiful old wood-burning cast-iron stove that lends itself to stewing and baking. It is the centerpiece of the kitchen and makes it a true country kitchen. As a result, I've begun to collect antique cooking utensils. A cast-iron corn stick pan will go a long way toward recreating the taste of this recipe even if you do not have a cast-iron stove. A quirk of my corn stick pan is that it makes only seven sticks, so this recipe is for seven sticks only. It can, of course be increased.

MAKES SEVEN CORN STICKS

¾ cup yellow cornmeal
¾ cup flour
2 tablespoons sugar
3 teaspoons baking powder
½ teaspoon salt
¾ cup milk
1 egg
3 tablespoons peanut oil
2 teaspoons or more minced preserved jalapeño chile

Place the cornmeal, flour, sugar, baking powder, and salt in a large bowl. Add the milk, egg, and peanut oil and beat for about 1 minute, or until the mixture is smooth. Add the minced jalapeño chile and stir to be sure the pieces are well distributed. Pour into a greased, seasoned cast-iron corn stick mold and bake in a 425-degree oven for 20 minutes. Serve hot, with butter.

GAMBAS AL AJILLO (SPAIN)

SERVES SIX

6 tablespoons olive oil
4 cloves garlic, sliced

2 dried red chile peppers with the seeds removed, cut in two pieces
¾ pound small or medium shrimp, shelled
2 tablespoons beef broth
2 tablespoons freshly squeezed lemon juice
Salt and freshly ground black pepper to taste
2 tablespoons minced parsley

Heat the oil, garlic, and chile peppers in a large, shallow earthenware casserole. When the garlic begins to turn golden, add the shrimp and cook over high heat for about 3 minutes, stirring constantly. Add the broth and lemon juice and sprinkle with salt, pepper, and parsley. Serve immediately.

GIGOT D'AGNEAU AU POIVRE VERT (UNITED STATES)

Although it has a French-sounding name, this leg of lamb dish is a favorite variation of mine on steak au poivre vert. The leg of lamb is coated with a mixture of white, black, and green pepper and seared, then done to a pink turn. It is excellent when served with a freshly made chutney (see index) or even with Jalapeño (see Chile Jelly, page 223).

SERVES SIX TO EIGHT

¼ cup green peppercorns and 1 tablespoon of the preserving liquid
1 tablespoon black peppercorns, cracked
1 tablespoon white peppercorns, cracked
1½ tablespoons salt
One 4-pound leg of lamb
1 clove garlic, slivered

In a bowl, pulverize the green peppercorns with the freshly cracked black and white peppercorns and the salt. Mix into a paste. Make ten small incisions in the leg of lamb. Insert the garlic slivers in the incisions, then cover the lamb with the pepper paste and allow it to stand for half an hour.

Meanwhile, preheat the oven to 450 degrees. Place the lamb on a roasting rack in a roasting pan. Set the pan in the heated oven and sear the lamb for 10 minutes. Then reduce the heat to 350 degrees and continue to cook the lamb. Allow 10 minutes per pound for rare meat, 15 minutes per pound for medium, and 20 minutes per pound for well-done. These times include the searing. Serve the leg of lamb with fresh green beans, new potatoes, and a homemade chutney.

PASTA WITH VODKA (ITALY)*

This dish, which places the accent on peppers, is a new favorite in Rome. Using either Petrovska (chile-flavored vodka) or Pepper Vodka (page 242) and crushed dried red peppers, the dish is a spicy addition to the Italian pasta tradition.

SERVES SIX

1¼ pounds penne
7 tablespoons unsalted butter
1 teaspoon hot red pepper flakes
1 cup Pepper Vodka
1 scant cup fresh, ripe, peeled, seeded tomatoes, or drained canned Italian plum tomatoes, puréed
1 scant cup heavy cream
1 teaspoon coarse salt
1 cup freshly grated parmesan cheese

Bring six quarts of salted water to a boil in a pasta pot. When the water is boiling, add the penne and cook until al dente. While the pasta is cooking, melt the butter in a large frying pan, add the pepper flakes and the vodka, and simmer for 2 minutes. Add the tomatoes and cream and simmer for an additional 5 minutes.

* From *Italian Cooking in the Grand Tradition* by Jo Bettoja and Anna Maria Cornetto. Copyright © 1982 by Jo Bettoja and Anna Maria Cornetto. Reprinted by permission of Doubleday & Co., Inc.

Then add the salt. When the pasta is ready, drain well and add it to the frying pan. Simmering over low heat, add the parmesan and mix thoroughly. Pour into a warmed bowl and serve.

SALSA BOLOGNESE WITH HOT ITALIAN SAUSAGE
(ITALY)

This is a variation of the traditional Italian meat sauce made with ground beef and hot Italian sausage.

SERVES FOUR

- 1 tablespoon olive oil
- 1 tablespoon Pepper Oil (page 221)
- 1 large onion, chopped
- 1 teaspoon thyme
- 1 teaspoon oregano
- 1 teaspoon basil
- ½ pound hot Italian sausage
- 1 pound ground chuck
- 1 (6-ounce) can tomato paste
- 1½ cups water

Heat the oils in a heavy frying pan. Add the onion and cook it until soft. Add half the spices (½ teaspoon of each) and stir well. Remove the sausage meat from the casings and add it to the frying pan, breaking it up with a fork. Brown the sausage. Add the ground chuck, breaking it up with a fork. Stir occasionally to be sure the meat is evenly browned. Add the other half of the spices and mix well. Then add the tomato paste and the water and stir well. Lower the heat and allow the sauce to simmer for 20 minutes. (You may need to add a bit more water if the sauce becomes too thick.) Check the seasoning and serve hot, over the pasta of your choice.

SALSA PUTTANESCA
(ITALY)

Salsa Puttanesca is a spicy southern Italian sauce. Roughly translated, the term means whore's sauce. As the story goes, the sauce was so quick to prepare that it could be whipped up in a few minutes between "jobs." It can be served over many varieties of pasta.

SERVES FOUR

- ½ cup olive oil
- 1 clove garlic, minced
- 2 large onions, chopped
- 2 large tomatoes, peeled, seeded, and chopped coarse
- ½ cup red bell pepper, chopped
- ½ cup green bell pepper, chopped
- 2 teaspoons crushed red hot chile
- ¾ cup sliced, pitted Italian-style black olives
- 1 small can anchovy fillets, chopped

Heat the oil in a heavy frying pan and add the garlic, the onion, tomatoes, bell peppers, and the crushed chile. Sauté the mixture for about 5 minutes. Add the sliced olives and the anchovies and cook just long enough for all the ingredients to be heated through. Serve hot, over pasta.

To spice up the dish a bit more, add more crushed hot chile.

STEAK AU POIVRE
(FRANCE)

This is a classic French pepper dish that can be prepared with either green peppercorns or a mixture of green peppercorns and cracked black and white peppercorns. When made with the former, it is a bit more piquant.

SERVES FOUR

- 4 tournedos (fillet steaks about ¾ inch thick wrapped in a strip of fat)

3 tablespoons cracked black and white peppercorns (or use 2 tablespoons mashed green peppercorns and 1 tablespoon cracked black and white peppercorns)
5 tablespoons butter
2 tablespoons peanut oil
1½ tablespoons shallots, minced
½ cup beef bouillon
⅓ cup brandy, cognac, or armagnac
Salt to taste

Dry the steaks, then crush the peppercorns coarsely in a pepper mill or in a coffee grinder that you use only for this purpose. Press the pepper into both sides of the meat and allow the steaks to stand, covered, to absorb the flavor of the pepper.

In a heavy frying pan heat 2 tablespoons of the butter and the peanut oil and sauté the steaks until they are done to taste. Remove the steaks to a hot platter and keep hem warm while preparing the sauce.

Pour out the fat remaining in the frying pan and add one tablespoon of butter and the minced shallots. Cook slowly for 1 minute. Add the bouillon and scrape up the meat bits from the bottom of the pan. Add the brandy and boil vigorously to reduce the alcohol. Remove the frying pan from the heat and stir in the remaining butter a half tablespoon at a time. Verify the seasonings and add salt to taste. Pour the sauce over the steaks and serve.

STEAK PEDRO'S
(SPAIN)

In Torremolinos on Spain's Costa del Sol there was, a few years back, a charming restaurant named Pedro's. There, on a balmy Mediterranean night, it was possible to sit at eleven in the evening and dine lavishly while overlooking the activity on Torremolinos' "main drag." One of the specialties of the house was a variation of steak au poivre known as Steak Pedro's.

You can create Steak Pedro's by diminishing the amount of pepper used in the Steak au Poivre recipe (page 232) to 2 tablespoons and adding two dashes of Tabasco sauce to the final mixture. Whisk it briefly and pour over the tournedos prepared as for Steak au Poivre.

STUCK-IN-A-SNOWDRIFT CHILE (MEXICO)

Even the finest chefs and the most dedicated becs fins *occasionally find themselves without enough time even to boil an egg—and, in any case, there are no fresh eggs within a five-mile radius. This is the time to get out your recipe for Stuck-in-a-Snowdrift Chile. Ground beef may be anathema to chile connoisseurs, but it's just right for this quick dish, which is perfect for impromptu occasions because most of the ingredients are staples of the larder. Pepper Wine, the item that provides most of the zing (see page 130), is easy to prepare and just might become a staple of your larder. The dish will be greeted with enthusiasm by guests when presented in pottery bowls with the suggested garnishes.*

SERVES SIX

- 2 tablespoons peanut oil
- 1½ pounds ground beef chuck
- 1 medium-sized onion, chopped
- 1 (6-ounce) can tomato paste
- 1 (8-ounce) can stewed tomatoes, chopped
- 1 (1-pound) can kidney beans
- 2 tablespoons chile powder
- 1 teaspoon or more Pepper Wine (page 130)
- ⅓ cup water

Heat the oil in a saucepan and brown the meat. Add the onion and cook until it is transparent. Add the other ingredients and stir to mix well. Cover and cook over low heat for about 10 minutes or until the meat is tender. Stir the chile occasionally to be sure it does not stick. Serve hot, with Jalapeño Cornsticks (see page 000). You may wish to garnish the top of the chile with a dollop of sour cream, grated cheddar cheese, and a sprig of fresh coriander. Serve with Mexican beer such as Carta Blanca or Dos Equis. You might even find yourself praying for a snowdrift to get stuck in.

BUFFALO CHICKEN WINGS (UNITED STATES)

When I first heard of this dish, I pictured a Pegasus-like buffalo winging its way through the air. In fact, these are spicy chicken wings as cooked in Buffalo, New York. They can be served as an appetizer or a main dish.

SERVES SIX AS AN APPETIZER

- 2½ pounds chicken wings
- 2 cups peanut oil for frying (You may use vegetable oil, vegetable shortening, or even lard supplemented with bacon drippings.)
- ¼ cup butter
- 2 tablespoons Tabasco sauce

Separate the chicken wings at the joints and reserve the tips. (You can use them later to make chicken stock.) Wash the pieces and pat them dry on paper towels. Heat the oil or shortening to 375 to 400 degrees in a heavy cast-iron fryer. Fry the chicken for 12 minutes until cooked through and crisp. Drain the chicken pieces on paper towels. (Torn brown paper bags are also excellent for draining the chicken.) Melt the butter in a small saucepan and mix in the Tabasco sauce. Toss the chicken wings in the sauce until they are well coated. Use any remaining sauce as a dipping sauce for the chicken. Serve the chicken hot as an appetizer.

MARYLAND CRAB CAKES (UNITED STATES)

My friend Mad Martha the weaver is partial to crab cakes from her native Maryland. These are just spicy enough to suit her fancy.

🌶🌶🌶 SERVES FOUR TO SIX

2 pounds fresh crabmeat
¼ cup peanut oil
2 medium-sized onions, minced
¼ cup celery, minced
1 teaspoon dry mustard
2 teaspoons crushed hot red chile
½ teaspoon thyme
4 tablespoons mayonnaise
2 eggs, beaten
1 teaspoon parsley, minced
Salt and freshly ground black pepper to taste
1 cup dry bread crumbs

If using whole crabs, remove the meat from the shells and place it in a small bowl. Heat 1 tablespoon of the peanut oil in a frying pan and cook the onions and celery until they are soft. In a large bowl, combine the crab, the onions and celery, and all the remaining ingredients except half the bread crumbs. Mix well to be sure all ingredients are evenly distributed and shape the mixture into cakes. Roll the cakes in the remaining bread crumbs. Heat the remaining oil in a frying pan and fry the cakes over moderate heat, turning once, until they are browned on both sides. The total cooking time is about 10 minutes. Serve with a bottle of Tabasco or Louisiana Red Hot Sauce on the side for confirmed lovers of hot stuff.

GRILLED SHRIMP (UNITED STATES)

These shrimp can be done in a broiler or on a charcoal grill. The dish is simple and can serve as the main course of any summer barbecue. One reminder: if grilling over charcoal, make sure the coals are thoroughly heated and covered with a gray ash before you begin to grill the shrimp.

SERVES FOUR

16 jumbo shrimp
½ cup olive oil
½ cup peanut oil
2 teaspoons minced hot green chile
1 teaspoon hot dried red chile, crumbled
½ cup freshly squeezed lemon juice
1 teaspoon freeze-dried green peppercorns, crushed
Salt and freshly ground black pepper to taste
Lemon wedges for garnish

Clean the shrimp and pat them dry on paper towels. Combine all the other ingredients with the exception of the garnish in a non-reactive bowl. Mix them well. Place the cleaned shrimp in the marinade, cover with plastic wrap, and marinate them in the refrigerator overnight. Heat the broiler or the charcoal to cooking temperature. Meanwhile, place the shrimp on metal skewers and arrange them on the broiler or grill rack. Cook the shrimp for 5 minutes on each side, basting with the marinade. When the shrimp are ready, serve on a platter garnished with lemon wedges.

DEVILED CRABMEAT (UNITED STATES)

When it's crab season in Maryland, my friend Martha Jones's sisters have been known to ride up from that state bearing a basket full of crabs for the delight of Martha and her guests. Here's one way she likes to serve them.

SERVES SIX

2 cups flaked raw crabmeat (If you use fresh crabs, reserve the shells for serving.)
2 hard-boiled eggs, chopped
2 tablespoons minced parsley
4 scallions, including 3 inches of the green part, minced
1 tablespoon Dijon-style mustard
½ teaspoon thyme
1 small hot red chile, minced
⅓ cup butter
⅓ cup flour
1 cup milk
1 egg, beaten
½ cup dry bread crumbs mixed with 2 tablespoons melted butter

Mix the crabmeat with the hard-boiled eggs, parsley, scallions, mustard, Tabasco, thyme, and chile. Melt the butter and stir in the flour; slowly add the milk. Cook the mixture over low heat, stirring constantly, until the sauce thickens. Add the sauce to the beaten egg. Mix in the crabmeat and stuff the mixture into porcelain crab shells. (If you have used fresh crabs for the crabmeat, you can reserve the shells and stuff them.) Sprinkle the top of the deviled crab mixture with the bread crumbs and bake in a 350-degree oven for half an hour. Serve hot.

SWORDFISH STEAKS WITH TARRAGON AND PEPPER (UNITED STATES)

This dish is a variation on the classic French steak au poivre. In it the swordfish steaks are marinated briefly in a lemon juice and vinegar mixture and then quick cooked. This is a good summer dish and goes well with String Beans with Garlic and Bell Pepper.

SERVES TWO

1 tablespoon white wine tarragon vinegar
1 tablespoon freshly squeezed lemon juice
2 teaspoons cracked black and white peppercorns
2 tablespoons light Italian olive oil
5 sprigs fresh tarragon
2 swordfish steaks
Salt to taste

Mix the vinegar, lemon juice, cracked peppercorns and olive oil in a small bowl. Snip the tarragon sprigs into small pieces and add them to the marinade. Place the swordfish steaks in the marinade and let them sit for five minutes. Remove the steaks and place them in a frying pan. Cook them 3 to 5 minutes on each side over medium heat, turning carefully so that they do not break. Remove from the frying pan and serve hot with white rice and String Beans with Garlic and Bell Pepper (page 227).

HOT PORK CHOPS (UNITED STATES)

In Louisiana, Cajun and Creole cooks love their pepper and their pork. Cooks season their meats with a mix of three different types of pepper, each of which brings its own savor to the dish. The saying goes that the black pepper adds the aroma, the red pepper the burn, and the white pepper the bite. This recipe for pork chops enhances the sweetness of the pork meat with all three peppers.

SERVES FOUR

1 tablespoon freshly ground black pepper
1 tablespoon freshly ground white pepper
1 tablespoon dried hot red chile, pulverized in a spice grinder
Four 1-inch-thick loin pork chops

Combine the peppers and the chile in a mortar and pound them to mix well. Rub both sides of each chop with a bit of the pepper mixture, coating them evenly. Cook the pork chops as you normally would, taking care that they do not dry out. Serve the pork with a green salad, rice, and a bottle of Tabasco sauce or Louisiana Red Hot Sauce for those who truly love pepper.

NAVAJO GREEN CHILE (UNITED STATES)*

I debated long and hard whether to include any recipes for chile in Hot Stuff. *After all, no one but its creator is ever satisfied with a chile recipe. I decided to include this recipe from Jane Butel's* Chile Madness *both as an acknowledgment of the wonders of chile and because it's the hottest chile recipe I've ever found. NOVICES BEWARE . . . if you're not a firm lover of hot stuff go easy on the chiles in this one.*

SERVES SIX

- 3 pounds boneless pork shoulder, fat and bone removed, cut into ½-inch cubes (reserve fat)
- ⅓ cup flour in a heavy paper bag
- 3 medium onions, chopped coarse
- 4 medium cloves garlic, chopped fine
- 2 (16-ounce) cans whole green chiles, drained, seeded, and cut into 2-inch slices
- 2 (16-ounce) cans whole tomatoes
- 1 (6-ounce) can tomato paste
- 3 cups water
- 2½ teaspoons salt
- ½ teaspoon dried oregano (preferably Mexican)

Melt the pork fat in a heavy skillet over medium-high heat. Coat the pork cubes with flour by shaking them in a paper bag with the flour. Add the cubes to the skillet a few at a time, stirring

* From *Chile Madness* copyright © 1980 by Jane Butel. Workman Publishing Company, New York. Reprinted with permission.

to brown evenly. Remove the cubes to a 5-quart dutch oven or other heavy pot. Continue browning the pork cubes in the skillet until all are browned.

Add the onions and garlic to the skillet. Cook, stirring occasionally, until the onions are translucent. Add to the pot with the pork.

Stir the remaining ingredients into the pork and onion mixture. Bring to a boil, then lower the heat and simmer, uncovered, for half an hour. Taste, adjust seasonings, and cook for half an hour longer.

STUFFED PEPPERS (ARMENIA)

This recipe was given to me by Violet Soghomonian, who says it is a traditional way of cooking peppers in her country. The difference in the stuffing is in the bulgur and in the sumac that is used as a seasoning.

SERVES EIGHT

- 8 medium-sized red bell peppers
- 1 pound ground lamb
- 1 cup canned tomatoes, drained, the juice reserved
- ¼ cup tomato paste
- 2 tablespoons minced red bell pepper
- 2 teaspoons salt
- 1 teaspoon cayenne pepper
- 2 tablespoons freshly squeezed lemon juice
- 1 teaspoon cumin
- 1 teaspoon basil
- 1 to 1⅓ cups bulgur (you may substitute rice)
- 3 teaspoons sumac (you may substitute 3 teaspoons freshly squeezed lemon juice) *
- 2 cups water

* Sumac can be found at some stores that sell Middle Eastern ingredients listed at the end of the book.

Core and seed the bell peppers and remove the membranes, but leave the peppers whole. Wash them thoroughly inside and out. Mix together the lamb, canned tomatoes, tomato paste, minced bell pepper, salt, cayenne, lemon juice, cumin, basil, and bulgar. Stuff the peppers with this mixture and arrange them side by side in a flame-proof casserole. Place a heavy plate upside down on top of the peppers to weight them. Prepare a cooking liquid of the sumac, water, and ½ cup of the reserved liquid from the canned tomatoes. It should cover all but ¼ inch of the peppers. (You may add more water if necessary.) Boil the cooking liquid in a small saucepan and then pour it over the peppers. Bring the peppers to a boil over medium heat, then lower the heat and allow them to simmer for 30 minutes, or until the bulgar is cooked. Serve the peppers topped with a dollop of yogurt and a sprinkling of sumac for an authentic Middle Eastern taste.

PEPPER VODKA
(RUSSIA)

This is a spicy vodka made with cracked black peppercorns. It is wonderful to drink chilled until it almost syrups, or in the recipe for Pasta with Vodka (page 230), or in a Bloody Mary (page 243). It is simple to make and will keep as long as the vodka lasts.

YIELD = 1 QUART

1 tablespoon freshly cracked peppercorns
1 quart unflavored vodka

Place the peppercorns in the vodka and allow them to remain there overnight. They will steep and give their flavor to the vodka. You may wish to leave them longer, depending on how peppery you want your vodka. When ready, strain out the peppercorns and decant the vodka into a fancy bottle. You may wish to add a few uncracked peppercorns to the vodka for decoration.

BLOODY MARY
(UNITED STATES)

This is the quintessential brunch tipple in most of the United States. Named for an English queen, it is a mixture of tomato juice, celery salt, Tabasco sauce, and other ingredients. Each bartender prepares the drink according to a well-guarded secret recipe. Here's mine.

SERVES ONE

½ cup tomato juice
1 jigger of vodka, or more to taste and capacity for alcohol
Juice of half a lemon
¼ teaspoon celery salt
1 teaspoon Worcestershire sauce
1 teaspoon or more Tabasco sauce
Freshly ground black pepper to taste
1 scallion, including 3 inches of the green top, for garnish

In a chilled, stemmed glass, mix all the ingredients well. Add two ice cubes and serve with the scallion as garnish.

BLUFFS BLOODY
(UNITED STATES)

Since I was nine years old, my family has spent a portion of every summer in Oak Bluffs on Martha's Vineyard, Massachusetts. Because our house is located just across the street from the tennis court, and I am a rabid non-tennis-player, we spend our early morning on the back porch enjoying our breakfast. Friends drop by when they see us out, and we greet one and all with a Bluffs Bloody, our house version of the Bloody Mary. Without the vodka, the drink becomes a Virgin Bluffs.

ꕥꕥꕥꕥ **SERVES ONE**

1 cup V-8 juice
1 tablespoon freshly squeezed lemon juice
2 tablespoons juice from any jar of hot peppers (Italian pepperoncini are preferred)
1 tablespoon Tabasco sauce
2 tablespoons Worcestershire sauce
Dash of celery salt
Vodka to taste
1 scallion, 1 pepperoncini pepper, and 1 strip of fresh zucchini for garnish

Mix all the ingredients except the garnishes in a glass and stir well. Add two ice cubes and serve with the garnish in a large, chilled, stemmed wine glass.

HOT MARTINI (UNITED STATES)

One day, while we were sitting on the back porch in Oak Bluffs sipping Bluffs Bloodies, the conversation turned to pepper (Guess why?) and an old friend of the family said that he came from one of the Hot States, an area that he defined as including Mississippi, Alabama, Arkansas, Texas, and, naturally, Louisiana. He remembered that when he moved to the northern part of the United States he had had to accustom himself to blander food. My mother remembered that his father-in-law had asked her if she ate pepper when she was planning to get married, and added, "A woman who doesn't eat pepper just isn't worth anything." If only to be "worth" something, try to have at least one Hot Martini a week. A Hot Martini is incredibly easy to make. Prepare a vodka martini according to your usual recipe, but use Pepper Vodka (page 242) instead of your usual tipple. When ready to serve, add a small hot chile as garnish. Use the milder Italian cherry peppers that are readily available, or the pepperoncini, unless your friends are true chile mavens. Serve your Hot

Martinis in chilled, stemmed glasses. Some people add a jalapeño strip and call the drink a Martinez.

FRAISES AU POIVRE (FRANCE)

Pepper and strawberries may seem unusual at best, but a few grindings of black pepper bring out the earthy sweetness of the strawberries. The recipe is excellent with the small, delicate strawberries known as fraises des bois (wild strawberries).

SERVES FOUR TO SIX

1 pint strawberries, hulled and sliced if they are large
1½ tablespoons brown sugar
2 tablespons mandarin liqueur
2 tablespoons armagnac
2 teaspoons freshly squeezed lemon juice
Freshly ground black pepper to taste

Place the strawberries in a glass or earthenware bowl and add the sugar, liqueurs, and lemon juice. Mix the ingredients by turning the fruit gently with a spoon. Cover the bowl with plastic wrap and chill it in the refrigerator for 1 hour. When ready to serve, transfer berries and liquid to individual champagne glasses and serve topped with a good grinding of black pepper.

STRAWBERRIES IN PEPPER CREAM (THE NETHERLANDS)

This is an adaptation of a dessert I first tasted at the Five Flies restaurant in Amsterdam. The time was just after I knew I would be writing Hot Stuff, *and I was thrilled to find this intriguing dish on the menu. I ordered it and was surprised to find that the pepper cream was whipped cream shot through with coarsely ground black pepper. The taste was delightful, and the pepper did not intrude at all on the delicate woody taste of the strawberries. It was the first recipe I collected for this book.*

SERVES FOUR TO SIX

1 pint fresh strawberries, hulled
1 tablespoon sugar
½ pint heavy cream
3 tablespoons mandarin liqueur
2 teaspoons black pepper, ground coarse
Preserved tangerine or orange peel for garnish

Place the strawberries in a glass or ceramic bowl, add the sugar, and set aside. In another bowl, beat the cream until stiff. Gradually add the mandarin liqueur and the black pepper to the beaten cream. To serve, place a spoonful of whipped cream in the bottom of a stemmed wine glass, add strawberries, and top with the remaining whipped cream. Garnish with a curlicue of preserved tangerine or orange peel. Serve immediately.

SPICY CHEVRE AU POIVRE (GENERAL)

Goat cheese is the quintessential nouvelle cuisine fromage. Here, it is preserved in a spiced olive oil until used. When ready to serve, it can be crumbled in a salad, served with toasted French bread, or simply nibbled with a glass of red wine.

SERVES EIGHT TO TEN

1 log of goat cheese (chevre) cut into 1-inch slices
½ teaspoon crushed red chiles
5 black and 5 white peppercorns
2 teaspoons green peppercorns, drained
1 bay leaf
4 whole allspice

2 whole cloves
Extra virgin olive oil to cover

Place the slices of goat cheese in a sterilized wide-mouth pint canning jar. Add the spices and cover the cheese with the olive oil. The olive oil must be at least ¾ of an inch above the cheese. Seal the jar and store it in a cool, dry place. It will keep for at least a month. As you use the pieces of cheese, be sure that the remaining cheese is covered with the olive oil to prevent spoilage.

◆§ Menus

COOKING IS a communal activity in many parts of the world where hot stuff is found. In Senegal or in India, for example, the whole family sits down to partake not only of food but of the particular warmth that comes from being with those they love and breaking bread with friends and family. For this reason, the food in *Hot Stuff* lends itself particularly to entertaining. Take out that serape from Mexico that's been hiding in the closet and use it as a tablecloth for a Mexican dinner. If you're too shy to wear a sari to your Indian supper, use it as a table covering or get small printed cotton scarves and use them instead of napkins. Polish your brass utensils and use them on a dark-colored tablecloth for your Moroccan meal. Spread a brightly colored piece of dashiki fabric on the floor and enjoy your Thiebou Dienne in the true Senegalese manner. Be adventurous; suggest eating with your hands. (Some say that you taste the food more intensely without the interference of the taste of the silverware.) In short, enjoy the recipes and share them with those you care about.

Because some of the foods in *Hot Stuff* will be unfamiliar to many readers, I have included a selection of menus that will enable you to create complete "pepper meals." These meals not only highlight the hot food of a particular region, they also offer an introduction to regional cooking. Most of the recipes for these menus are included in *Hot Stuff*. The remaining, usually simple, dishes can be found in other cookbooks. In many cases the countries where hot cooking is found do not have a special talent for desserts; therefore, the desserts are in most cases fresh fruits or fresh fruit salads. If you wish to choose another, feel free. These menus are simply guidelines and should be thought of as departure points. Recipes that are included in *Hot Stuff* are marked with an asterisk (*).

AFRICA

A SIMPLE SUPPER

Peanut Soup*
Biokosso*
Gombos à la Senegalaise*
Watermelon Slices

A NORTH AFRICAN DINNER

Crudités à la Tunisienne*
Couscous de Poulet*
Moroccan Pepper Salad*
Fresh Melon Slices with Orange Water

A GALA LUNCHEON

Akkra*
Hot Sauce for Akkra*
Boulettes de Poisson*
Thiebou Dienne*
Pickles pour Thiebou Dienne sous Verre*
Fresh Mangoes

A LIGHT MEAL

Avocat Epicé
Poulet Yassa*
White Rice
Green Salad
Fresh Fruit

THE PORTUGUESE INFLUENCE

Oeufs Diablo*
Camarao Grelhado Piripiri*
Green Salad
Quindins*

FROM THE SLAVE COAST

Yam Fritters*
Oysters Azi Dessi*
Spicy Rice*
Melon Slices

A COCKTAIL PARTY

Crudités à la Tunisienne*
Oeufs Diablo*
Akkra*
Hot Sauce for Akkra*
Spicy Oysters*
Spicy Tomato Sauce*
Boulettes de Poisson*
Banana Snacks*

A TRADITIONAL IVOIRIAN MEAL

Soupe d'Avocat*
Foufou*
Sauce Claire*
Summer Fruit Salad

EAST AFRICAN CURRY DINNER

Vindaloo Curry*
Cucumber Sambal*
Carrot Sambal*
Apricot-Plum Chutney*
Kenya Corn*
Fresh Fruit

AN ETHIOPIAN DINNER

Doro Wat*
Sik Sik Wat*
Mixed Salad
Berberé*
Injera (These are thin buckwheat crepes on which Ethiopian food is traditionally served. Many people who do not have the time to prepare the crepes in the traditional way use Aunt Jemima buckwheat pancake mix to make a large thin crepe that is an approximation of the injera.)

LATIN AMERICA

A BRAZILIAN SATURDAY LUNCH

Feijoada*
Farofa*
Molho de Pimenta e Limão*
White Rice
Fruit Salad

A GUADELOUPEAN LUNCHEON CHEZ CLARA

Calalou aux Crabes*
Chiquetaille de Morue*
Piment-Confit*
Colombo de Mouton*
Fresh Tomato Salad
Tropical Fruit Sorbets

A BAHIAN DINNER

Acarajé*
Sauce for Acarajé
Moqueca de Peixe*
Salada de Quiabo*
White Rice
Farofa Amarela*
Black Beans
Quindins*

A MEXICAN MEAL

Guacamole*
Tortilla Chips*
Nachos*
Huachinango Yucateco*
Arroz Verde*
Tequila with Sangrita*

A HAITIAN DINNER

Plantain Chips
Coconut Crisps*
Griots de Porc*
White Rice
Sauce Ti-Malice*
Mixed Green Salad
Melon Slices or Tropical Fruit Sorbets

A CARIBBEAN LUNCHEON

Spicy Pumpkin Soup*
Peppery Hens*
Baked Tomatoes*
Mixed Green Salad
Bananas Flambé

A LATIN AMERICAN COCKTAIL PARTY

Acarajé*
Sauce for Acarajé*
Guacamole*
Tortilla Chips*
Nachos*
Curry Crisps*
Cerbiche*
Green Mango Souskai*
Bacalaitos*
Salsa por Bacalaitos*

A GALA JAMAICAN LUNCHEON

Red Pea Soup
Curried Goat*
White Rice
Tomato and Onion Salad
Fresh Fruit Salad

A QUICK SUPPER

Stuck-in-a-Snowdrift Chile* garnished with sour cream and grated sharp cheddar cheese

A SUNDAY BREAKFAST FOR TWO

Huevos Rancheros*
Tequila with Sangrita*

ASIA

A GALA INDIAN DINNER

Mint Coriander Dip*
Poppadoms
Vindaloo Curry*

Raita*
Katchumber Salad*
White Rice
Nectarine-Mint Chutney*
Apricot-Plum Chutney*
Raisins
Coconut Flakes
Peanuts

A SINGAPORE BRUNCH

Jook with assorted accompaniments*
Green Tea

A SINGAPORE FOOD STALL COCKTAIL PARTY

Beef, Lamb, and Chicken Saté*
Saté Sauces*
Saté Babi*
Sauce for Saté Babi*
Spicy Plantain Chips*
Vinegared Green Chiles*
Cucumber Salad*
Chile Crab*

AN INDIAN LUNCHEON

Mint Coriander Dip*
Poppadoms
Lamb Tikka*
White Rice
Onion Relish*
Bhindi Bhaji*
Fresh Mangoes

A CHINESE DINNER

Spicy Bean Curd served as an appetizer*
Hunan Lamb*

Spicy Sesame Chicken*
White Rice
Orange Sections

A MACAO LUNCHEON

Cozido de Peixe*
White Rice
Mixed Salad
Melon Salad

A VEGETARIAN FEAST

Mint Coriander Dip*
Poppadoms
Lentil Curry*
Vegetarian Stuffed Peppers*
Mixed Salad
Fresh Fruit

A SINGAPORE SUPPER

Spicy Plantain Chips*
Beef Saté*
Saté Sauce*
Cucumber Salad*
Onion Sambal*
Sambal Udang*
Spiced Summer Fruit Salad*

☙ THE WESTERN TRADITION

AN ITALIAN SUPPER

Antipasto with Marinated Cannelli Beans*
Pasta with two sauces—Salsa Puttanesca* and Salsa Bolognesa with Hot Italian Sausage*
Fruit Salad

AN OAK BLUFFS COCKTAIL PARTY

Spicy Ham Spread*
Mules*
Hot Cashews*
Chile Almonds*
Pepper Dip with Crudités*
Bluffs Bloodies*
Bloody Marys*
Hot Martinis*

A LIGHT SUMMER LUNCHEON

Buffalo Chicken Wings*
Colette's Salad*

A QUICK SNACK

Spicy Chevre au Poivre*
Oven-Warmed French Bread

A FORMAL DINNER

Minted Yogurt Soup*
Gigot d'Agneau au Poivre Vert*
String Beans with Garlic and Bell Pepper*
Carrots
White Rice
Hot Plum Chutney*
Green Salad
Fraises au Poivre*

A SOUTHERN STYLE DINNER

Hot Pork Chops*
Okra and Tomatoes*
White Rice
Jalapeño Cornsticks*

A QUICK LUNCH

Arugula Salad*
Spicy Chevre au Poivre*
Oven-Warmed French Bread

A LATE NIGHT SUPPER AT PEDRO'S

Gambas al Ajillo* served as an appetizer
Steak Pedro's*
White Rice
Mixed Green Salad

Mail Order Sources

THE WORLD OF HOT STUFF is growing closer every day. Where once the mere mention of an item like yellow bell peppers in a recipe was enough to send the cook searching for sources, these ingredients are now available to many supermarkets. Jalapeño peppers packed in brine are sold almost everywhere, as are red bell peppers, various hot sauces, and chile preparations. But for those who must search out special items like Brazilian malagueta peppers and for those who live a bit off the beaten path, the following list gives sources for some of the peppers and other ingredients called for in *Hot Stuff*. Suppliers are listed by geographical area for the reader's convenience. If the supplier specializes in a particular item, this information is included in parentheses. Suppliers who provide mail order service have an asterisk beside their names. When ordering by mail, it is recommended that the reader write for a catalog and price list before placing an order.

In addition, many large department stores throughout the country have gourmet departments that offer a variety of the special ingredients called for in *Hot Stuff*. Chile powders, spices, preserved hot peppers, and the like are sometimes no farther away than your local Macy's, Bloomingdale's, or Marshall Field's.

There are also a growing number of mail order gourmet supply houses, such as Williams Sonoma, that supply items such as chile *ristras* and the like.

◆ NORTHEAST

Annapurna (Indian ingredients) *
127 East 28 Street
New York, N.Y. 10016

Aphrodisia Products, Inc.*
282 Bleecker Street
New York, N.Y. 10014

Cambridge Coffee, Tea and Spice House
1765 Massachusetts Avenue
Cambridge, Mass. 02138

Casa Moneo (Latin American ingredients) *
210 West 14 Street
New York, N.Y. 10011

Casa Pena
1636 17th Street, N.W.
Washington, D.C. 20009

K. Kalustyan (Indian and Indo-Caribbean ingredients)
123 Lexington Avenue
New York, N.Y. 10016

Little Indian Store (Indian ingredients) *
128 East 29 Street
New York, N.Y. 10016

Paprikas Weiss
1546 Second Avenue
New York, N.Y. 10028

Pecos River Spice Company (Texas-style chile products)
P.O. Box 680
New York, N.Y. 10021

H. Roth & Son
1577 First Avenue
New York, N.Y. 10028

Sahadi Importing Company (Middle Eastern and North African ingredients)
187 Atlantic Avenue
Brooklyn, N.Y. 11201

Southeast Asian Trading Company
68-A Mott Street
New York, N.Y. 10013

Spice and Sweet Mahal (Indian ingredients)
135 Lexington Avenue
New York, N.Y. 10016

The Spice Corner
904 S. 9th Street
Philadelphia, Pa. 19147

The Spice Market
94 Reade Street
New York, N.Y. 10013

Syrian Grocery Import Company (Middle Eastern and North African ingredients)
270 Shawmut Avenue
Boston, Mass. 02118

Wing Fat Company, Inc. (Asian ingredients) *
33–35 Mott Street
New York, N.Y. 10013

Zampognaro (Franco-Italian ingredients)
262 Bleecker Street
New York, N.Y. 10014

☙ THE SOUTH

Asia House Grocery (Asian ingredients) *
2433 Saint Paul Street
Baltimore, Md. 21218

Asia Trading Company (Asian ingredients)
2581 Piedmont, N.E.
Atlanta, Ga. 30324

Central Grocery*
923 Decatur Street
New Orleans, La. 70116

Giant Foods of America (Indian ingredients)
100 Oaks Shopping Center
Nashville, Tenn. 37204

Gourmet Shop (Creole ingredients) *
D. H. Holmes Company, Ltd.
819 Canal Street
New Orleans, La. 70116

Greek American Grocery Store (Middle Eastern ingredients)
2961 Coral Way
Miami, Fla. 33134

Haddy's Food Market
1503 Washington Street
Charleston, W.Va. 25312

Rahal & Sons, Inc. (Middle Eastern ingredients)
1615 S.W. 8th Street
Miami, Fla. 33135

Raj Enterprises (Indian ingredients)
881 Peachtree Street
Atlanta, Ga. 30309

South and Eastern Food Supply (Asian ingredients) *
6732 N.E. 4th Avenue
Miami, Fla. 33138

Super Asian Market (Asian ingredients)
2719 Wilson Boulevard
Arlington, Va. 22201

Frank A. Von der Haar (Creole and Arcadian ingredients) *
4238 Magazine Street
New Orleans, La. 70115

Wang's Company (Asian ingredients)
800 Seventh Street, N.W.
Washington, D.C. 20001

Morris Zager*
230 Fourth Avenue, N.
Nashville, Tenn. 37219

◈ THE MIDWEST

Athens Imported Food (Middle Eastern ingredients) *
City Market 84–84
Indianapolis, Ind. 46204

Antones (Indian ingredients) *
2606 Sheridan
Tulsa, Okla. 74129

Delmar & Company (Caribbean ingredients)
501 Monroe Avenue
Detroit, Mich. 48226

El Nopal Food Market (Latin American ingredients) *
544 N. Highland Avenue
Indianapolis, Ind. 46202

Far East Company (Asian ingredients) *
247 W. McMillan Street
Cincinnati, Ohio 45219

India Groceries (Indian ingredients) *
5022 N. Sheridan Road
Chicago, Ill. 60640

India Spice Company (Indian ingredients) *
437 South Boulevard
Oak Park, Ill. 60302

King's Trading (Asian ingredients) *
3736 Broadway
Kansas City, Mo. 64111

La Preferida, Inc. (Latin American ingredients) *
3400 W. 35th Street
Chicago, Ill. 60632

Sheik Grocery Company (Middle Eastern ingredients)
652 Bolivar Road
Cleveland, Ohio 44115

Supermercado Maria Cardenas
1714 W. 18th Street
Chicago, Ill. 60680

THE SOUTHWEST

Antone's Import Company*
4234 Harry Hines Boulevard
Dallas, Tex. 75219

Antone's Import Company* '
South Boss Road
Houston, Tex. 77027

Ashley's, Inc.
6590 Montana Avenue
El Paso, Tex. 79925

Bricenos Corn Shop (Latin American and Southwestern ingredients)
1611 E. Grant Street
Phoenix, Ariz. 85034

Bueno Mexican Foods (Latin American and Southwestern ingredients) *
P.O. Box 293
Albuquerque, N.M. 87103

Simon David Grocery Store
711 Inwood Road
Dallas, Tex. 78207

Jim Jamail and Son (Caribbean ingredients) *
3114 Kirby Drive
Houston, Tex. 77006

Josie's Best Mexican Foods (Latin American and Southwestern ingredients) *
1731 2nd Street
Santa Fe, N.M. 87501

Pier L Importers
5402 South Rice Avenue
Houston, Tex. 77006

Theo Roybal Store (Latin American and Southwestern ingredients) *
Rear 2120216 Galistero Street
Santa Fe, N.W. 87501

Santa Cruz Chile & Spice Company (Latin American and Southwestern ingredients)
P.O. Box 177
Tumacacori, Ariz. 85640

THE WEST

Angelo Merlina & Sons (Middle Eastern ingredients) *
816 6th Avenue, South
Seattle, Wash. 98134

Ann's Dutch Import Company (Southeast Asian ingredients)*
4537 Tujunga Avenue
North Hollywood, Calif. 91604

Bankok Market (Southeast Asian ingredients)*
4804–6 Melrose Avenue
Los Angeles, Calif. 90029

Bazaar of India (Indian ingredients)*
1131 University Avenue
Berkeley, Calif. 94702

Beaverton Foods (Latin American ingredients)*
P.O. Box 104
Beaverton, Ore. 97005

Bezjian Grocery (Indian ingredients)*
4725 Santa Monica Boulevard
Los Angeles, Calif. 90029

The Chinese Grocer (Chinese ingredients)*
209 Post Street
San Francisco, Calif. 94108

Del Ray Spanish Foods (Latin American ingredients)
Central Market Stall A-7
317 Broadway
Los Angeles, Calif. 90013

El Mercado (Latin American ingredients)
1st Avenue and Lorena
Los Angeles, Calif. 90063

House of Rice (Indian ingredients)*
4122 University Way, N.E.
Seattle, Wash. 98105

Mediterranean & Middle East Import Company (Middle Eastern ingredients)*
223 Valencia Street
San Francisco, Calif. 94103

Mexican Grocery (Latin American ingredients)
1914 Pike Place
Seattle, Wash. 98101

Porter's Foods Unlimited (Indian ingredients) *
125 W. 11 Avenue
Eugene, Ore. 97401

Sing Chong and Company (Chinese ingredients)
800 Grant Avenue
San Francisco, Calif. 94108

Naturally, in addition to these there are local specialty shops, greengrocers, and grocery stores that may also have local and ethnic specialties that feature or highlight hot stuff.

☙ Index

A native New Yorker, JESSICA HARRIS has a Ph.D. in Performance Studies from New York University and is an assistant professor teaching English and French at Queens College.

She writes for *Travel Weekly*, and has covered food and travel subjects for *Essence, Elan, Vogue, Black Enterprise,* and other magazines. A world traveler, Ms. Harris collected most of the recipes for *Hot Stuff* in their country of origin.